RESPECTABILITY
ON TRIAL

RESPECTABILITY
ON TRIAL

Sex Crimes in New York City, 1900–1918

Brian Donovan

Published by State University of New York Press, Albany

Printed in the United States of America

For information, contact State University of New York Press, Albany, NY
www.sunypress.edu

Production, Ryan Morris
Marketing, Fran Keneston

Library of Congress Cataloging-in-Publication Data

Names: Donovan, Brian, 1971– author.
Title: Respectability on trial : sex crimes in New York City, 1900–1918 /
  Brian Donovan.
Description: Albany : State University of New York Press, 2016. | Includes
  bibliographical references and index.
Identifiers: LCCN 2016000438 (print) | LCCN 2016012982 (ebook) | ISBN
  9781438461953 (hbk. : alk. paper) | ISBN 9781438461946 (pbk. : alk. paper)
  | ISBN 9781438461960 (e-book)
Subjects: LCSH: Sex crimes—New York (State)—New York—History—20th
  century.
Classification: LCC HQ72.U5 D66 2016 (print) | LCC HQ72.U5 (ebook) | DDC
  364.15/3—dc23
LC record available at http://lccn.loc.gov/2016000438

10 9 8 7 6 5 4 3 2 1

For Natalie

Contents

Acknowledgments

I am grateful to Ellen Belcher from the Lloyd Sealy Library at the John Jay College of Criminal Justice for helping me acquire material from the Trial Transcript Collection. This book would have been impossible to write without her help. I need to thank several colleagues for their helpful comments and encouragement, including Sherrie Tucker, Michael Baskett, Cathy Preston, Akiko Takeyama, and Marta Vicente. Lynn Davidman delivered critical feedback on the manuscript as well as timely support. William Staples and Joane Nagel gave me a needed kick in the pants to finish the project.

The Hall Center for the Humanities at the University of Kansas provided a wonderful space for me to present and discuss my research. I am especially thankful for Victor Bailey, Kathy Porsch, Ann Schofield, and Kim Warren. Others gave me generous help at different stages of the project. Tori Barnes-Brus proved to be an excellent collaborator, and her research help on chapter 4 was invaluable. Aislinn Addington conducted important research for chapter 3. I am forever indebted to her friendship and support. Nicole Perry and Jane Webb are two young scholars whose research helped sharpened my own. I am appreciative of others who have given me support and inspiration, often without knowing it: Jason Barrett-Fox, Rebecca Barrett-Fox, Matt Burke, Kelly Chong, Christy Craig, Kerry Donovan, Mary Donovan, Robin Henry, Meredith Kleykamp, Randy McAvoy, Trudy McAvoy, Stephanie Russell, David Smith, Christian Watkins, and Janelle Williams. Substantially revised versions of chapters 2 and 4 were published in the journal *Law and Social Inquiry*. A research fellowship from the National Endowment for the Humanities funded this project during a crucial stage of its development. Finally, I would like to thank my editor at State University of New York Press, Beth Bouloukos,

and her assistant Rafael Chaiken for their efforts in bringing this project
into existence. This book is dedicated to Natalie Donovan, my wife and best
friend of fifteen years, for her unwavering love and companionship. I could
not have done this without her.

~

A previous version of chapter 2 appeared as "Gender Inequality and Criminal
Seduction: Prosecuting Sexual Coercion in the Early Twentieth Century,"
Law and Social Inquiry 30 (2005): 61–88. A previous version of chapter
4 appeared, coauthored with Tori Barnes-Brus, as "Narratives of Sexual
Consent and Sexual Coercion: Forced Prostitution Trials in Progressive-Era
New York City," *Law and Social Inquiry* 36, no. 3 (2011): 597–619. Both
are used with permission of John Wiley & Sons.

Introduction

In January 1906, a young woman named Margaret Peters testified in the New York City Court of General Sessions that a man named Julius Bloch raped her in the cigar factory where they both worked. Peters and Bloch were alone in the factory when the attack occurred. Bloch allegedly pushed Margaret Peters onto a wooden box and forced himself on her. Peters testified that the assault was so traumatic that she "lost her mind" and was rendered temporarily unconscious (an account that the defense attorney used against her later in the trial).[1] She returned home, told her family what had transpired, and was escorted to a police station where a charge of first degree rape was filed against Julius Bloch.

In the trial, Julius Bloch's defense attorney attacked Margaret Peters's sexual respectability. He insinuated that Margaret Peters told "smutty stories" at work. Although the judge snapped at the attorney for improperly discussing the "girl's unchastity," other witnesses testified that she was disreputable and, therefore, fabricating her account of sexual assault.[2] Peter's coworker, Frida Gail, testified for the defense, and she affirmed that Peters "talked very smutty" and said inappropriate things "about men's privates, and about ladies [sic] privates."[3] When the defense attorney asked her to elaborate, she demurred, fearing that her own reputation would be sullied by repeating the vulgar details. The judge reassured her that her testimony "is not anything against you." Next, Julius Bloch sat in the witness stand and described how he and Peters developed a flirtatious relationship at work. He told jurors that he did not assault her but, rather, their sexual encounter was consensual and that Margaret Peters allegedly "made a bed" with the wooden box. Finally, Jennifer Bloch, Julius's wife, took to the witness stand and testified that he always came home on time from work and always brought home his full salary. She told the jurors that she forgave him for his transgressions.[4] The jury deliberated for thirty minutes before acquitting Bloch for the crime of first degree rape.

1

The trial of Julius Bloch encapsulates the tensions and contradictions in early twentieth-century notions of sexual respectability. New York women like Margaret Peters were increasingly working outside of the home, exploring romance on their own terms, and engaging in frank sexual talk that was once deemed the exclusive domain of men. By the 1920s, the "New Woman" and the "flapper"—images of a confident and assertive womanhood—would become staples of popular culture and accepted by wide swaths of American society. In the years leading up to World War I, however, the criterions of respectable womanhood were in flux, and women were often held to standards of behavior we associate with the stereotypes of Victorianism: women were expected to be chaste, modest, and pure. Their sexuality was supposedly signified by their lack of sexual passion and their focus on the hearth and home.

As a theater of respectability, the criminal courtroom throws into bold relief the contested nature of gender and sexuality in early urban America. In *People v. Bloch*, the trial participants engaged in various performances of proper manhood and womanhood. The defense attorney and several witnesses claimed that Margaret Peters was sexually assertive and inappropriate. Frida Gail did not want to tarnish her reputation by uttering the supposedly vulgar comments made by her coworker. Julius and Jennifer Bloch testified that Julius met hegemonic standards of masculinity with his paycheck and attention to home life. The fact that he had developed an attraction to, and possibly raped, his coworker did not damage his respectability in the eyes of the all-male jury, but his alleged victim was consider dishonorable and unwomanly because she engaged in bawdy workplace banter.

This book examines sex crime trials in New York City that occurred during the so-called "first sexual revolution" (approximately 1900–1920). The opening decades of the twentieth century were a volatile period in US sexual history. New forms of leisure, romance, and marriage challenged sexual Victorianism, especially in major cities like Chicago, Los Angeles, and New York City. Although "flappers"—sexually assertive young women from the Jazz Age—symbolize, to some extent, the first sexual revolution, they actually embody its end stages. Elizabeth Clement notes, "By the late 1890s, conditions were ripe for revolution in working-class understandings of the appropriate sexual behavior of women."[5] Betsy Israel observes, "Much of the Jazz Age imagery we associate with the 1920s—driving, incessant dancing, loose-fitting clothes—actually took shape around 1913."[6] Historians have described these changes with contrasting images of revolution and repression. Historian James McGovern said the years leading up to World War I "represented such visible departures from the past and are so commonly practiced as to warrant calling them revolutionary."[7] The first sexual revolution gave young men and women opportunities to control their romantic lives.[8]

On the other hand, men and women had differential access to new work and leisure opportunities, and they experienced the so-called revolution unevenly. Young women encountered a heightened risk of acquaintance rape as they pursued sex, love, and romance in an era of unsupervised dating. Young women who took advantage of new social and sexual opportunities also faced state surveillance and social control. For instance, women were arrested for "chastity" offenses for flirting with servicemen near military bases.[9] Also, new employment prospects put women at risk for exploitation, and shady employment agencies sometimes drew unsuspecting women into sex work. Women, who may have entered sex work on their own volition, encountered abuse by both pimps and customers.

The first sexual revolution reflected inequalities between racial and ethnic majorities and minorities, sexual minorities and majorities, and members of different socioeconomic classes. The resistance to sexual revolution disproportionately targeted sexual minorities, the working-class, women, immigrants, and racial minorities. For instance, subcultures of men who had sex with other men had more chances to congregate in new urban spaces like boarding houses and bathhouses, but they also found themselves the target of new police scrutiny. Also, the "white slavery scare"—the concern that white women were being abducted and sold into prostitution—was used by reformers to vilify African Americans and immigrants. Immigrants were deported or denied entry for being suspected of prostitution, and the most aggressive police surveillance occurred in neighborhoods of concentrated ethnic and racial minorities like the Tenderloin and Chinatown.[10]

The trials considered in this book uncover the contradictory features of early twentieth-century gender and sexual ideologies. In particular, these trials show how constructions of social respectability shaped how sex crimes were understood by attorneys and jurors. Judgments and distinctions about proper masculine and feminine attributes and behaviors enabled and constrained the justice-producing capacity of New York City's criminal justice system. Conflicting gender ideologies—widely shared ideas about manhood and womanhood—shaped how the trials unfolded. Consequently, my analysis of these trials reveals the tensions between sexual revolution and counterrevolution, and social control and social justice, in the early twentieth century.

This book focuses on four categories of sex crime: seduction, rape, sodomy, and compulsory prostitution. Each category entailed a different set of claims about sexual respectability that alternately drew on declining "Victorian" notions of gender and sexuality and emergent notions of gender and sexual progressivism. Seduction, rape, sodomy, and compulsory prostitution trials produced stories of violence and transgression that expose the importance of culturally constructed standards of social and sexual respectability to explain how the law and criminal justice system worked during the early twentieth century.

The criminal trials analyzed in this book were referendums on sexual respectability, and they were sites of sexual revolution and counterrevolution. Sex crime trials offer a powerful vantage point for understanding gender and US history. Sharon Ullman, in her analysis of early twentieth-century sex trials, notes how "courtroom conflicts became a mechanism that drove the shift in sexual attitudes."[11] Historian Dawn Flood contends, "Sex crime trials, where for many years the only female participants were likely to be the victims, present an expansive opportunity to explore how the gendered nature of the courtroom inhibited some social challenges even while encouraging others."[12] Criminal law is a central arena where gender inequality is perpetuated and alleviated, and a close reading of trial transcripts can illuminate how gender ideologies (like Victorian passionlessness or masculine chivalry) and material inequality (such as unequal work opportunities) shape how the law works. Conversely, such an approach has the capacity to show how the legal sphere—its texts, practitioners, norms, and practices—directs how people think about gender and sexuality.

Eavesdropping on Sexual Revolution

Trial transcripts offer insight into immigrant and working-class life in early urban America, but the pages contain a web of conflicting and self-interested narratives. As sociologists Patricia Ewick and Susan Silbey have noted, "The strategic use of narrative is nowhere more developed than in legal settings where lawyers, litigators, judges, and juries all participate in the telling of tales."[13] The American criminal courtroom is, above all else, an arena of storytelling.[14] One approach to a trial transcript is to evaluate the truthfulness of the stories recounted therein and to arrive at an accurate description of the events surrounding the criminal indictment. When reading a transcript, I strove to understand what happened during the alleged crime by juxtaposing different stories, making reasonable inferences about them, and applying my understanding of the historical time period to the courtroom accounts. Except for a few, these trials received no press coverage.

Presenting excerpts from trial transcripts invites readers to act as an extra jury member, to evaluate the testimony in front of them, and to draw conclusions about the alleged crime. Using the transcript to piece together the series of events that ultimately led to the arrest and indictment, however, is tricky and potentially misleading. Versions of reality compete against one another without providing points of neutral adjudication, and the reconstruction of a coherent story out of a single trial transcript will necessarily exclude some points of view. Use of court documents to construct an accurate and seamless portrait of reality often obscures the legal exigencies that led to the documents' creation, and it removes the documents from their historical and institutional context.[15] Furthermore, storytelling in the courtroom often resists closure and coherence. It has the character of postmodern narrative with fragmented images sketched through the unique question-and-answer format of witness questioning and testifying.[16] Therefore, the trial transcripts considered in this study are less valuable as records of "what happened" and are more valuable as imprints of particular ideas about sex, gender, men, and women. At the same time, however, it is naïve to think that the transcripts are incapable of conveying past events and experiences. The dual quality of transcripts as both an imprint of ideology and as a record of "what happened" requires careful consideration as to the possibilities and limitations of these documents.

The trial transcripts considered in this book survived by chance. In 1972, the John Jay College of Criminal Justice received a shipment of boxes from the New York Supreme Court containing verbatim transcripts from trials conducted in New York City's main criminal courthouse from 1883 to 1927. The transcripts—hundreds of thousands of typewritten pages—decayed in storage for over a decade until an enterprising group of historians and librarians at John Jay College recognized the documents' importance and created the Trial Transcript Collection in the early 1980s.[17]

Trial transcripts offer a rich source of historical material, and they better capture the tone and tempo of courtroom activity compared to other accounts and records. The transcripts present plaintive pleas for understanding and heated exchanges between trial participants. As historical documents, trial transcripts contain a wealth of information about the culture and practices of ordinary New Yorkers, but the process of transcribing, and the criteria used by officials to selected court proceedings for transcription, impose constraints on what the transcripts reveal and what questions they can address.

The collective labor of stenographers allows us to glimpse into early twentieth-century sex crime trials. Court stenography was a well-paying occupation that employed increasing numbers of women in the first two decades of the twentieth century. Salaries for New York City court stenographers were $2,300 a year in 1901, but stenographers had the ability to make from $5,000 to $7,000 a year selling their transcripts.[18] Before the introduction of stenotype machines, New York court stenographers used shorthand to record the verbal proceedings of criminal trials, but they were not required to create typed transcripts from their notebooks unless a judge or attorney requested it. Pretrial statements and prosecutors' records archived at the New York City Municipal Archive, while often valuable, sometimes do little more than reiterate a synoptic version of events usually recounted in greater detail by individuals on the witness stand. I drew from these other sources, but the transcripts, and the stories they convey, took the center stage in this study.

At the start of this project, I collected, read, and analyzed seduction, compulsory prostitution, sodomy, and first degree rape trial transcripts for the years 1900–1919.[19] Altogether, I printed seventy-five trial transcripts from the John Jay College Trial Transcript Collection, totaling approximately sixteen thousand pages. I read the transcripts at least twice, a process that took years.[20] The cases discussed in depth in this book, therefore, are a subset of the Transcript Collection that I consider important or representative. The wealth of information contained in the documents necessitated a procedure or method to condense the material while somehow preserving its relevant details. For every transcript, I typed—sometimes with the help of research assistants—extensive notes. These trial notes included summary information about the trial and the attorneys' strategies, lengthy excerpts from the direct and cross-examination of witnesses, and other relevant information. The notes recorded the family and work histories of the defendants and complainants, the character evidence for or against them, and the incriminating or exonerating details about their recent past unearthed through attorney questioning. The notes also contained excerpts from judges' instructions to jurors, questions jurors asked during the trials, cases cited by attorneys and—in the rare instances where they are available in the transcripts—*voir dire* (juror questioning and selection), and attorneys' opening and closing statements. The trial notes included all testimony related to sexual consent, sexual coercion, and social and sexual respectability (the major theme that emerged as I read the transcripts). Moving back and forth between the trial notes and the transcript text allowed for a reading of the trials that zoomed out to a trial's sociohistorical context and zoomed in for the you-are-there experience of line-by-line dialogue.

Three bodies of scholarship from the late twentieth and early twenty-first centuries guide the theoretical and methodological framework of this study: feminism (particularly research on gender and "respectability"), cultural histories of crime, and sociolinguistics (specifically, "conversation analysis"). Feminism, broadly conceived, frames the overall approach to the transcripts, from the initial selection of trials to the analysis of participants' discourse. Cultural history examines the courtroom as a site of clashing ideologies. This approach views the action in a trial as emanating from sometimes incompatible cultural systems that extend outside the courtroom and beyond the immediate creation of the participants. Understanding the ideologies expressed in a sex crime trial reveals the context of gender and sexual inequality in which the trial occurs. The third influence, a type of discourse analysis, examines the courtroom as a site of verbal exchange. The conversation analysis approach studies the dynamics of trials from the inside, as an interactive process whereby trial participants create legal meaning through conversation and talk. The effects of language and representation are especially clear in legal settings (consider the power of a judge stating "I hereby sentence you"). The institutional force of law expresses itself through pronouncements of guilt and innocence. The legal arena shows that discourse—whether it is witness testimony, the language of statutes, judges' orders, or juror discussions—enacts power relations and has concrete effects on the lives of courtroom participants.

Gender and Respectability

This study holds gender and sexuality as fundamental aspects of social life. In the late 1980s, scholarship in gender history marked a shift in perspective. Whereas feminist historians in the 1970s and '80s challenged male-centered historical narratives by showing the underappreciated role of women in politics and society, the new generation of feminist scholarship made gender a central category of historical analysis.[21] In the 1980s and '90s debates between self-described proponents of "women's history" and "gender history" mirrored wider academic conflicts about poststructuralism and feminism. Contemporary discussions of feminism have emphasized intersectionality, or the interdependency and mutual constitution of inequalities marked by sexuality, social class, race, and ethnicity.

Anthropology, history, sociology, and other academic disciplines have shown how gender shapes, and is shaped by, distinctions about who meets culturally approved standards of respectability.[22] Beverley Skeggs emphasized women's use of cultural, social, and economic capital to cultivate respectability.[23] According to Skeggs, respectability is "an amalgam of signs, economics and practices, assessed from different positions within and outside of respectability."[24] The concept of respectability is important for several different reasons. Respectability has dual quality: individuals can generate standards of respectability, and standards of respectability can be imposed from the outside onto individuals.[25] Illustrating the latter, historical scholarship emphasizes the controlling force of respectability discourse in women's experiences of work and home life. Davidson, for example, analyzed women's employment on the Pennsylvania railroad in the early twentieth century to reveal "the power that conceptions of sexual respectability held over women's lives."[26] Illustrating the former, scholars have shown how claims to respectability function as a resource that individuals can use to their advantage. The role of respectability as a resource is particularly clear in the research on the "politics of respectability" in African American history. Evelyn Higginbotham describes the complex role that respectability played in the discourse of black Baptist women in the late 1800s to early 1900s. Claims to respectability legitimized black women's fight for equality.[27] In short, respectability is a powerful discourse that can be both imposed on others and drawn upon as a personal and collective source of strength.

The concept of respectability is also significant because it reveals the connections among intersecting inequalities like class, race, ethnicity, and gender without reducing inequality to a single source. For instance, Kate Boyer's analysis of Victorian Montreal emphasized the importance of respectability: "To make their social worlds comprehensible, determining respectability became an inexact, but ubiquitous science."[28] Boyer explained that "far more than a shorthand for class, then, respectability was a way of speaking about and organizing gendered, racialized and sexed bodies."[29] Alison Phipps argued that respectability is gendered but that the "concept is undeniably also classed, and therefore the division between 'good' rape complainants and 'bad' ones may be partly drawn via the embodied symbolic economy of social class, as well as that of gender."[30] The language of respectability interlocks different dimensions of social inequality and, for the purposes of this study, the concept of respectability provides a vantage point to address how gender inequality intensifies, mitigates, or otherwise relates to other social divisions like race, ethnicity, and social class. Representations of gender hinge on performances and judgments of respectability, and those judgments had concrete consequences in New York City's criminal courtroom. The trials analyzed in this book were anchored in discourses about respectability, and claims to masculine and feminine respectability formed an important foundation for attorneys' strategies and jurors' decision making.

Cultural History and Crime

Cultural history is the second theoretical and methodological tradition underpinning this study. Clifford Geertz's cultural anthropology largely inspired the birth of "new cultural history," what historical sociologist Richard Biernacki refers to as "the cultural history 'revolution' of the 1980s."[31] Geertz showed how untangling the semiotics of a given cultural form could reveal the webs of meaning that held societies together. Geertz's regard for the importance (and relative autonomy) of cultural meaning led historians to analyze what they once regarded as cultural effluvium. According to historian Sarah Maza, Clifford Geertz's collection of essays *Interpretation of Cultures* "inspired, more than any other work, the first generation of 'new cultural historians.'" Seemingly trivial cultural practices revealed something important about a society and its social institutions. Peasants' jokes, parades, and celebrity scandals became objects of historical analysis, and historians drew connections between seemingly disparate phenomena, like credit debt and fear of masturbation, or between animal massacres and class conflict, to show a society's underlying cultural logic.[32]

The growth of cultural history in the 1980s and '90s expanded the range of proper subjects for studies of law and society, and what seemed of marginal interest to the older brand of social history—like sensational trials and mysterious murders—now took the spotlight. Historian Natalie Davis's 1987 study of "pardoner tales," letters prisoners wrote to magistrates in sixteenth-century France, demonstrated the value of studying crime and criminals as an entry point into wider sociohistorical questions.[33] Petitioners drafted "letters of remission" as a way to defend their criminal behavior and (they hoped) avoid a death sentence. Almost always, individuals created and submitted letters of remission when faced with a possible death sentence. Supplicants recounted their story before a royal notary in the hope that they would show them mercy. Davis provided a methodological manual for cultural historians, and she opened new terrain for studies of law and culture. In discussing Davis's approach, Conley and O'Barr write, "By analyzing what these stories say, how they say it, what they include, what they leave out, and how they were received, we can learn a great deal about the dynamics of the society that produced them. Of particular interest to us is what we can learn about the relations between men and women and their respective interactions with the law and its power."[34]

The documents analyzed by Natalie Davis proved valuable in understanding life in sixteenth-century France insofar as they gave information about customs, holidays, and aspects of the criminal justice system. Yet, Davis showed how the "fictional" qualities of these appeals for mercy better reveal the social fabric of early modern France compared to the strictly "factual" information found in these texts. The value of pardoner tales lays not so much in their descriptions of reality as in their ability to express the mentalities, ideologies, and worldviews of men and women in early modern France.[35] The lesson from Davis is that even fictional claims like one would find in a criminal trial can reveal the mentalities, ideologies, and cultural standards of a certain time and place.

Following this general mode of historical inquiry, scholars have demonstrated how crime, criminals, and legal battles crystallized and condensed the cultural underbelly of specific historical epochs. Crime and punishment reveal social fault lines and anxieties. Judith Walkowitz showed how responses to the Jack the Ripper murders provide a cultural mapping of the gender and class trouble that animated social tensions in late-Victorian England. Walkowitz writes: "Response to the Ripper murders, then, reveals significant class divisions and class-based fantasies. It also exposes deep-seated sexual antagonism, most frequently expressed by men toward women."[36] Likewise, Angus McLaren used different criminal trials to sketch from the "negative definitions" of manhood a social portrait of hegemonic masculinity in order to arrive at "a clearer notion of the social and cultural anxieties of the age."[37] Amy Srebnick analyzed the murder of Mary Rogers, a woman whose battered body was discovered in the Hudson River in 1841, to chronicle "the modernization of urban antebellum culture."[38] Lisa Duggan used Alice Mitchell's 1892 murder of Freda Ward to show "the work of sex and violence in making the state and the nation."[39] In these analyses, criminal trials are about more than sex and murder. They reflected outward to grander claims about modernity, gender, and society.

With its wide aperture, cultural history shows how criminal trials reflect and condense general rubrics of meaning. Cultural historians opt for distinct literary choices that correspond to different modes of argument. Their reading and representation of the transcripts connects the trial and gender relations like a synecdoche, a literary trope that describes a part-whole relationship where the part represents a larger totality. The trial, in turn, is an embryonic representation of those historical, cultural, or ideological currents. Analyses of criminal trials often rely on the synecdoche. Historical writing generically uses the synecdoche when writing about any event that is representative of a larger era, age, or epoch. Histories of criminal events and criminal trials often make a manifest appeal to the synecdoche, claiming that the crime or the trial represents a cultural or social whole.[40]

The cultural history approach is useful for my analysis of sex crime trials because it excavates the broad interpretive schemas that oriented trial participants and provided external cultural coherence for their trial narratives. This book examines courtroom stories about illegal sex and violence voiced during an unstable transition in the American sexual landscape, and the trials offer a front-row perspective for understanding the wider contests over gender and sexuality that engulfed the nation at the turn of the century; one can read the trials as miniaturizations of the first sexual revolution. The courtroom struggles illustrate, in microcosm, a clash between competing ideological frameworks: well-established ideas of feminine respectability and emerging ideas about women's sexual agency, manhood defined by marriage and responsibility, and new freedoms available to bachelors and men who exhibited nonhegemonic ideals of manhood. This course of inquiry looks outside the trial—to history, culture, ideology, or other concepts we generally think of providing *context*—to ascertain the meaning and importance of the verbal exchanges occurring inside the courtroom.

Toward a Bifocal Reading

Finally, this study is influenced by sociolinguistics and, in particular, "conversation analysis," a line of scholarship that analyzes the minutiae of human communication. Conversation analysis is a type of social science that analyzes how everyday conversations create social order. Conversation analysis (CA) shares similarities with ethnomethodology, sociolinguistics, and formal discourse analysis. Ian Hutchby and Robin Wooffitt contend that CA is more than a methodological approach; it "represents a distinctive sociological vision, a way of seeing the world and of approaching data."[41] The CA approach derives from a number of lectures delivered by sociologist Harvey Sacks in the 1960s and early '70s. During the years when Geertz created a new way to do anthropology, Sacks fashioned a new way to do sociology, and both theorists had vastly different understandings of where and how to analyze the enduring building blocks of society, or what is commonly referred to as "social structure." Cultural anthropology and cultural history view social structure as external to individuals and having its own logic and inertia, expressed through social interaction and embodied in institutions, rituals, and cultural practices. Conversation analysts locate the creation of social structure from the inside out, through interpersonal communicative exchanges. Conversation analysts emphasize human agency. Hutchby and Wooffitt contend that conversation analysis starts "from the assumption that participants are active, knowledgeable agents, rather than simply the bearers of extrinsic, constraining structures."[42] They explain, "CA takes the view that 'structure' is a feature of situated social interaction that participants actively orient to as *relevant* for the ways they design their actions."[43] Social structure is a context for interpersonal interaction; it is not the independent variable that explains interaction.

Conversation analysts demonstrate the force of turn-taking sequences, question format, and verbal corrections to uncover otherwise fleeting or invisible aspects of talk, conversation, and speech. From the tight aperture of conversation analysis and formal discourse analysis, scholars have focused on courtroom participants' verbal tactics and exchanges as a way to illuminate the linguistic and discursive foundations of gender inequality in different legal settings.[44] Word choice and sentence structure have legal consequences because they shape how jurors and other courtroom participants understand the facts in a given case.

Conversation analysis and sociolinguistics have made great strides in understanding the dynamics of sexual assault trials. They have helped address why, for instance, women often experience a second layer of trauma as complaining witnesses in these trials despite the nationwide adoption of rape shield laws in the late twentieth century that barred defense attorneys from introducing evidence about the victims' sexual past. Legal scholar Gregory Matoesian uses conversation analysis to show how defense attorneys in rape trials subtly undermine complainants' testimony without explicitly questioning their prior sexual experience during cross-examination. Attorneys linguistically evade rape shield laws and introduce testimony that those laws were designed to preclude.[45] For instance, Matoesian deconstructs the transcript of the 1991 William Kennedy Smith rape trial to show how—despite Florida's relatively tough state rape shield law—Smith's defense attorney managed to cast doubt on the accuser. In her book on acquaintance rape, anthropologist Peggy Sanday described the defense attorney as advancing "subliminal messages" about the complainant during the trial.[46] Matoesian's piercing study reveals that what Sanday refers to as "subliminal messages" were patterned questioning techniques. What made them seem subliminal was that their efficacy appeared distinct from their content. The defense attorney blamed the victim in the form of the question, not in the question's substance. For instance, the defense attorney asked the complainant's friend a long string of questions to make it seem like she was more interested in the location of her shoes than the welfare of her friend. The defense attorney's rhetorical moves—"creative and improvisational poetic structures, such as repetition, direct quotes, and parallelism"—made it seem like the complainant consented to Kennedy's sexual advances.[47] Barely perceptible linguistic maneuvers in the courtroom have real consequences.

Similar research has examined the syntax of different testimony in the 1995 O. J. Simpson trial. In her analysis of the Simpson trial, Cotterill shows how litigants attributed blame and motive by exploiting the gap between the denotational and connotational meaning of specific words, that is, the space between a word's strict definition and the meaning it carries in a particular cultural context. She writes, "Through the skillful exploitation of layers of lexical meaning, it is possible for lawyers to communicate subtle and partisan information about the victims and alleged perpetrators, without falling foul of the rules of evidence and without appearing to subvert the intended function of the opening statements."[48] For instance, whereas the prosecutor spoke of the "domestic violence" or "cycle of violence" to which Simpson allegedly subjected Nicole Brown Simpson, the defense referred to the assaults as "incidents" or "altercations."

Conversation analysis is valuable for understanding the contests over sexual and social respectability during the first sexual revolution. Core concepts in conversational analysis provide a method to explain the institutionally mediated and culture-bound forms of communication that Ludwig Wittgenstein termed "language games."[49] The game metaphor allowed Wittgenstein to theorize the relationship between rule-governed human interaction as well as the pragmatic and creative spaces within those rules. CA reveals how people play different legal language games within the limits posed by the asymmetrical constraints, opportunities, and institutional practices of the courtroom. For example, attorneys may ask witnesses questions, but witnesses may not ask attorneys questions in return. If the opposing side objects to a question or line of questioning, judges can expressly allow or forbid those queries. The courtroom imposes rules, and courtroom participants choose among different moves within set frameworks established by the codes of criminal procedure and the norms of courtroom behavior.

To be clear, this book does not engage in formal conversation analysis. Although this book excerpts and analyzes lengthy segments of courtroom dialogue, the transcripts lack the detail and notation that enable a conversation-analytic reading. The practice of conversation analysis hinges on the ability to record segments of conversation and then to transcribe the recorded material in a way that permits the analyst to discern the normative rules of seemingly spontaneous or chaotic conversation. Segments of conversation are precisely transcribed with the length of pauses indicated to the tenth of a second. Conversation analysis transcripts reveal when speakers take an audible in-breath and when they stretch specific syllables. This method of transcription allows the researcher to see the configuration of different conversational moves, and it can reveal patterns of preferred moves that people tend to make in similar social contexts.

Although my analysis does not engage in conversation analysis, a "conversation analytic mentality" guides my reading of the transcripts.[50] In this spirit, I pay added attention to word choice, repetition, question sequencing, sentence structure, and how some questions encourage certain responses and foreclose others. Although orthodox conversation analysis rejects context-based interpretations of conversational data, I argue that talk and speech give traction to the preexisting social fractures and power imbalances outlined by cultural historians.[51] Along these lines, Max Travers argues that conversation analysis and ethnography are useful approaches to study legal practices, but their respective proponents talk past each other and resist incorporating the insights of the other into their own analyses. He bemoans the lack of a "third way" that harnesses the fine-grained gaze of conversation analysis in conjunction with context-sensitive ethnographic observation. This book attempts to navigate a third way between the micro-level of verbal exchange and the macro-level of historical context.

Therefore, the analysis of sex crime trials offered in this book is bifocal. It toggles between the interior dynamics of the trial and the external power relations that allow those dynamics to have legal consequences. Trial testimony reflects American culture, the US legal system, and prevailing notions of gender and sexuality, but it reflects those bigger dimensions of social history only insofar as they reveal themselves in the back-and-forth dialogue of courtroom talk.[52] Zooming in, the line-by-line dialogue within a single transcript allows for an in-depth reading of how attorneys and witnesses negotiated the meaning of sexual respectability, consent, and coercion. Zooming out, the trial transcripts show how stories and accounts of sexual practices capture social change occurring in the first two decades of the twentieth century. A bifocal reading combines the value of understanding the trial narratives as part of a larger story (or set of stories) existing in American culture and understanding the trial narratives as comprised of in-the-moment interaction and argumentation. The tension between conversation analysis and cultural history offers a potent way to assess the scholarly and social value of sex crime trial transcripts. Zooming in to glimpse attorneys' verbal tactics, and zooming out to the historical and cultural context in which those tactics are intelligible, represents the lives of ordinary New Yorkers in a unique and powerful way. Social structure, as historian and social theorist William Sewell Jr. explains, comprises language games as well as a built environment that provides inertia and stability to the game-playing.[53] The trial transcripts and the stories of working-class life recorded therein sketch the connection between the actions of the courtroom participants and the structural constraints they faced in early New York City.

~

Chapter 1 considers the national and statewide changes in work, leisure, and courtship that fueled sexual revolution in New York City in the early twentieth century. The chapter also explains how cases arrived in New York City's main criminal court (the Court of General Sessions) and the basic elements of criminal sex crime trials. The Court of General Sessions handled all felonies tried in New York County and was, by the early twentieth century, the busiest criminal court in the world. The path to the criminal courthouse was a long process that began with a complaint brought by a private citizen or law enforcement agent. Defendants were arraigned in magistrate's court and, if there was sufficient evidence against them, felony indictments were presented to a grand jury. Once approved by a grand jury, defendants were tried in the Court of General Sessions in front of a jury of twelve men. Considering the type and diversity of sex crime cases it processed, New York City's Court of General Sessions was a central site of sexual revolution and counterrevolution.

Chapter 2 focuses on seduction trials. The criminal category of "seduction" has a long history in the United States that stretches back to the 1830s. Chapter 2 shows how seduction prosecutions were used as an instrument to secure marriage proposals from reluctant suitors, and they were also used to punish men who committed what we would recognize today as acquaintance rape. New York's seduction statute forbade, "seduction under promise of marriage," which occurred when a person "seduces and has intercourse with an unmarried female of previous chaste character."[54] The law was designed to punish men who robbed women of their virginity based on a false pledge of future matrimony. Successful prosecution of seduction cases required specific performances of respectability from complaining witnesses. Victims of seduction were prompted to give testimony that they physically resisted their suitor's sexual advances and that they mentally clung to future marriage as the sole reason they consented to sex. Additionally, the law required that the victims be "of previous chaste character." In the argumentative space of the courtroom, "chastity" was often understood to be synonymous with moral uprightness, not simply physical virginity. In these ways, claims of feminine respectability harkened back to the Victorian stereotypes of feminine passionlessness, docility, and marriage-mindedness, corresponding to an understanding of womanhood in place during the law's creation in 1848. Progressive-Era seduction trials, however, revealed new courtship practices and new ideas about manhood and womanhood. Unsupervised dating was a relatively new practice in the early twentieth century, and seduction trials often revolved around the conflicting reports about what happened during these dates. In several trials, testimony about seduction revealed accounts of what, today, we would call "date rape." In this way, seduction prosecutions were a response to sexual violence and a community's desire to promote marriage for young adults before they had children out of wedlock. Seduction prosecutions show the countervailing forces of sexual revolution: The law embodies the nineteenth-century perspective on women as weak and needing protection from seducers, but it was used to address modern circumstances like unsupervised courtship.

Chapter 3 analyzes early twentieth-century rape trials in New York City. Like seduction prosecutions, rape trials in Progressive-Era New York City demanded specific performances of respectability from the complainants. Similar to seduction trials, claims to womanly respectability required that complainants resisted their attackers during their assault. Yet, the "resistance test" was more than a legal strategy; it was part of the formal requirement of the law. New York's law against first degree rape had strict standards for successful prosecution. A third party needed to verify the attack, and the resistance test mandated that complainants "fiercely resist" their attackers. As a result, successful prosecutions for rape were rare, and typically involved instances where the attack entailed extreme violence when, for instance, the victim was beaten to unconsciousness. In fact, in many of the rape trials examined, victims testified that they lost consciousness during their attack. Testimony of unconsciousness worked to satisfy the implicit standard that the rape involved extreme physical violence, but it gave defense attorneys an opportunity to question complainants' memories of the attacks. A woman faced a potential double bind in these trials because she had to recognize and describe her assault, but she also had to make claims about her lack of consciousness in order to assure the jury she did not consent. The dynamic in rape trials—requiring women's agency in reporting their victimization but equally requiring a denial of the capacity for agency—is emblematic of the tensions in the first sexual revolution. Women were simultaneously encouraged to assert their independence but punished if they did.

Chapter 4 follows the prosecution of pimps and procurers under New York's "compulsory prostitution" statute. New York's law against compulsory prostitution addressed instances of grievous sexual exploitation where pimps and procurers of prostitutes profited off of the sex trade. The statute made it a crime to "place any female in the charge or custody of any other person for immoral purposes or in a house of prostitution with intent that she shall live a life of prostitution."[55] The law was created and designed to address the supposed problem of "white slavery" where devious men drugged and abducted white girls and forced them into prostitution. Stories of white slavery asserted a distinctly nineteenth-century understanding of womanhood where women, particularly white women, would not practice prostitution unless they were forced into it. Popular stories of innocent women coerced into white slavery shaped expectations as to how courtroom participants told and heard stories of forced prostitution. Jurors anticipated accounts of innocent and naïve young women abducted and forced into brothels, but witnesses often recounted experiences that ran counter to the stereotypical portrayals in books and film.

In practice, many of the prosecutions addressed instances of ordinary sex work that did not include the elements of the popular image of white slavery. Pimps used psychological, financial, and physical coercion on women sex workers, but witness testimony in these trials uncovered scenarios that were vastly different from the stories of white slavery found in books, film, and magazines. Testimony about compulsory prostitution in the courtroom routinely lacked the hallmarks of popular white slavery narratives that included stories of forcible abduction, physical brutality, drugging by hypodermic needles, and locked doors. Nonetheless, both prosecutors and defense attorneys selectively drew from the white slavery scenario and its imagery of forced abduction and enslavement. Prosecutors emphasized the parallels between the story of prostitution uttered by witnesses and the stock tropes of the Progressive-Era white slavery scare. Defense attorneys, on the other hand, described the ordinariness of the crime and its disconnection from the stories of white slavery to which jurors might have been exposed. The melodramatic and stylized white slavery narrative formed a discursive resource for both sides of the case. In this way, compulsory prostitution trials expose the tensions in Progressive-Era gender ideology between, on one hand, understanding women as capable of consenting to prostitution and, on another hand, viewing women (especially white women) as naturally pure and unwilling to engage in sex work without brute force.

The sodomy trials in the Transcript Collection document a bathhouse raid, an interracial street solicitation in Harlem, and an intimate pairing between an older married man and a young male boarder. Chapter 5 examines various applications of New York's sodomy law during the first two decades of the twentieth century to reveal how sodomy was, alternately, a catch-all concept referring to deviant sexual practices as well as a category-specific crime associated with "fairies," "inverts," and others whom we would classify in the early twenty-first century as gay or queer. New York's sodomy law set a punishment of up to twenty years in prison for "[a] person who carnally knows in any manner any animal or bird; or carnally knows any male or female person by the anus or with the mouth; or voluntarily submits to such carnal knowledge; or attempts sexual intercourse with a dead body."[56] Unlike the other trials considered in this study, sodomy trials did not typically produce testimony about sexual coercion and physical violence, and they did not focus on a complainant's sexual agency and consent. All the same, the defendant's social and sexual respectability were on trial. Of particular interest was the extent to which the defendants were engaging in a vice as opposed to acting on an internal disposition toward same-sex intimacy. In one of the trials, for example, the defendant rebuffed accusations that he solicited a male prostitute in Harlem by emphasizing his drunkenness. The defendant acted immorally because of his intoxication, not his homosexuality; he might have been engaging in "sodomy," but he was not a "sodomite." Defendants and witnesses used other strategies to suggest that their crime was on par with gambling and drinking but not reflective of their identity or sexuality. They testified about their marriages, their religiosity, and their contributions to society in order to create an image of morality and respectability.

Sodomy trials are important to examine because they occurred during a time when the meaning of same-sex desire was undergoing a significant shift. Same-sex relations in the nineteenth century were considered deviant, but their deviance did not originate from an internal homosexual disposition. Only in the 1890s did the term "homosexual" emerge as a description of an individual who is psychologically and physiologically the "opposite" of "heterosexuals."[57] As Michel Foucault, George Chauncey, and other scholars have explained, same-sex sexual encounters in the nineteenth century reflected what individuals "did," not who they "are." Working-class Italian immigrants in New York City, for instance, could have sex with other men without jeopardizing their perceived masculinity or respectability. By the 1930s, the understanding of an oppositional binary between heterosexuality and homosexuality was firmly in place in the United States, but sodomy trials during the first sexual revolution occurred during a time when the meaning of same-sex desire was in flux. Defendants drew upon the older nineteenth-century understanding of sodomy as an immoral act equivalent to other immoral acts like adultery or being drunk. Prosecutors strove to suggest that the defendants were degenerate men who were inherently abnormal.

The concluding chapter revisits the tension between sexual revolution and counterrevolution in early twentieth-century New York City. The chapter considers the force of respectability in creating the state-sanctioned bundle of sexual freedoms and constraints referred to as "sexual citizenship."[58] Rights to sexual citizenship protect the negative and positive freedoms that comprise true sexual autonomy. Rights of sexual autonomy and expression fortify sexual citizenship, but sexual citizenship does not guarantee legal citizenship. The process of becoming a "good citizen" in the United States meant that the individual displayed signs of respectable sexual behavior. Ethnic assimilation required sexual assimilation. Sex crime trials demonstrate that discourse about sexual respectability had decisive consequences for who was considered American and un-American.

Chapter 1

Trials of the First Sexual Revolution

The Progressive Era (1890–1918) created the modern United States. Historian Matthew Guterl has noted that "the United States was transformed from an uncivil, rough-and-tumble backwater to a world power and the very seat of 'civilization.'"[1] In the decades leading up to World War I, America experienced a series of contradictory impulses. Labor unions made gains in membership and legal status but faced opposition from powerful monopolies and business interests. The era saw the proliferation of settlement houses and immigrant communities but also gave birth to a xenophobic and racist backlash, culminating in the 1910 report from the Dillingham Commission, which purported to offer scientific evidence of the inferiority of new immigrants from Southern and Eastern Europe. The dual nature of the progressivism has vexed historians for decades. Barbara Antoniazzi described the double quality of the period: "Celebrated and condemned by historians of each generation, the age of reform has been praised for its forward-looking spirit and genuinely emancipatory accomplishments as well as criticized for its conservative undertow and class-inflected paternalism."[2] The Progressive Era was a time of ongoing, and sometimes explosive, tension between social progressivism and social control.

New York holds a special place in the modernization of the United States during the Progressive Era. According to historian Angela Blake, "Between 1890 and 1924, New York became the nation's metropolis, the de facto capital of the United States."[3] New York City skyscrapers, the tallest buildings in the world at that time, symbolized the growth and commercial character of the city. Meanwhile, the influx of new immigrants coming into New York City reflected the progressive and conservative contradictions that roiled the nation. The rapid growth of capitalism in the early twentieth century was due, in part, to the expansion of immigration. John Bodnar's research has shown how "neither immigration nor capitalism as it emerged in the United States would have been possible without each other."[4] The birth of modern New York City, and of the United States as a whole, was fueled by the synergetic mix of immigration and corporatization.

New immigrants, while powering economic growth in different ways, struck fear in the minds of older American citizens. Guterl observes, "The idyllic Victorian past—a world of presumed pristine neatness and order—had been ruined by the scale and type of immigration."[5] Between 1880 and 1919, over twenty-three million immigrants came to the United States, and almost three-quarters of them arrived in New York. By 1910, immigrants comprised about 40 percent of the city's population.[6] In contrast to earlier waves of immigration, most of the new arrivals were from Southern and Eastern Europe, and so-called "native-born whites" and "Anglo-Saxons" viewed them as racially inferior and potentially catastrophic additions to the American population. Although native-born whites placed African Americans at the bottom of the racial hierarchy, they considered Italians, Russians, Hungarians, and other immigrant groups as not quite "white." Although they were white by law, many "old-stock" Americans questioned their morality and fitness for citizenship.[7]

Immigration reshaped the landscape of New York City's boundaries and communities. By 1900, New York City's Lower East Side—bounded by 14th Street, Broadway, the Brooklyn Bridge, and the East River—was the most densely populated place in the world and home to tight-knit Chinese, Jewish, Greek, and Italian groups. In 1910, over 1.25 million Jews from Eastern Europe lived on the Lower East Side.[8] In the early twentieth century, Harlem housed approximately seventeen thousand Russian Jews. Jewish organizations and benevolent societies played an important role in the city's social and economic life, but to speak of a single "Jewish community" in New York City is overly simplistic.[9]

Likewise, Italian immigrants gathered with others from the same province or village, and therefore settlements were internally divided based on the regional dialects and affiliations. Whereas the Yiddish press worked to bridge some interethnic divisions within the Jewish community, widespread illiteracy among Italians impeded a widening sense of community. The presence of Italian immigrants, however, represented a threat because of their supposed penchant for violence and criminality, especially those from Southern Italy. New York City was a locus for anxiety about Italians. In 1890, Italian immigrants made up about 5 percent of the city's population, but they were over 10 percent of the population by the 1910s.[10] Despite deep variations within New York City's immigrant groups, native-born whites regarded them as an unwashed mass that threatened to overturn the country's stability and morality.

During these same years, African Americans moved from southern to northern American cities, and the population of African Americans in New York City rose from over twenty-three thousand in 1890 to almost ninety-two thousand in 1910.[11] In the early 1900s, African Americans settled in Harlem and, by 1914, approximately fifty thousand were living in the neighborhood.[12] Whites responded to the changing racial makeup of the community with racial hostility. Organizations like the Anglo-Saxon Realty Corporation and the Harlem Property Owners' Improvement Corporation pressured white home owners not to sell their homes to African Americans, enforcing "restricted covenants" in a losing effort to keep Harlem "white."[13] Race relations in New York City sometimes resulted in mass violence and, in 1900, a race riot erupted the city.[14] The proximate cause of the riot was a white police officer who fought with a man named Arthur Harris after Harris accused the officer of mistreating his common-law wife. The woman was waiting for Harris on a street corner when the officer accused her of soliciting for prostitution. In early twentieth-century New York City, racism and racial tensions explosively combined with changing understandings of gender, sexuality, and public space.

The First Sexual Revolution

In the early twentieth century, norms of gender and sexuality underwent a dramatic shift on diverse fronts. Various social groups confronted and worked to overturn the nineteenth-century image of feminine submissiveness and inherent moral purity. Working-class women adopted new courtship practices that defied earlier norms of feminine propriety and blurred the boundaries between respectable and scandalous behavior. Gay men, lesbians, transgender persons, and other sexual minorities created their own social worlds in New York City's cafés and saloons. Gay men, in fact, were more visible and integrated into city life during the decade preceding World War I than they were during the decades immediately following World War II.[15] During the first two decades of the twentieth century, teenagers and young adults overhauled the standards of sexual conduct governing earlier generations, and they faced and fashioned a cultural landscape fundamentally different from the one experienced by their parents. Writing about the early years of this cultural shift, historian Kevin White noted that "young men and women gained the freedom to enjoy themselves as never before."[16] Historian Joanne Reitano stated, "Theaters, movie houses, restaurants, dance halls, and hotels spelled the demise of the Victorian restraint."[17] Historical research has added layers of complexity to the Victorian-to-modern story of American sexuality, and many have documented how Americans were never really "Victorian" in the way that the stereotype suggests.

As early as the 1970s, historians have cautioned against characterizing the Victorian era (approximately 1840–1900) as a time of sexual puritanism. For example, Kushner argues: "The assumption that most nineteenth-century Americans were puritanical about sex has led, in turn, to a second confusion: that the increased public discussion of sexual matters in the early twentieth century signaled a 'sexual revolution.'"[18] Victorians' proscriptions against pornography, masturbation, and nonmarital intimacy revealed a society obsessed with sex, not one that was sexually reticent. This was an essential part of Foucault's argument in *The History of Sexuality*.[19] More recently, Horowitz hopes that her research "will lay both the concept and the term [Victorian sexuality] to rest."[20] For Horowitz, abortion, prostitution, obscenity, and the emergence of men's "sporting culture" were flash points in nineteenth-century urban America that strain any characterization of a unanimous Victorian culture or an uncomplicated turn-of-the-century shift.

There is little doubt, however, that those living in the early years of the twentieth century, in small towns and in large cities, witnessed an upheaval in sexual manners and mores. The first sexual revolution popularized and institutionalized modern notions of gender and sexuality. To a great extent, the first sexual revolution was a consequence of large-scale industrialization and urbanization that refigured urban space and changed the economic basis of family life.[21] Americans had big families in the 1800s as an economic strategy, but the average family size plummeted over the course of the century. In 1800, a typical married couple had over seven children, and, in 1890, an average household had an average of four children.[22] Preindustrial labor was divided and managed within families, but the rise of the factory system undermined the place of the family as a singular economic unit. Raising many children no longer held economic advantage. Breakthroughs in science, medicine, and public health decreased infant mortality and the need for families to have many children to maintain economic solvency. The economic place of children in family life was forever altered. A sentimental understanding of children and domesticity took hold of the middle and upper classes. During industrialization, children became symbols of couples' romantic love instead of additional labor power.[23] Love and romance, once considered secondary (if at all) to the economic and social dimensions of marriage, became central. The idea of "companionate marriage," once controversial in the nineteenth century, was the mainstream by the early twentieth century.[24]

Changes in families corresponded with new employment opportunities for young adults. Young unmarried working-class women, including many immigrants or the daughters of immigrant parents, heavily populated the female labor force. The rapid growth of corporations and retail markets created sales and clerical positions. Women filled a rising demand for saleswomen, clerks, and stenographers, and many were hired into jobs that had been the exclusive domain of working-class men.[25] In 1890, there were 3.6 million women in the paid labor force, representing about 19 percent of the female population. By 1910, almost a quarter of the US female population worked outside the home. In Manhattan and Brooklyn, the total number of women in the workplace almost doubled between 1880 and 1900.[26] Income from the rising employment opportunities gave working-class women a growing public presence in New York City, and the arrival of mobile and uprooted populations of immigrants and wage-earning women generated innovative ideas about companionship, romance, marriage, dating, sex, and childrearing.[27]

Compared to those living in the nineteenth century, city dwellers in the first two decades of the twentieth century had greater time away from work and more money to spend. An expanding leisure culture allowed an unprecedented degree of intermingling among unmarried men and women. Moving picture shows, telephones, automobiles, amusement parks, and new dance crazes set the tone for an emerging ethos that celebrated sexual expression set free from the exigencies of childbirth and domesticity. Major American cities made enormous investments in entertainment and recreation, creating urban architecture to cradle new subcultures, sexual norms, practices, and identities.[28] New amusements such as movie theaters and dance halls gave young city dwellers opportunities to socialize and form attachments away from parents and guardians.[29] Movies captured the imaginations of thousands of New Yorkers. From 1900 to 1908 the number of motion picture theaters in New York City grew from fifty to five hundred, and twenty to forty thousand New Yorkers attended the theaters daily.[31] *The Outlook* observed in 1914, "There is no doubt that the motion-picture show is America's most popular form of recreation."[30]

Movies were a popular form of cheap entertainment in New York City, but dancing was extraordinarily attractive to young women. Historian Kathy Peiss observed, "Of all the amusements that bedazzled the single working woman, dancing proved to be her greatest passion."[32] In 1911, New York City had over five hundred registered dance halls, and it appeared to those living during the era that a "storm of dance madness has come over the young people of New York."[33] Civic activists portrayed dance halls as a moral threat because it placed young men and women in dangerous proximity. They criticized popular dance styles—and the accompanying ragtime music—as promoting immorality. New York reformer Julia Schoenfeld reported in 1914 that she "found that vulgar dancing exists everywhere, and the 'spiel,' a form of dancing requiring much twirling and twisting, and one that particularly causes sexual excitement, is popular in all."[34] "Spieling," where the male partner hugs and twirls his female partner across the dance floor, was a form of "tough dancing" popular among immigrants and the working class. Civic activists, anti-vice societies, and moral reform organizations viewed the spaces that catered to these intimate dance styles as dens of iniquity. In 1913, for example, a grand jury presented findings to Justice Edward Swann "condemning the turkey trot and kindred dances." Swann accepted the grand jury's presentment, noting that "Rome's downfall was due to the degenerate nature of its dances" and complaining that "even the moving pictures show these dances in their most exaggerated forms."[35]

The alleged threat of "tango pirates" loomed over the social dancing scene in New York City. In a gender inversion of the "gold digger" threat that would alarm Americans in the 1920s and 1930s, tango pirates were lower-class men who exploited the trust of, and lived off of the generosity of, rich women. New York newspapers described tango pirates as using cocaine to ensnare unsuspecting victims who patronized cafés. One New York district attorney described them as "ignorant, ill-born fellows who have acquired a mere veneer of good manners and small talk."[36] The fear of the tango was not unique to New York City. In 1914, at the height of the tango pirate scare, Massachusetts lawmakers considered outlawing the dance.[37]

Dancing as an entertainment spectacle also drew intense criticism. In the Dance of the Seven Veils, a woman adorned in gauzy fabric interprets a Biblical scene. The dancer uses her body to express sensuality as she removes her clothing little by little during the course of the routine. The dance was inspired by Oscar Wilde's play and Richard Strauss's opera describing the young woman who presented John the Baptist's head to Herod. The dance was supposed to be carnal and spiritual, seductive and classical. Salome dancers were a common feature of early twentieth-century vaudeville, circuses, and dime museums.[38] Despite its claims to respectability in reproducing a Bible story, the "Salome craze" that swept popular and high-brow theater from 1907 to 1908 drew criticism for its supposed promotion of lust and lasciviousness.[39] In 1908, a physician warned that the "intense, abnormal passion stimulated by the dancers must reach across the footlights and take hold of the nervous systems of hysterical women in the audience."[40] Salome dances were placed under observation by the New York City police and were, for a time, banned in New Jersey and Brooklyn.[41]

The transition from dancing as an act of degeneracy to dancing as a form of healthy exercise occurred in the early decades of the twentieth century. It is not an exaggeration to say that Irene and Vernon Castle, a husband-wife dancing team, were almost entirely responsible for the revived respectability of close partner dancing in the years before World War I.[42] The Castles acted as trendsetters by coopting and "taming" African American dance styles and making them fashionable among the middle and upper classes. They owned a New York City club that became, according to their biographer, "*the* hotspot for high society and tourists alike."[43] In their best-selling dance instruction book they compared dance favorably to other amusements, like movies: "Surely there cannot be as great moral danger in dancing as there is in sitting huddled close in the darkness of a sensational moving-picture show or in following with feverish interest the suggestive sex problem dramas."[44] Although the Castles defended partner dancing against its moral critics, they drew a sharp boundary between the refined steps that they taught and popular dances like the Turkey Trot, Grizzly Bear, and Bunny Hug. The Castles carved a space of respectability for modern dance, but the dances and the dance halls popular among working-class and immigrant communities remained morally suspect well past the 1920s.[45]

Hand in hand with movies and dancing, new housing opportunities encouraged women's independence and sexual autonomy. At the end of the nineteenth century, approximately half of the unmarried women in the city lived with private families.[46] In 1900, the vast majority of wage-earning women in New York were single and living outside the confines of parents and guardians.[47] During these years, boardinghouses and large commercial lodgings sprang up in major urban centers to give women some escape from familial constraints. Proponents of boardinghouses argued that they helped preserve female sexual purity by replicating the domesticating influences of the family dwelling, including their offerings of religious service, affordable lodging, and respectable leisure activities. The Young Women's Christian

Association (YWCA) and other charitable agencies envisioned themselves as recreating a protected domestic space within the maelstrom of city life.[48] They catered to rural women perceived as adrift in New York City, but they were less charitable to immigrants, racial minorities, and women who did not fit their profile of respectability.[49] The labor of immigrant women, however, worked to inadvertently protect the respectability of so-called native-born whites. Lynn Weiner notes, "Many of the homes barred domestic servants, laundry workers, black women, and factory operatives, reflecting their concern with the white native-born women dispossessed of their status by the need or desire to work. For the native-born women, the homes acted as a buffer between the urban environment and the domestic ideology. Although they worked for a living, they still lived 'at home,' and so their bodies, reputations, and status remained protected."[50]

"Furnished rooms" were another housing option for independent wage-earners in the city, but women who wanted to live in these accommodations often faced suspicions about their morals, and so landlords preferred to rent to men. Although the "furnished room districts" of major US cities offered wage-earning women independence and freedom, members of the middle and upper classes viewed them as notorious hotbeds of immorality for that very reason.[51] Like the distinction between the supposedly respectable dances taught by the Castles and the supposedly degenerate dancing found in popular dance halls, the distinction between acceptable and unacceptable housing for working women had more to do with class, race, and ethnicity than the inherent features of the room or building.

In this historical context, middle- and upper-class civic activists maintained older standards of sexual respectability, but working-class men and women in early twentieth-century New York did not view virginity as the definitive sign of moral worth and did not see premarital intercourse as akin to prostitution.[52] Moreover, many working-class women cultivated relationships with men where they traded sexual favors for gifts or an evening's entertainment. Although upper- and middle-class reformers saw little difference between prostitutes and so-called "charity girls," the practice of "treating" changed the working-class sexual economy. Historian Elizabeth Clement writes, "Treating emerged as an intermediate category, a line somewhere between the morally gray area between prostitution and the premarital intercourse that often occurred in courtship."[53] Working-class women refashioned the economics of courtship, and they challenged traditional codes of sexual morality within the constraints imposed by their class position and immigrant status.

Criminal Law and Sexual Counterrevolution

The early twentieth-century United States witnessed sexual revolution, but it also experienced state-sponsored sexual repression and moral reform. The sexual revolution encapsulates the tension between social control and social justice characteristic of the era. Criminal law enforcement counteracted the sexual revolution in two main ways: vulnerable populations were overexposed to the harshest elements of criminal law enforcement, and they were under-exposed to its justice-producing potential. Counter to the image of sexual revolution, historical accounts show how police and prosecutors enforced sex crime laws in ways that hurt the working class, women, gays, and racial and ethnic minorities. Progressive-Era courts and police were instruments of social control that enforced a version of white middle-class sexual morality on immigrants and workers.[54]

The criminal justice system overexposed racial and ethnic minorities, women, and men who departed from a white middle-class ideal to the most coercive aspects of the criminal justice system. Racist and anti-immigrant attitudes were entrenched in the upper leadership of the New York City police force. William McAdoo, who served as the New York City police commissioner from 1904 to 1905, said, "One of the most troublesome and dangerous characters with which the police have to deal is the Tenderloin type of negro," whom he described as violent gamblers who go "heavily armed."[55] In 1905, he formed a five-person "Italian Squad" designed to root out the influence of the Italian mafia, or what was called "the Black Hand."[56] McAdoo's successor, Theodore Bingham, greatly increased the size of the Italian Squad and claimed in 1908 that Italians committed at least 20 percent of all crime in New York City.[57] Bingham also asserted that Jews committed over half the crime in New York City, a comment for which he later apologized due to pressure from Jewish community leaders.[58] McAdoo and Bingham counted among the many native-born whites in New York's criminal justice system who conflated foreignness and criminality.

While law enforcement overexposed vulnerable groups to the coercive dimension of the criminal justice system—raids, arrests, and surveillance—it underexposed the same populations to the justice-enabling force of the law. Women, in particular, faced a series of barriers to justice. Women had a limited presence in New York's criminal justice system. Maude Miner became New York's first female probation officer in 1906.[59] In 1912, Isabella Goodwin was appointed as the first woman detective in New York City.[60] Jean Norris was the first woman appointed as magistrate judge in 1920.[61]

Women had made gains in the legal world, especially after World War I,[62] but men had overwhelming power in New York's criminal justice system, and women told their stories in court in front of male attorneys, an all-male jury, and a male judge.

Women also faced a series of challenges embedded in sex crime case law and its prevailing interpretations by judges and jurors. Rape, seduction, and forced prostitution prosecutions effectively required victims to fiercely resist their attackers. New York's rape law had explicit criteria that the victim resist her attacker, and the seduction law required complainants to be "of previous chaste character." Defense attorneys challenged women complainants about their prior sexual experiences and thereby assaulted their reputation, morality, and respectability when they sat in the witness chair. To embrace the image of the early twentieth-century as a time of sexual revolution ignores the ways in which the criminal justice system responded to and processed sex crime allegations.

The Enforcement of Sex Crime Laws

New Yorkers accused of sex crimes traveled through a complicated bureaucratic and political maze, beginning with police and ending with a possible prison sentence. New York City police conducted investigations that led to arrests, but most sex crime cases in the early twentieth century originated with a complaint made by a private citizen or member of a legal aid society. From there, police arrested the suspect or suspects, often in the presence of the victim and (if necessary) an interpreter.

Municipal police officers carried out the vast majority of arrest in New York City, but agents from preventative societies exercised lawful arrest power for specific problems and populations. For example, representatives from the Society for the Prevention of Cruelty to Children (SPCC) had police power in apprehending suspects accused of crimes against minors. The SPCC was one of a handful of important crime preventative societies in New York City, including the American Society for the Prevention of Cruelty to Animals (ASPCA), the Society for the Prevention of Crime (SPC), the City Vigilance League (CVL), the Committee of Fourteen, and the New Society for the Suppression of Vice. As historian Gilfoyle explains, "Preventative societies were major vehicles of power by which purity-minded New Yorkers redefined appropriate sexual behavior, and, most importantly, transformed sexual politics in New York."[63] Reform societies acted as enforcers of a white middle- and upper-class version of sexual and social respectability.

New York anti-crime societies had a vexed relationship with local police. Sometimes the two groups worked hand in hand, but, during times of municipal reform or anti–Tammany Hall activism, the crime societies regarded police corruption as part of the city's dysfunction. By 1900, Reverend Charles Parkhurst presided over the City Vigilance League, which took fierce aim at the Tammany Hall Democratic machine and a system of graft and corruption entrenched among police.[64] Parkhurst wrote, "People are even yet sometimes expressing surprise that I have so little admiration and respect for our police force! I believe that from top down, with some splendid exceptions, they are the dirtiest, crookedest, and ugliest lot of men ever combined in semimilitary array outside of Japan and Turkey."[65] In response to critics like Parkhurst, New York City cycled through waves of municipal police reform. The first major effort was the 1894 Lexow Committee, commissioned by New York senator Clarence Lexow and led by Reverend Parkhurst. The committee examined over six hundred witnesses and uncovered evidence of rampant police corruption, extortion, bribery, and brutal force. The instituted reforms aimed to make the criminal justice system less prone to political influence, but police brutality and political corruption persisted.[66]

After arrest, suspected criminals were held in detention rooms or "pens" until they could be arraigned in magistrate's courts. The magistrate's court, formerly known as the police court, played an important role in the New York criminal justice system. In 1911, New York Supreme Court justice Alfred Page described it as "the court of first instance for all grades of criminal offenses."[67] As the first face of justice from crimes ranging from speeding to homicide, magistrates saw a cross-section of New York life. A majority of the defendants, however, were poor immigrants. Given the disproportionate number of immigrants in the magistrate's court, observers viewed the courts as important vehicles of ethnic assimilation.[68] A former chief city magistrate described the court as "the greatest educational institution in the US."[69] Former New York City police chief Theodore Bingham declared that "it is in the police court and in the lower civil courts that the millions of ignorant foreigners gain their first and, for the most part, only impressions of our government and our boasted liberty."[70] In this way, the court system was a major, albeit coercive, force of Americanization. By 1920, there were thirty-one magistrate's courts in New York City processing about two hundred thousand arraignments a year.

Accused criminals had the right to produce witnesses on their behalf, but court reformers described the arraignment process as harsh and alienating. In 1912, Robert Ferrari, a private lawyer and criminology lecturer at New York University, described the typical scene: "The immigrant is at the prisoner's bar before the Police Court Justice. He is bewildered, lost. He has no friends, no one to aid him. He is not represented by counsel."[71] Although defendants could call witnesses in their defense, they were largely powerless. The magistrate's court processed so many cases, and such a variety of cases, that magistrates rarely had an opportunity to delve into the intricacies of any single circumstance.

The architecture of the typical magistrate's courthouse contributed to the psychological and physical estrangement experienced by so many accused criminals. Before court reforms in 1910, a wide space separated the defendant from the magistrate. The prisoner was often kept in the back of the court, unaware of the proceedings until the magistrate made a decision. Police and other witnesses were separated from the magistrate by a few inches, and the crime was discussed in low tones. William McAdoo, who served as New York City's chief magistrate from 1910 to 1930, said, "There was an air of privacy about the court."[72] The audience was separated from the bar by a ten-foot-tall wire screen. Policemen, lawyers, and court stenographers stood on a small platform in front of the judge's bench called a "bridge."[73] Defendants' alienation was reinforced by their physical separation from the court's decision-makers. The prisoner was placed in the back while the lawyers and magistrate discussed and negotiated his or her fate.

A magistrate's first task was to evaluate the seriousness of the charge facing the suspect. For minor offenses such as public drunkenness, a sanitary code violation, disorderly conduct, or violation of the Sabbath law, magistrates had complete power to try the case, determine guilt, and impose a sentence. For more serious crimes, magistrates assessed if there was enough evidence against the suspect to produce an indictment. The magistrate had the power to discharge the case if he judged the evidence as insufficient. In some instances, if a suspect faced a felony trial, the district attorney could override the magistrate and submit the indictment to the grand jury. In most instances, the magistrate had power (if there was enough evidence against the suspect) to prepare an indictment for either the grand jury of the Court of Special Sessions (for misdemeanors) or the grand jury for the Court of General Sessions (for felonies).

After a magistrate issued an indictment, a representative from the district attorney's office, typically an assistant district attorney (ADA), presented grand jurors with evidence of the defendant's crime. Grand juries did not render a judgment of guilt or innocence, but they evaluated whether or not the evidence presented in the indictment was sufficiently compelling to go before a jury. Twenty-three men served on the grand jury, and members were drawn from the same jury pool as regular jurors. Because their service could last over a month (with some serving for multiple years) jurors tended to be wealthy businessmen.[74] Therefore, an early stage of the criminal justice system was controlled by wealthy white men who, with precious few exceptions, had more resources and privileges than the accused prisoner.

In fact, the majority of arrested criminals in early twentieth-century New York City were immigrants. In 1910, the imprisonment rate for foreign-born immigrants was more than double the rate for native-born whites. Immigrants coped with the criminal justice system in multiple ways.[75] Legal aid societies provided support for immigrants who were poor and could not speak English, but other defendants secured legal counsel with the help of "runners" or "steerers." Runners and steerers were paid by trial attorneys to solicit plaintiffs in civil cases and defendants in criminal cases. In the realm of civil law, runners practiced "ambulance chasing."[76] They used police accident reports to locate victims at their home and then persuade them to use their services. In the realm of criminal law, runners loitered around jails and bail bond vendors looking for people who needed legal assistance. They promised freedom to those facing criminal charges as long as the suspects contacted the attorney listed on their referral cards and paid a requisite fee. Runners also told suspects that a long prison sentence awaited them if they failed to follow their advice. Runners often worked in tandem with bail bondsmen, corrupt police, and court reporters to gain clients.[77] After they secured legal representation, persons charged with felonies had their day in court at New York's Court of General Sessions.

The Court of General Sessions conducted felony trials in the Tweed Courthouse in lower Manhattan, about one-half mile from the current location of the World Trade Center Freedom Tower. When it closed in 1962, the Court of General Sessions was the oldest American legal institution. The court was created in 1683 and met four times a year. It was known as the Court of Quarterly Sessions in the nineteenth century and it had jurisdiction over civil and criminal matters. Records show one of the earliest cases held in the court was a man charged with burglary. He was found guilty, a "B" was branded on his forehead, and he was given eleven lashes.[78] Over the course of the nineteenth century, courts largely abandoned sentences of physical punishment in lieu of prison terms and, by the early twentieth century, had the common features of a modern US criminal trial.

Criminal trials in the early twentieth century resemble contemporary US trials in their basic structure. A Court of General Sessions trial began with jury selection and opening statements from the prosecutor and the defense. The prosecution had the privilege of calling the first witnesses. In the trials examined in this book, the first witness was often the alleged victim, or "complainant," and sometimes the attorneys and judge referred to a female complainant as a "prosecutrix." After the prosecutor questioned each individual (direct examination), the defense attorney offered their own line of questioning (cross-examination). After examining the complainant, prosecutors often called the arresting officer, witnesses, and relatives of the complainant. Defense attorneys typically began their case with the direct examination of the arresting officer or officers and finished their case with an examination of the accused. After the defense "rested" (finished their witness questioning), prosecutors had the opportunity for a rebuttal, allowing them to call new witnesses or recall old witnesses. Defense attorneys, in turn, had a chance to give a "sur-rebuttal" in response to the prosecutor. After the final individual left the witness stand, the prosecuting attorney and the defense attorney gave closing statements summarizing the important arguments for each respective side. Judges presiding over criminal trials read to jurors a series of instructions about the concept of reasonable doubt and the key factual issues to which they should ignore or pay attention.

Trials in the Court of General Sessions required twelve jurors. New York State mandated jurors to be English-speaking American males between the ages of twenty-one and seventy years old who owned at least $250 worth of property.[79] The commissioner of jurors maintained the pool of eligible men who could serve, and in 1902, the trial juror list had about six thousand names. Despite criteria designed to produce an educated jury pool, critics claimed that too many jurors were foreign-born or middle or lower middle class. Robert Ferrari asked, "Do you find any doctors upon the jury, any engineers, or any teachers, architects, contractors, reporters, editors? The people who serve on the jury are on a dead level of mental inferiority. As I have already said, they are small shop keepers, and clerks, with very little intelligence, very little education, very little learning, and very little experience of life."[80] A former juror complained, "The majority of our most intelligent citizens seldom serve," and juries were populated by "foreigners unacquainted with our language and ignorant natives."[81] Laments about the quality of New York jurors reflect anxieties about race and social class rampant among middle- and upper-class whites in the early twentieth century.

Jurors had a formal role as neutral fact-finders, but they also had understandings of crime, police, men, women, and sex that shaped how they interpreted the facts of a case. Often drawn from the same social milieu as the defendants and complainants, jurors represented their home and neighborhood as much as the state. A New York City prosecutor complained in 1908 that jurors "want to be not only jurors, but district attorney, counsel for the defendant, expert witness, and judge into the bargain."[82] Unlike contemporary juries, jurors in early twentieth-century courts routinely interrupted the flow of cross-examination to ask questions that were neither solicited by attorneys nor screened by judges. Vested with the responsibility of being neutral fact-finders, jurors frequently stepped out of their passive role to shape trial narratives.[83] Besides their verdicts, two types of evidence reveal jurors' legal consciousness: questions they asked witnesses during the trial and questions they asked the judge during their deliberations. These practices suggest jurors played a more active role in criminal trials than many scholars have assumed. Counter to the view of jurors as a passive audience that evaluates competing stories, jurors in the early twentieth century helped create the stories that witnesses and attorneys told to them.

Jurors often asked questions that seemed to alter prosecution or defense strategies and prompt judges to intervene and offer a different or more substantial explanation of the crime or the law. The legal sphere, as a broker of sexual respectability, was not just a place for the imposition of the law from above, but a place where judges, defendants, complainants, and jurors actively negotiated the terms and parameters of acceptable sex and sociality. Trial transcripts of alleged seducers, rapists, pimps, and sodomites reveal the dynamics of these negotiation processes.

Chapter 2

Date Rape and the Crime of Seduction

From 1830 to 1860, moral reform and anti-vice organizations campaigned for laws against "seduction." In the nineteenth century, the word "seduction" described situations where men leveraged economic resources for sexual gratification. The term carried an inherent ambiguity because the victims were complicit in their supposed downfall. These were acts of "seduction," not rape or abduction. The victims of seduction exercised free will, but the wealth, reputation, or rhetoric of the seducer skewed the decision making of the victim. Nineteenth-century reformers viewed seduction laws as necessary to protect working-class women from the exploitation of wealthy men.

New York's Female Moral Reform Society petitioned the state legislature for laws to punish seducers in the late 1830s.[1] In 1848, New York lawmakers passed the nation's first seduction law. Other states followed New York's lead, and, by the early twentieth century, thirty-five states had criminal seduction statutes.[2] Seduction laws criminalized sexual betrayal, making it a crime to have sex with a woman on a false promise of marriage. Lawmakers established seduction statutes alongside age of consent laws and laws against coercive prostitution as part of a broad effort to mitigate male sexual violence.

New York's seduction law defined "[s]eduction under promise or pretense of marriage" as a "person, who under promise of marriage, or by means of a fraudulent representation to her that he is married to her, seduces and has sexual intercourse with an unmarried female of previous chaste character."[3] The law punished seducers by imprisonment for "not more than five years, or by a fine of not more than one thousand dollars or both."[4] New York's law was similar to most states in that the crime of seduction rested on three essential elements: the suspect's promise of marriage preceding sexual intercourse, the complainant's unmarried status, and the complainant's prior chastity.[5]

The crime of seduction turned on whether the defendant promised to marry the complainant. In twelve states, including New York, lawmakers included a provision in their statutes that barred seduction prosecutions if the perpetrator agreed to marry the complainant.[6] In this way, seduction laws represented a legal means to restore the virtue and class status of unmarried women. In 1921, a University of Kansas law professor explained how the threat of prosecution might "give strength to weakening knees on the way to the marriage altar."[7] The law created a mechanism for women to restore their social respectability. As Lawrence Friedman explained, "If a (respectable) man had a 'right' to a woman with an 'unstained name,' it followed that a name-stain would be utterly devastating to any woman who hoped to occupy a respectable niche in society."[8] Seduction prosecutions were a mechanism to repair the family unit and to compel the man to marry. Pregnancy accelerated public pressure to marry because it was the only way to give the child legal recognition. Seduction prosecutions promoted marriage to restore a woman's honor and to give her child a good name.

The seduction trials in the Transcript Collection expose the dual social function of seduction laws: the encouragement of reputational repair and the prosecution of sexual coercion. These trials show the prosecutorial hurdles needed to sustain a seduction prosecution, particularly the implicit demand that complainants resist their attacker as a sign of nonconsent, and the explicit requirement that the complainant be of "previous chaste character."

Criminal Law and the Seduction Genre

Criminal seduction laws originated from the seduction genre in nineteenth-century popular culture. Seduction stories described men with wealth and status preying upon the economic insecurity of working-class women, having sex with them, and betraying them. Publications from the burgeoning purity movement such as *The Advocate of Moral Reform* and *The Friend of Virtue* routinely explored these themes.[9] Moral reformers used these stories as a cultural resource with which to make political claims, and the seduction narrative of the nineteenth century carried an explicit critique of class and gender inequality. Vicious practices from the upper classes were seen as the greatest threat because rich men could hide their immorality behind their wealth and refinement.[10] Reformers considered seduction a central cause of prostitution, which they believed ensured the victim's early death.

Seduction narratives were a popular feature of small newspapers called "penny presses."[11] The story *The Beautiful Victim*, originally published in 1862 by the *National Police Gazette*, is a good representation of the popular seduction genre.[12] *The Beautiful Victim* described how a working-class girl fell victim to the wiles and adulation of her employer and then found herself pregnant and abandoned. Although the story epitomizes the genre, the story would strike twenty-first-century readers as an account of rape, not seduction. Kirkpatrick's plight, however, demonstrates the nineteenth- and early twentieth-century conflation between rape and so-called seduction. As the rest of this chapter will make clear, the lines between rape and seduction were not clear-cut to people living in earlier eras, and incidents we now think of as "date rape" were considered "seduction" well into the twentieth century.

The Beautiful Victim chronicled the betrayal of seventeen-year-old Mary Kirkpatrick from New Jersey. Kirkpatrick epitomized the common victim of seduction narratives. Her heritage was of "English origin," and the Kirkpatrick family "sprung from a most respectable source."[13] Mary was described as having an "alabaster-like forehead" that gave her an "exceedingly youthful appearance."[14] *The Beautiful Victim* noted, "Her manners are lady-like, and her language as grammatical and carefully expressed as that of any young lady graduating from the best boarding schools."[15] Her beauty and refined comportment drew the lecherous attention of her boss, a local mill owner named Alfred Inglis.

Alfred Inglis had status and power, but his outward respectability belied his deceit and aggression. *The Beautiful Victim* described how "he flattered her and told her that his wife was too stale; he offered her money and told her that she could have money whenever she wanted."[16] Inglis commented on her pretty legs, gave her apples, and increased her weekly wages from $2.50 to $3.00. One day, ignoring her protests, he raped her on top of a table in the machinery room. He turned on the machinery to drown out the sound. She resisted "with all her might," but to no release.[17] Mary Kirkpatrick became pregnant, and Inglis offered to take her to New York City for an abortion. She strenuously objected and eventually gave birth in a lying-in hospital where the child died several days later.[18] After winning $1,800 in a civil suit against Inglis, her family pressed criminal charges against him. The prosecutor argued that Alfred seduced Mary with "his confectionaries, his papers, his apples, his extra pay, his flattering, his blandishments."[19] The jury deliberated for fifteen minutes before finding Inglis guilty of the relatively new crime of seduction.[20]

Nineteen-century moral reformers created and disseminated seduction narratives as part of a broad effort to raise public awareness of the age of consent, prostitution, and the dangers of unrestrained male sexuality.[21] Seduction was an entry point into wider discussions about the place of women in society, and the popularization of the seduction issue fueled the early women's movement a full decade before suffragists petitioned states for women's voting rights.[22] Activism against seduction took shape under a gender ideology that extolled women's innate virtue. The dominant Victorian ideology of femininity emphasized the inherent moral purity of women that stemmed from their sexual modesty and passivity. Historians have shown how proponents of feminine domesticity used a strategic discourse to advance political aims. Suffrage and temperance activists adopted a language of domesticity and separate spheres precisely because that was the best starting point for demanding more public roles for women. For instance, Frances Willard, guiding light of the Woman's Christian Temperance Union in the nineteenth century, masterfully deployed the rhetoric of "home protection," using women's position as the "natural" protectors of the home as a reason to give them economic and political power with which to best protect the domestic sphere.[23] According to historian Nancy Cott, "The belief that women lacked carnal motivation was the cornerstone of the argument for women's moral superiority, used to enhance women's status and widen their opportunities in the nineteenth century."[24] Although outwardly restrictive, this ideology of femininity allowed middle- and upper-class women to make a strong claim for political power in the name of "social housekeeping" or "home protection."[25] Women's supposed lack of sexual passion ensured domestic harmony, and white Victorians saw this as a foundation of national strength.

Finding it doubtful that white women would willingly engage in nonmarital or nonreproductive sex, moral organizations pressed for laws regulating sexuality with the assumption that men were natural predators and women were naturally docile. Yet the laws that they helped passed were used decades later to address situations largely unaccounted for in the archetypical nineteenth-century seduction narrative.

State legislatures passed criminal seduction laws in the 1840s, but the tort of seduction existed as common law since the colonial era, standing as one of the most widespread forms of civil litigation in the nineteenth century.[26] The tort of seduction permitted fathers to sue over their daughters' lost chastity and their subsequent inability to provide services for their family. Poor and working-class families brought the largest number of suits. Premarital sex had severe economic consequences for these families because it limited their access to the marriage market and took women away from their economic role in the family. The legal framework that allowed a father to recover money for the lost labor power of his daughter presupposed a master-servant relationship within the patriarchal household. A woman's sexual consent, therefore, was immaterial to successful seduction suits.[27] The campaign to establish seduction in the realm of criminal law marked an early feminist recognition of the public harm caused by sexual violence. Social activists reframed seduction from a problem of men exploiting the property of other men to a problem of men exploiting women.[28]

A series of precedent-establishing cases laid the groundwork for seduction as a criminal category. These cases sketched a category of sexual coercion with a relatively low burden of proof compared to the stringent requirements of rape law.[29] By midcentury, courts began to distinguish sharply between rape and seduction, viewing them as mutually exclusive crimes. In fact, given the higher standards of proof required for rape prosecutions and the law's collaborative relationship with male interests, men in the nineteenth century accused of seduction often pleaded to rape as a way to avoid seduction suits. Defendants used rape as an affirmative defense in seduction torts. If they could successfully prove that the harm to the complainant was the public crime of rape rather than the private wrong of seduction, they would be protected from having to pay exorbitant fees. Legal scholar Lea VanderVelde noted, "These defendants must have thought they had less to fear from pleading to the use of force than they did from a damage judgment for seduction. Repeated attempts to invoke this defense suggest that this was a conscious legal strategy rather than a mere error in pleading."[30]

The creation of criminal seduction laws dovetailed with other legal changes that restructured relations between men and women in the nineteenth century. The common law notion of coverture granted a husband full ownership of his wife's property, allowed him total control over her real estate, and vested him with the power to block any legal action taken by his wife without his permission. Mirroring a national trend, New York lawmakers and appellate decisions challenged the absolute rights of husbands over their wives.[31] For example, New York's 1848 Married Women's Property Act, passed the same year as the seduction statute, weakened coverture by granting women property rights. Also, in 1864, the New York Court of Appeals held that husbands had no legal remedy against those who helped their wives leave them. Here, the court articulated the idea that wives had rights apart from those bestowed to them within the marriage covenant.[32]

Seduction and Sexual Coercion

Stories of violence and coercion were an important part of testimony in early twentieth-century seduction trials. A number of seduction trials showed striking similarities between contemporary accounts of acquaintance rape and early twentieth-century accounts of "seduction." In several of the examined trials, victims' testimony revealed that, although they had an intimate relationship with the defendant, they did not consent to sex. In this way, seduction laws acted as a proxy for laws against acquaintance rape; the complainant's resistance to the act of intercourse signaled their "seduction" in the absence of legal categories that recognized these scenarios as rape. Eight of the fifteen seduction trials in the John Jay Trial Transcript Collection contained testimony about overt acts of physical sexual coercion. Seduction trials in New York City demonstrate a range of alleged sexual violence addressed by prosecutors, defense attorneys, judges, and juries.

In a 1910 case, a complainant testified that the defendant lifted up her dress and forced himself on her as she tried to fight back.[33] In the 1917 seduction trial of Edward Millinger, a twenty-six-year-old dressmaker named Fannie Salmanowitz testified that she "pleaded and begged" with Millinger to stop his advances before they had sex. In another case, eighteen-year-old Freda Smilowitz said in her pretrial statement that a man named Charles Weintraub encouraged her to get drunk and then he sexually assaulted her. She said, "He tried to get me into that house where he was living; and he pushed me into the hallway, and put his hand over my mouth so I could not scream."[34]

In *People v. Abraham Cohen*, New York's seduction law acted as a substitute for rape laws in a literal sense.[35] Seventeen-year-old Sarah Gross brought statutory rape charges against Albert Cohen after he had sex with her in November 1915. Cohen took her to the City Theater, and after he accompanied her back to her apartment she "begged him to go home," but he insisted that she take off her corset.[36] Gross filed statutory rape charges, but the police department could not legally establish her age because she was a recent Russian immigrant without the proper documentation. Instead, Gross filed seduction charges against Cohen, but he was later acquitted.[37]

Seduction Trials as Reputational Repair

Successful seduction prosecutions rested on proof of the seducers' promise of marriage. Prosecutors strove to show that the guarantee of future matrimony acted as the guiding motivation for victims to have sex with their seducers. The creators of seduction laws assumed that the promise of marriage acted as the force most likely to cause women to fall for the "employment of the seductive arts against them by the man."[38] Complainants in seduction trials repeatedly claimed that the promise of marriage had a powerful effect on their minds. Prosecutors took pains to show that not only did defendants promise to marry to victims, but the act of intercourse would not have taken place without the man's promise. Judges instructed juries that the complainant's thoughts of marriage and yearnings for domesticity were more important than the woman's feelings of romance or lust on behalf of the seduced. In a 1918 seduction trial, for example, the judge instructed the jury before their deliberations that they could find the defendant guilty only if "the prosecutrix yielded because of the promise of marriage, and not merely from a mutual desire or lustful reason."[39]

The 1905 trial *People v. Krakauer* shows how community involvement shaped the use of the seduction law to restore the respectability of the complainant and her associates. Arthur Train, a thirty-year-old assistant district attorney for New York, made his opening remarks to the jury. By all accounts, Train had a masterful command of storytelling conventions. As Arthur Train stood in front of the jury, he was already preparing for the next stage of his career as a writer. He had his first novel accepted for publication in 1905, the year of the Krakauer trial. By 1920, Arthur Train left the district attorney's office to embark on a prolific writing career.

Arthur Train was wary of female witnesses. In one of his nonfiction works he cautioned that women are led by emotion and are unreliable narrators. In most cases, no major miscarriages of justice occur because of this, but, Train warned, in circumstances involving women making sexual charges against men, jurors and judges needed to exercise "extreme caution."[40] His sexism and inherent skepticism of women led him to doubt the fundamental basis of the seduction law. He cited what he termed "an ordinary example" of a young woman from the East Side, a Polish or Russian Jew, who brings charges against a man she has been dating. He questioned the moral standing of laws that governed the conduct between young men and women. In describing what seems like a seduction prosecution, Train declares, "Her real motive is revenge upon her faithless fiancé. In nine cases out of ten the fellow is a cad, who has deliberately deserted her after getting her money, but it is doubtful whether any real crime is involved."[41] In his estimation, these cases "largely turn on the girl's physical attractiveness."[42]

In court, on February 15, 1905, Arthur Train made his best case for a young Hungarian Jew betrayed by a faithless fiancé. Train read New York's seduction law to the jury and described seduction as "a crime as old as the world."[43] He depicted nineteen-year-old Lillie Schlosser as a hardworking immigrant "who is a girl of peculiarly innocent mind."[44] Lillie Schlosser came to New York from Hungary after her parents died. Her brother emigrated from Hungary to the United States, worked in New Jersey, and sent her money to make the journey. The prosecutor described how, after arriving in New York City, she went to live with German immigrants, "two honest, worthy people by the name of Freedman" who "stood to her in the position of father and mother."[45] At the time of the trial, Lillie Schlosser had worked for five years in a cigar factory and helped Rosie Freedman with the housework at night.[46]

Lillie Schlosser's trouble began when she visited a dentist about a toothache. The dentist, Max Krakauer, became attracted to his patient, and he peppered her with questions about her family. Arthur Train stated that Krakauer "extracted from her not only her tooth but a great deal of information as to her circumstances in life."[47] After learning her brother was the only relative in the country, and that he lived out of town, Krakauer "seized the opportunity" and asked to call on her.[48] She declined, but he made a casual visit by the Freedmans' front stoop a few days later. Max Krakauer introduced himself to the couple and became a frequent visitor of their tenement. His interest in Lillie Schlosser grew, but so did the suspicions of the Freedmans. They wondered why someone of relatively high social status would show so much attention to a poor young woman. Rosie Freedman confronted Max Krakauer about her fears. She told asked him, "Do you know she is a poor girl? You are a doctor. What do you want to keep company with her for?"[49] Krakauer assured her he harbored an honorable attraction to Schlosser and that he intended to marry her. Arthur Train emphasized that the promise of marriage was the only condition under which the custodians of Lillie Schlosser would let her consort with Max Krakauer. Train declared, "having entered into this relationship of betrothed, which, in some countries is more important than the ceremonial of marriage itself—then and then only did the Freedmans permit Lillian Schlosser to go out with this defendant."[50] Max Krakauer announced his intention to marry Lillie Schlosser on Thanksgiving Day, 1903. Thereafter, the Freedmans hosted an engagement party and Max presented Lillie with an engagement ring.

The seduction started in Max Krakauer's dentist office where the couple initially met. Krakauer asked her to attend a dance, and he had her meet him at his office. While Lillie waited in the main room, Max stood in an interior room to adjust his attire. In the prosecutor's rendition of the events, Max Krakauer called out, "Lillian, come in and help me tie my tie." She entered the room and he put his arms around her, caressed her, reminded her they were engaged, and "asked her, in what language I know not, to allow him to enjoy her."[51] Schlosser was "horrified" at the idea, but Krakauer overcame her resistance: "He kept her there and cajoled her for some time but she refused repeatedly and persistently to allow him to have sexual intercourse with her."[52] His manipulative pleas gratified Lillian's "young girlish mind," which "finally persuaded her to allow him to have sexual intercourse with her in the hallway."[53] Afterward, Schlosser insisted that Krakauer take her home. On the way home, he "told her that his passion for her was so strong that if she did not consent to allow him to have sexual intercourse with her he would commit suicide, that he would go with other women and so forth and so forth."[54] Later that evening, Rosie Freedman found Lillie crying in the hallway and demanded that Krakauer leave.[55]

Weeks later, when it became apparent that Schlosser might be pregnant, Krakauer told Philip Freedman—Lillie Schlosser's guardian—that he had changed his mind about marrying Lillie. Krakauer said that she could not offer him enough money, and that he needed two hundred dollars. The prosecutor described Krakauer as greedy and manipulative and told jurors how he took money from her "on various pretexts."[56] Over time, Lillian Schlosser faced the truth that she was pregnant. According to the prosecutor, Max Krakauer revealed his utter lack of character when, upon learning the news, he convinced Schlosser to have an abortion.

If the jurors viewed the abortion narrative in the trial as incriminating, they likely blamed Krakauer and the doctor, not Lillie Schlosser. Abortion was an illegal, but common, practice in the early twentieth century. Although most abortions were among married women, and although women were asserting greater control over their reproductive futures, female victimization was the primary trope of early twentieth-century abortion narratives. Historian Leslie Reagan notes that "the image of the seduced and abandoned unmarried woman dominated turn-of-the-century newspapers and popular thinking."[57] Abortion was practiced by every racial, ethnic, and religious group.

Surveys of women in the 1920s estimated that 10 to 23 percent of women had abortions.[58] Women freely discussed methods for ending pregnancy and disseminated information about private physicians who performed abortions. Legally and socially, however, the abortion claims implicated the doctor and the male husband or lover. In New York State, a woman could be imprisoned for a year for taking "any medicine, drug, or substance," or if she "uses or submits to the use of any instrument or other means, with intent thereby to produce her own miscarriage."[59] Persons convicted of abortion faced up to four years in prison.[60] In *People v. Krakauer*, the prosecution raised details about the abortion to impugn the respectability of the defendant.

According to the complainant's testimony, Max Krakauer accompanied her to meet with a doctor. During direct examination, Schlosser described a horrific scene. Krakauer held her mouth and hands while the doctor operated on her with scissor-like instruments, causing her to become "full of blood."[61] Weeks later, Schlosser was sick and convinced that she was still pregnant. Krakauer insisted that Schlosser visit the doctor again and paid him a dollar for the procedure. This time, the doctor told her, "I will give you something for your stomach" but performed the same operation on her after giving her a drink that made her dizzy.[62] Schlosser testified that "at the second time he hurted [sic] me terrible. I was very sick."[63] The second abortion kept her ill for three weeks, prompting the doctor to make several house visits. Krakauer's attorney objected to the questioning about the abortion because it was "not binding upon the defendant," while the prosecutor countered by stating that "the conspiracy to commit abortion" spoke to the defendant's character and conduct.[64] The jury ultimately convicted Krakauer of seduction.

Lillie Schlosser faced severe stigma and hardship from her pregnancy and abandonment, and the seduction prosecution presented a way to restore her reputation. For her parents' generation living in Hungary, the relationship Lillie Schlosser had with Max Krakauer would be arranged, guided by a matchmaker, carefully supervised, and secured with a dowry. These practices began to wane in nineteenth-century Europe, and new Jewish immigrants to early twentieth-century New York City largely abandoned traditional courtship in favor of new norms of dating.[65] Young American Jewish women had some freedom to base marriage decisions on mutual attraction and love instead of family demands. Young Jewish women coming of age in the Progressive Era, however, faced traditional pressures to marry. Historian Melissa Klapper documents that the expectation of future marriage was "a near inevitability for Jewish women during this time period."[66] Community members assumed Jewish women would marry suitable Jewish men (in 1910, more than 98 percent of Jewish women married Jewish men).[67] The community used seduction prosecutions to support endogamy. In this context, landladies and guardians were the eyes and ears of the tenements, and these women were critical witnesses in seduction trials. Historian Elizabeth Clement notes that the respectability of the landlady was also at stake in seduction trials.[68] They occupied a difficult position where their reputations were reflected in the moral upkeep of their tenants. The trial of Max Krakauer called into question the morality of the defendant and complainant but also members of the community charged with maintaining marriage norms.

Seduction prosecutions promoted reputational repair for women accused of having sex outside of marriage. Seduction prosecutions offered a path to respectability for working- and middle-class women in the early twentieth century. In the 1918 trial *People v. Handsman*, for instance, a twenty-two-year-old sales clerk named Sadie Marsa claimed that she began a relationship with a twenty-three-year-old man named Morris Handsman. Handsman worked at a cigar store on the Lower East Side. Like most Jewish immigrant women in New York City, Marsa worked in textiles.[69] Morris Handsman said he "became acquainted with the complaining witness through flirtation" when she visited him in the cigar store. Marsa first met the defendant when she used the phone in the cigar store to call her parents to tell them that she was going to arrive late that particular evening. Marsa visited Handsman at work for about two months before he met her parents. They began dating, seeing each other twice a week, and, one evening, the intimacy between them was "getting overheated."[70]

Sadie Marsa told the grand jury, "He put his arms around me and kissed me passionately, and he has made love to me about fifteen or twenty minutes. Hugging me, holding me close to him, until he must have gotten that way."[71] Her phrase "made love" did not refer to sexual intercourse, as it would later in the century, but it referenced petting and caressing that were part of the seduction process. Morris Handsman allegedly told her, "No matter what happens, I am going to screw you, and I don't care what happens," as he picked up the front of her skirt.[72] After midnight, and after nearly two months of dating, Sadie Marsa and Morris Handsman had sex in the back of the cigar store.[73] Marsa said she was ashamed to return to face her parents, so Handsman took her to the Bridge Hotel on Bowery and Delancey. The couple knew that the hotel clerk would not let them stay without baggage, so Marsa wrapped her coat in paper and pretended it was a bundle of clothes. They signed in as Mr. and Mrs. Herman from Boston, retired to their room, and had sex three more times before falling asleep at two in the morning.[74]

In the weeks following her alleged seduction, Sadie Marsa feared that she was pregnant. She also feared that Morris Handsman had no interest in marrying her and would dodge his moral and legal responsibility to offer support for her and her future child. Marsa made an appointment with the justice of the peace and voiced her concerns to him. The justice comforted Marsa and told her that they needed to arrest Handsman to compel him to do the right thing, and so they created a plan for his capture. The justice instructed her to persuade Handsman to go to the Bridge Hotel again and, soon after they arrived in their room, to request he take her home. The police planned to grab Morris from the streets as the couple left the hotel. The first part of the plan went smoothly, and Morris Handsman and Sadie Marsa entered the hotel room under false names like they did once before. They were in a hotel room and, as planned, she asked him to take her home, "But something seemed to go through him" and he became suspicious.[75]

Sadie Marsa saw doubt creep across his face and, knowing that the sting operation was ruined, she told him that she would scream if he refused to take her home. He said, "Holler, I don't care whether you holler or not. I won't take you home."[76] At this point, she started to have misgivings about arresting Handsman. She said in her pretrial statement, "So, I thought and considered the matter over, and thinking that he was a fellow of a fine family and that I would tell him in a nice way. It would hurt my feelings to see him arrested." She told him about the plan and he started to cry and pull at his hair. Their conversation, as recounted by Marsa in her pretrial deposition, is as follows:

Handsman: What am I going to tell my folks?

Marsa: I looked the same way. Tell your folks that you met me, and cared for me, and married me. Not everybody knows each other's folks. Bigger people than you go off and get married, and don't say anything to their folks.

H: I like to go with you for another few months and give your ring. I will tell you what I'm going to do. I will take you to a doctor and have the doctor look you over and see if he can do anything for you. Then we will get married right away, if he can't do anything for you.

M: I won't go to any doctor. Furthermore it is criminal to do anything like that. Why should I suffer when you're the man that did it? I want to get chance with my life. You have done it. I think you should stand by me.

H: Well, I'm willing to pay expenses whatever it would cost. Go and see what the doctor says, if you have to go under an operation, or perhaps he can give you some pills.

M: I won't take anything of that kind. Do as you have said before. I want to go home.

H: All right, I will marry you. As long as you are going to be my wife, you can stay with me overnight again. You need not worry as long as you are going to be my wife.[77]

She said Handsman cried and said, "I will marry you tomorrow morning. We will take out a license." They then retired to bed together and had sex two or three times before falling asleep together.[78] Morris Handsman escaped the police, but he remained concerned that he could be in trouble, and he was resolved to not marry her.

The next day, Handsman went into a café next to his barber shop to talk to an Italian man. Marsa, suspicious about the meeting, heard the Italian assure Morris that he will secure him a lawyer to fight any legal problems caused by dumping Sadie. After the meeting, he acted cold toward Marsa and continued to insist that she see a doctor to have an abortion. Marsa called the justice of the peace again. This time, he confronted Handsman. Handsman told him that he changed his mind and, "Nobody can force me to marry when I don't want to marry. If it costs me all the money in the world, I am going to get out of it."[79] Morris ran from his store after the meeting, and Sadie called her mother. The two of them went to the first district magistrate's court and a detective was assigned to the case. Handsman was arrested a week later, and Sadie miscarried about three months after the arrest.

In some cases, seduction prosecutions worked as both a prod toward matrimony and as a proxy rape trial. For instance, the 1913 trial *People v. Isaac Cohen* recounted the ordeal of Sara Habif, a twenty-two-year-old Jewish woman who emigrated from Turkey to the United States in order to be with her intended husband, Isaac Cohen. Habif gave Cohen's parents a two-hundred-dollar dowry upon her arrival in November 1912. They moved into a small apartment with Cohen and his parents on East 102nd Street, and

Habif spent her days helping his mother with housework. Cohen asked her "many a time" to have intercourse with him, but she refused, claiming that she "wanted to be married just like every other girl."[80] Eventually, he made a formal promise to marry her and told a number of friends and acquaintances. Habif wrote to her parents in Turkey and told them of their wedding plans.

As their wedding day approached, Sara Habif said that Cohen repeatedly pressured her to have sex and told her that he would only marry her if she became pregnant. In early March 1913, he threatened to tear up their newly printed wedding invitations if she refused. She testified that when he grabbed her she "didn't wish to scream nor to defend" herself because his parents sat in the adjoining room.[81] She claimed, "He took hold of me and I could not move, although I cried some, and felt very much pain."[82] Her deposition notes that she "did consent (under great pressure and strain) to have said Isaac Cohen have sexual intercourse with her."[83] Habif discovered she was pregnant in June.

Sara Habif and Isaac Cohen's community had a common agreement about what constituted seduction, as well as a shared understanding of the role of law in enforcing marriage norms. Mrs. Jessurun, the landlady, said in her statement that she knew Sara's brother and had received a letter from him discussing his sister's engagement. Jessurun spoke to Isaac about it, and he assured her that the wedding would take place "pretty soon" and that they intended to print invitation cards. She recalled their conversation:

"Why have you treated this girl this way?" Jessurun asked.
"I didn't send her away," he said.

"Why don't you get married to this girl?"

"She told me she was not decent."

"Why so? How do you know that this girl is not decent; you have no proofs."

"Yes, I have my proofs."

"That is nonsense; you will have to get married to that young lady; there is a court here and there are so many people to look out for this girl."

"You are not the Judge; you have nothing to do with it; I can't marry the girl."[84]

Marriage agreements were public actions that had community consequences. Jessurun's comment that "there is a court here and there are so many people to look out for this girl" invoked both the power of the community and the power of law in compelling the marriage, and Cohen's reply underscored the limits of Jessurun's authority. The community members lacked the power of the judge and jury in the courtroom, but they exercised lateral power by using sex laws for ends not intended by the creators or enforcers of the law. Legal institutions functioned as agents of social control in early twentieth-century working-class communities, but, in this instance, the community discussed and negotiated how to use the law to protect the interests of Sara Habif, her reputation in the community, and the social standing of her child. The law—its agents and institutions—is exercised in webs of power relations that are neither entirely top-down (the courts and police impose order on the working class) nor bottom-up (the working class use the police and courts as instruments).

Sara Habif and Isaac Cohen also understood the law and the types of evidence required to prove (in a legal sense) sexual connection. After intercourse, Sara Habif cleaned herself with a handkerchief and kept the bloodstained cloth as proof that Cohen took her virginity. Isaac Cohen somehow discovered that she possessed the bloody cloth and he flew into a rage. He screamed at her and, according to Sara Habif, threatened her with a revolver. Cohen forced her to write a note that said that the stains "were caused by my monthlies, and were put there on June 23rd. I did this because of fear of my mother."[85] The note and the circumstances surrounding it were used by both the prosecution and the defense. Cohen's attorney entered Habif's note as a defense exhibit to prove that Sara Habif was not a virgin. The prosecuting attorney questioned Habif about the revolver presumably to expose Cohen's violent tendencies and to defuse the influence of the note on the jurors. Before the jury had a chance to discuss the conflicting testimony, the judge instructed the jury to acquit the defendant due to a lack of corroborating evidence.

The trials of Max Krakauer, Morris Handsman, and Isaac Cohen revolved around conflicting claims about intimacy and personal promises, but the courtroom battles illuminated large-scale changes in Progressive-Era New York City. Lillie Schlosser and Sara Habif were working-class immigrants who did not speak English. Sadie Marsa had no high school education and modest future prospects. The seduction trials represented a path to repair their reputation by casting a bright light on the bad behavior of their dating partners. The trials functioned as community social control in a context where traditional standards of matchmaking and supervised courtship were in decline.

In the Progressive Era, the physical and psychological harms of sexual violence and sexual betrayal were compounded by the reputational loss or "name-stain" incurred by premarital sex. Seduction prosecutions allowed New York City ethnic communities to maintain traditional marriage standards, rehabilitate the respectability of the aggrieved woman, and police sexual violence. Seduction trials were shaped by community expectations, and witnesses often showed keen awareness of the relevant law and the evidence needed to prove that a crime of seduction had occurred. Seduction prosecutions helped women's economic and social security by protecting them from violence and betrayal, but these progressive impulses were kept in check by two popular defenses in seduction prosecutions. Defendants and their attorneys argued that the complainants consented to sex and that they were unchaste. To prove that a complainant consented to sex, a defense attorney elicited testimony about the woman's lack of physical resistance to the alleged seducer's advances. To prove that a complainant was unchaste, a defense attorney drew forth testimony about the complainant's prior sexual experience. Both defense strategies deployed language that invoked older norms of female passionlessness and inherent purity.

The "Resistance Test" in Criminal Seduction Trials

Seduction prosecutions suggest how, absent a textual prerequisite of victims' resistance, cultural conceptions of proper femininity effectively placed a "resistance test" on complainants. New York's seduction law did not carry an explicit requirement that the victim resist her attacker, but attorneys questioned victims about their physical struggles with defendants to evaluate their consent. The resistance test was used in a variety of circumstances.

People v. Handsman, the case about the cigar store clerk who seduced Sadie Marsa, illustrates the centrality of the resistance test in seduction trials. In *Handsman*, Marsa testified that she became pregnant, initiated an aborted sting operation, and had Handsman arrested after he refused to marry her. Joseph Weber, Morris Handsman's attorney, questioned Marsa about the details of the crime during cross-examination. Weber used a question format that limited the types of responses Sadie Marsa could use. Handsman's defense attorney countered Marsa's story with a pointed linguistic strategy:

> *Defense attorney Michael Driscoll*: You let him have sexual intercourse with you?

> *Complainant Sadie Marsa*: I resisted at first; I didn't want it. He said, "What do you care? I am going to marry you just the same." I loved that man dearly.

> *Q*: You didn't fight, did you?

> *A*: Yes, I did fight, pushed him away and everything.

> *Q*: Did you scratch?

> *A*: What do you mean, did I scratch? Do you think I am a cat?

> *Q*: Did you try to force him away?

> *A*: Yes, I tried to get away, and he said, "no, I am going to have it; I feel that way, and I am going to have it."[86]

The defense attorney used a question format that constrained and simplified the complainant's response. The attorney's second question is what practitioners of conversation analysis call a "tag question" (questions demanding a yes or no response) instead of open-ended "Wh" questions. Tag questions contain the scope of the victim's answer.[87] Wh questions—such as "What was going through your mind while you were being seduced?"—permit the witness to provide context and explanation. With their either/or logic, tag questions restrict the respondent's answer to a yes/no response. Attorneys' use of a closed question format to maintain control over cross-examination is a common oratorical move, but its use in seduction trials is particularly relevant. Tag questions foreclose a resolution of the perceived ambiguities of criminal seduction and acquaintance rape; she loved him, but he raped her; he forced her to have intercourse, but there was no great physical struggle. The either/or logic of tag questions allows defense attorneys to deny sexual violence occurring on a continuum between extreme and nonexistent.[88]

Sadie Marsa's cross-examination worked to establish the criteria by which the jury should judge her resistance (fighting, scratching, or using force). The defense attorney asked about the circumstances of her resistance to show that her failure to force him away signified her consent. For her part, Marsa broke from the expectations of feminine decorum and talked back to the attorney. Marsa's question—"Do you think I am a cat?"—pointed to a double bind imposed by the resistance test. Women were deemed as consenting to sex if they did not exhibit extraordinary resistance against it, yet fierce opposition (scratching like a cat) violated norms of feminine passivity.[89]

Sadie Marsa knew how to use the law. Despite her relative lack of social power, she sought help from the justice of the peace and city police to protect her respectability and possibly compel Handsman to marry her. But Marsa was constrained by the defense tactic that required seduction victims to fiercely resist their attackers. Handsman and his attorney were also familiar with the tacit requirements of successful seduction prosecutions, and they subsequently questioned her about fighting Handsman in order to discount her story of seduction and duplicity.

The transcript of *People v. Bogden* shows how defense attorneys characterized a woman's lack of resistance as signifying her consent.[90] Julia Witowski worked as a domestic servant in New York City after arriving in the United States in 1906 from Poland. Sometime in July 1909, she began dating a man named John Bogden and, after a few months, they discussed the prospect of marriage. After returning from a ball late at night, they had sex in her bedroom. Bogden's defense attorney questioned Witowski's willingness to sleep with his client:

Defense attorney: Did you repel him, throw him off, or what, what did you do?

Witowski: Yes, sir, I have thrown him off—well, I could not.

Q: Did you pick the dress up yourself or did he do it?

A: He did it.

Q: Did you let him do that, did you?

A: No, sir.

Q: You did not?

A: No, sir.

Q: Fighting around with him—answer my question now, please.

A: I did not permit him to do so but he swore he would marry me and he said he was excited.

Q: Who was excited?

A: He was.

Q: Did you know what he intended to do to you?

A: Yes sir, I knew.[91]

Against Witowski's assertions that she physically could not ward off Bogden's advances, the defense attorney insinuated that she consented to having sex because she knew his intentions and did not mount a fight against it. In the preceding segment, the defense attorney challenged Witowski's denial that she consented to intercourse with the defendant. After she rebuffs his yes-or-no question (*Q*: "Did you let him do that, did you?" *A*: "No, sir."), he pressed her on the point once more. His statement, "Fighting around with him—answer my question now, please," conferred agency to the victim. He did not fight against her; rather, she fought with him. Likewise, the attorney's clarifying question ("Who was excited?") paired with his follow-up question ("Did you know what he intended to do to you?") suggested to the jury that she, too, was sexually excited by the circumstances. This string of questions attempted to create an image of the couple as sexual equals engaging in playful intimacy.

In another trial, *People v. Sochinsky*, witnesses described how a nine-teen-year-old Polish immigrant named Sophie Gregorwich met John Sochinsky, a twenty-one-year-old bartender, at the wedding of a mutual friend.[92] Gregorwich worked as a servant since immigrating to New York City in 1910. Thereafter, he visited her every second week at Gregorwich's sister's house in Brooklyn, and he proposed to her in March 1914. Months later, on New Year's Day, he had sex with her in the tenement house where she lived. Gregorwich pressed seduction charges against Sochinsky after he refused to marry her.

Gregorwich's testimony indicated that Sochinsky raped her. She stated that Sochinsky fought with her, threw her down on the bed, and implored her to keep quiet. Using a strategic set of questions, Sochinsky's defense attorney interrogated Gregorwich about her lack of resistance against her attacker:

Q: Did he pull your clothes up or did you push them up yourself?

A: He did.

Q: Did you fight with him or consent?

A: Yes sir; I told him that I am a decent girl, that I didn't have anything to do with a man in the world, and I don't see why he should do that to me.

Q: But did you consent?

A: No, sir; I did not; I did not.

Q: Did he fight with you?

A: Yes sir; he threw me down on the bed.

Q: Did you scream out so that anybody could hear you?

A: Yes, sir; he told me to keep quiet, don't be hollering.[93]

In this exchange, the defense attorney attempted to downplay the assault by establishing a sharp dichotomy between consent and coercion. The defense attorney's question "Did you fight with him or consent?" implied that physical resistance stood as the only way to signal nonconsent. When Gregorwich tried to complicate the distinction between fighting back and consent, the attorney persisted in his interrogation ("But did you consent?"). The defense attorney's follow-up questions ("Did he fight with you?"; "Did you scream out . . . ?") posited an unbreakable link between sexual coercion and physical violence, suggesting that the former cannot occur without the latter. Police arrested Sochinsky three months after the initial assault occurred, and after deliberating for fifteen minutes, the jury found him guilty of seduction.

The defense attorney for John Nicholas also used the resistance test to measure the complainant's sexual consent. John Nicholas first arrived in the United States in 1904 when he was twenty-three years old. After a brief stay, he spent five years in Greece and then returned to New York City in 1910 to work as a florist. Katina Contogianni was a thirty-five-year-old when she met Nicholas and his wife through a mutual friend. Contogianni, also a recent Greek immigrant, found friendly company with the Nicholases and frequently visited their residence.[94] Nicholas's wife was pregnant, became extremely ill, and died on December 17, 1913. At the time of her death, Nicholas had already developed an attraction to Contogianni. Various witnesses testified that Nicholas initiated a sexual relationship with Contogianni shortly after his wife's death, and many suggested that the two were having an affair in the weeks before she died. He proposed to Contogianni on Christmas day, about a week after his wife died. He was going to marry her, he said, but needed a forty-day mourning period following Greek custom.

The prosecutor called Katina Contogianni as the first witness, and she told her story through a court-appointed interpreter. Contogianni arrived in New York in August 1913 after a nineteen-day voyage from Greece. She met John Nicholas about ten days after her she landed in the United States. The alleged seduction occurred about two weeks after the death of Nicholas's wife. One evening, he invited Contogianni to his apartment. John Nicholas moved across the room and sat next to her. He initiated an emotional conversation with Katina and restated his love for her. He reasoned that she was "already his wife" and begged her to sleep with him.[95] She said, "I was crying and he said, 'Don't cry, the day is nearing when you will be my wife.'"[96] On cross-examination, the attorney asked, "Did you cry loud?," and she replied, "I cried and I shouted."[97] The follow-up question for Katina Contogianni revealed the contested meaning of "consent" in seduction trials:

Defense attorney: [Y]ou knew that you were doing was wrong at the time that you say you had intercourse with him on the 10th of January?

Contogianni: I certainly did.

Q: Did you walk to the bedroom with him or did he drag you?

A: He dragged me.

Q: Do you know what he wanted?

A: Well, he told me. He said, "We might just as well do it now or later; it makes no difference."

Q: And did you consent?

A: I did.

Q: Then why did he drag you, if you consented? [objection—sustained].[98]

The attorney raised the contradiction that she consented to sex, yet Nicholas had to drag her to the bedroom. The series of questions imposed the resistance test, but the scenario she described in the preceding dialogue would not persuade a jury in the early twentieth century of a rape charge. Rape trials in early twentieth-century New York City typically involved extreme violence, multiple attackers, and testimony about the victim's unconsciousness. However, the idea that Contogianni somehow consented and yet was dragged to the bedroom was consistent with a popular understanding of seduction.

Like other seduction trials, the landlady's testimony proved important. Catherine Lantry, Katina Contogianni's landlady, testified for the prosecution. She said that she confronted the defendant and asked, "'How dare you bring that girl from my house, and destroy her?' He said, 'Why, I don't know what you're talking about, madam.'"[99] Their discussion grew heated, and Lantry intimated that she could have him deported. She told him, "'Well, I don't see how you are going to get out of it. I think there is an emigration law that punished the likes of you,' and he said 'Oh, I can get ten Greeks to swear she is a bad woman,' and I said 'You can get ten Greeks to perjury themselves.'"[100] Katina Contogianni, John Nicholas, and Catherine Lantry knew how to use the law for their own purposes. They showed awareness of the criminal court system and the standards of proper testimony. Like the *Krakauer* and *Handsman* cases, the prosecution of John Nicholas showed the intracommunity exercise of legal power. The landlady threatened Nicholas with legal action, but Nicholas's defense could invoke community as well and question Katina Contogianni's alleged lack of resistance in the sex act.

The extent to which the complainant resisted her attacker was a pivotal issue in the 1919 case *People v. Brennan*.[101] Irene Grork testified that she began dating a man named Peter Brennan, and that he proposed to her three months after their first meeting. Grork, a twenty-year-old department store salesperson, claimed that Brennan pressured her to have sex after they had returned from a burlesque show. Irene Grork said on direct examination: "We were sitting in the front room, and he was sitting on the arm of my chair, and he embraced me, hugged me and kissed me, then he asked me if I wouldn't give in to him, if I wouldn't give him what he wanted, and I told him no, and he said 'why?' and I said 'just simply no,' and he said he didn't see no cause for me to refuse him."[102] Brennan's defense attorney asked Grork a series of questions designed to reveal her sexual consent:

Defense attorney: And then as you were going in to get a drink, then he grabbed you?

Irene Grork: Yes sir.

Q: And what did you do when he grabbed you?

A: I couldn't do anything. He grabbed me and threw me in on the bed.

Q: Did you do anything?

A: No.

Q: Did he strike you?

A: No.

Q: Did he put his hand over your mouth?

A: No.

Q: Well, was there a struggle?

A: No.

Q: What?

A: No.

Q: He pulled you onto the bed, and you laid right there?

A: Yes, sir.

Q: When he pulled you on the bed, did you lay right there without offering any resistance?

A: Yes.[103]

The attorney's questioning implied that, absent of a physical struggle, Grork gave herself to Brennan on her own volition. The defense attorney asked a series of questions in order to assess Grork's willingness to have sex with Brennan. The yes/no answers demanded by his question format led Grork to deny several times that Brennan used force against her. The defense attorney used a technique legal scholar Gregory Matoesian calls "detailing to death," whereby an attorney asks a string of questions about a single event in order to compel jurors to focus on putatively odd or inconsistent testimony.[104] In the *Brennan* case, the defense attorney's repetitious questions forced Grork to repeatedly negate and deny that different forms of assault took place.

Grork discovered that she was pregnant and, as she described during the trial, "he said he would go to this druggist and see what he could do."[105] Delia Grork, Irene's mother, testified in direct examination:

Assistant district attorney: Did Brennan say anything to you at the time about the condition of Irene?

Delia Grork: Yes sir.

Q: What did he say?

A: He told me he took her to a doctor to have—to do away with the baby, so it wouldn't be born, because they didn't want me to know about it, and he gave so much money to the doctor to operate on Irene, and Irene didn't go back to the doctor the next day, when she should have gone back, with the arrangements that he made with this doctor.[106]

These questions impose male-centered criteria on what counted as coercion by making a contradiction between a broadly defined category of consent and a narrowly defined category of force.

Prosecutors elicited testimony about the complainant's physical struggles with the perpetrator, and prosecutors stressed that some mixture of trust and coercion, instead of lust and free will, guided the victim's behavior. In turn, defense attorneys focused on the sequence of behaviors immediately leading up to the act of intercourse in order to highlight the complicity of the victim in her alleged seduction. Absent any evidence of struggle, defense attorneys insinuated that the victims willingly had sex with their seducers. Defense attorneys asserted a binary conception of consent; either the victim fully agreed to have intercourse, or she steadfastly refused. By framing consent and refusal as a dichotomized choice, defense attorneys obscured the role of male privilege and power in shaping this decision making. The seduction narratives solicited by defense attorneys masked the context of seduction, both the larger dynamic of gender inequality and the sexual circumstances wherein inequality becomes visible.

Proving Chastity in the Courtroom

Seduction laws were designed to protect unmarried women, but this protection was tempered by the unwritten requirement that victims of seduction resist their seducers. Perhaps the largest barrier to redressing gender inequality through seduction prosecutions was the condition of prior chastity required of the victim. In first degree rape trials, an uncodified chastity requirement hampered prosecutors because juries, judges, and legal scholars read victims' prior sexual experience as signifying consent.[107] In seduction prosecutions, the chastity requirement explicitly determined whom the law protected. Under the nineteenth-century seduction tort, the presumed proprietary right of the father over his daughter meant that the daughter's lost chastity amounted to the father's lost labor. This understanding of seduction did not require the courts to assess the character of the seduced victim because it—like her consent—was legally irrelevant.[108] As seduction moved into the realm of criminal law, legal adversaries argued over its scope.

New York was one of eighteen states that required the seduced woman to be of "previous chaste character." Other states limited prosecutions to cases where the woman was "virtuous" or "of good repute," while others argued that chastity was a moral condition reflected in one's virtuous reputation.[109] New York case law reflected the ambiguity of the "chaste character" criterion. Some claimed that chastity was a physical fact, *virgo intacta*, ruined by penetrative sex and a ruptured hymen. Other decisions held that New York's seduction law applied to widows and divorced women. A judge in a 1912 case reasoned that a narrow, physical, reading of "chaste character" precludes rape victims from receiving legal protection.[110]

New York City attorneys heatedly debated the meaning of chastity in seduction trials. Judges tried to introduce clarity by offering a stable definition of "chaste," but these efforts had mixed results. For example, the judge in a 1918 case explained to the jury, "The term 'chaste character' does not mean reputation for chastity, but means actual personal virtue as a moral and physical fact, and The People must affirmatively prove such reputation beyond reasonable doubt."[111] The instructions highlight the ambiguities of the "chaste character" clause. Chastity was, at once, a physical, moral, and reputational status.

Consistent with the definition of physical chastity, prosecutors solicited statements from their complainants early in direct examination to show that the act of intercourse with the defendant was their first. Testimony about blood played a large role in New York City seduction trials. Prosecutors tried to establish that the act of intercourse caused the victim to bleed, indicating their prior virginity.[112] In three of the fifteen trials, prosecutors sought doctors' testimony that their physical examination of the complaining witnesses revealed that the defendant and plaintiff had been sexually intimate.[113] In these trials, the medical testimony was challenged because doctors could not establish that the defendant was responsible for rupturing the victim's hymen, nor could they ascertain the date when the alleged intercourse occurred.

On the other side of the courtroom, defense attorneys argued for a higher standard of chastity. In *People v. Handsman*, the trial of cigar store worker, Sadie Marsa said she resisted at first, but Handsman assured her that he was going to marry her. Morris Handsman's defense attorney presented a completely different picture of Sadie Marsa. Handsman's defense attorney portrayed Sadie Marsa as hungry for sexual gratification. During the trial, a police officer recalled a conversation he had with the complaining witness Sadie Marsa.[114] Marsa reportedly told him that while spending time with Morris Handsman in a hotel room, she was so overcome with passion that she started masturbating. When the prosecutor objected, Handsman's attorney pleaded with the judge: "The law provides that [*sic*] a woman of previous chaste character. That means that she has got to be chaste in body as well as in mind, and the Court of Appeals said she must be free from

any taint. That is the kind of girls [*sic*] that gets protection."[115] The suggestion that Marsa was sexually passionate and excited, coupled with details
about her hotel room trysts with Handsman and her defiant attitude on
the witness stand, likely weakened the prosecutor's case in the eyes of the
jury. They found Handsman not guilty.

In *People v. Nicholas*, the trial of the Greek florist, Nicholas's defense
attorney assailed her morality. Nicholas's cook, Basilica Theophanes, testified that she saw Katina Contogianni wearing a negligee in bed with
the defendant. Theophanes testified that, while working as Nicholas's cook,
she witnessed Nicholas and Contogianni in bed together while Nicholas's
wife lay sick in the adjacent room. She castigated Katina Contogianni
for her behavior but said nothing to Nicholas or to his dying wife. The
defense attorney used Theophanes's testimony to suggest the immoral and
unchaste behavior of Contogianni, yet the prosecution's cross-examination
of Theophanes questioned Nicholas's morality and respectability:

> *Defense attorney*: You testified that you chided Katina about
> misbehaving herself with the defendant, because the defendant's
> wife was sick, is that right?
>
> *Theophanes*: I told her that she ought to be ashamed of herself
> to do that.
>
> *Q*: And did you tell the defendant that he ought to be ashamed
> of himself for committing adultery?
>
> *A*: I didn't think it was my place to talk to him.
>
> *Q*: You didn't think it was your place to talk to the defendant, but
> you did think it was your place to talk to the girl; is that right?
>
> *A*: I really couldn't because he was paying me and I didn't feel
> warranted in talking to him.[116]

Theophanes's statement highlights the sexual double standard that allowed
Nicholas to escape unscathed from his affair while Contogianni bore the
brunt of criticism. Her testimony also points to the gendered nature of economic inequality; her economic vulnerability prevented her from confronting
her employer, thus perpetuating the double standard.

In challenging the previous chaste character of the victim, defense attorneys often tried to despoil her reputation with various character witnesses. This was the favored strategy in *People v. Brennan*. In this case, the prosecutor argued that Peter Brennan took Irene Grork to a burlesque show, and then, when they returned to her rooming house, he promised to marry her and the couple had sex based on that promise. Grork discovered that she was pregnant and Peter Brennan pressured her to have an abortion. At that point, Grork worked with the police to have him arrested for seduction.

Peter Brennan's defense attorney called several witnesses who testified that Irene Grork and her friend Helen Spaulding spent time with men in an inexpensive rooming house, or "furnished room." The fact that Grork spent time in a furnished room might have indicated to the jury that she was immoral. The furnished room districts gave working-class women independence, yet these spaces drew suspicion for the same reason.[117] Other testimony challenged Grork's virtue. Grork's former coworkers testified that Grork and Spalding took a hermaphrodite up to Spalding's room, restrained him, pulled down his pants, and spanked him.[118] Also, a woman that worked with Grork testified:

> [Grork] told me that life wasn't long, that she didn't care what she had to do for a good time, she was going to enjoy life while she had it. Then her and Helen Spalding—Helen Spalding lived in a furnished room, and she said the lady was very nice, that Helen stayed with, that she didn't care what time or what fellows she took up to her house, and they used to have fellows up there and had a good time.[119]

The judge in this case told the jury before their deliberation, "A woman cannot be said to be seduced at the time of the alleged seduction if she was then leading a lewd and lascivious life."[120] Although accounts of her sexual expressiveness might have been a point of contention in the jury room—they deliberated for over an hour—the jury eventually found Brennan guilty of seduction.

The trial of Harry Rosenberg provides another vivid example of how defense attorneys used negative character evidence to attack the chastity of the complainants. Rosenberg met a twenty-one-year-old dressmaker named Sadie Cohen in February 1900 and promised to marry her four months later. Sadie Cohen testified that they exchanged gifts and love letters during their courtship. Rosenberg was Cohen's date for her sister's wedding.

Perhaps caught up in the romantic atmosphere of the wedding, Rosenberg declared his everlasting love to Sadie Cohen, and he voiced his matrimonial intentions in front of her parents and other family. Sometime in July, they had sex in her parents' house where she lived.

In a pretrial statement she made at the city magistrate's court, Cohen said that Rosenberg pressured her to have sex: "I still declined to consent, but he said I didn't trust my intended husband. I thereupon yielded and Harry Rosenberg took my virginity and maidenly purity."[121] On the witness stand she said, "I refused and finally after his persuasion I yielded and I had sexual intercourse with him while I was sitting on his lap and I shrieked and I said, 'Oh, Harry, you hurt me,' and he said, 'Keep still I don't want the whole family to come in.' That was the first time I had sexual intercourse with him."[122] Rosenberg assured her that his finances would improve and he would be able to marry her but, until then, they should keep their sexual relationship a secret.[123] Cohen brought a civil suit against Rosenberg for breach of promise and brought criminal charges against Rosenberg after she learned that he was seeing another woman named Nellie Hymes.

Rosenberg's defense attorney tried to dispel the image of Sadie Cohen as a virtuous woman who was concerned about her moral purity. The defense called Nellie Hymes, Rosenberg's new girlfriend, to the witness stand to suggest the immoral nature of Sadie Cohen. Nellie Hymes testified that Cohen went to her apartment to confront her about Harry. Cohen warned Hymes that Rosenberg would probably discard her, too, after they dated for a short time. Hymes, purportedly said, "'Miss Cohen, that can never happen to me for I know my place.'"[124] Hymes continued to underscore her moral superiority to the complaining witness:

> I said, "Miss Cohen, how did this thing happen, how could you allow anyone to do anything like that?"
>
> "You know I went to an affair and when I came home we stood in the hall, you know, as girls do, and he caressed me and fondled me and of course it happened—I don't know how it happened."
>
> "That would never have happened to me because I would not have allowed anything like that. I have stood in the hall many a time and a thing like that has never happened to me."[125]

Nellie Hymes claimed that Sadie Cohen harassed her by mailing "lots of annoying letters, printed pieces that came out of the newspaper."[126] When asked about her relationship with Rosenberg, Nellie Hymes drew a strong distinction between her behavior and that of the complainant: "The defendant did no more than kiss me; as long as we are engaged, we are allowed to kiss; I am a lady and I know my place and I can always keep my place."[127]

Harry Rosenberg told an acquaintance that he backed away from his promise with Cohen because her loss of virginity made her unfit for marriage. Testifying for the prosecution, a man named Saul Dickerson said, "One of his reasons for not marrying the girl was this, he [Rosenberg] said, 'If I married this girl, I don't know—how do I know she will be true to me as a wife, because if she submitted to me now how do I know she won't submit to someone else?'"[128] Rosenberg declared, "[S]he had no business to yield to me" and that "things have gone too far; I cannot marry her."[129] During his testimony, Dickerson said that he told Rosenberg, "'Well, you certainly ought to marry the girl under those circumstances.' He said, 'I cannot, it is too late, I am sorry for the girl, very sorry for her.'"[130] In Rosenberg's response, the sexual double standard structured the terms of his courtship with Sadie Cohen. It was something outside of his control and, although it made him sorry for Sadie, he claimed he was powerless to change it.

For his defense, Harry Rosenberg took the stand and leveled a serious charge against Sadie Cohen. He accused her of attempted abortion, and he made this accusation while simultaneously placing his motives above reproach. Rosenberg said that he visited Cohen in Staten Island while she was staying with her aunt. Rosenberg testified that she said, "'Harry, I don't know what to do, that medicine the girl friend of mine gave me don't seem to cure me,' and I said to her, 'That is all right Sadie, if I am the cause of your being in the family way I will marry you.' She said, 'Yes, you say that now, but what have I got to show?' So I said, 'Now, never mind, you will see.'"[131] Rosenberg told the jury that Cohen "suggested to me that the best thing to do would to have an abortion performed. I said, no, Sadie, I won't stand for that; I won't be a party to it and then I turned around and I said, 'If the worst comes to the worst I will marry you."[132]

The defense strategy in *People v. Hawkins* centered on the idea that chastity constitutes a moral condition instead of a physical fact.[133] In *Hawkins*, a twenty-six-year-old woman named Mary Keegan brought seduction charges against a forty-year-old clerk named Thomas Hawkins. Hawkins met Keegan in the summer of 1917 while visiting a saloon owned by her family. According to Keegan, Hawkins promised to marry her and soon thereafter took her to the Hotel Theresa in Harlem.[134] Her pretrial statement records that she "permitted [the] defendant to perpetrate an act of sexual intercourse with her."[135] He was arrested and released on two hundred dollars bail.

The defense attacked Keegan's claim to prior chastity by suggesting that she led an immoral life. Hawkins's attorney questioned Keegan about claims that she drank alcohol with other men and sat on Hawkins's lap in the saloon.[136] She denied these incidents took place, but a few witnesses testified that she visited several roadhouses with Hawkins's uncle and cousin. In challenging Keegan's chastity, Hawkins's attorney elicited testimony from some of the witnesses that Mary Keegan drank whiskey and danced to piano music. William Ricer, Hawkins's cousin, delivered perhaps the most damning testimony against Keegan when he described their car ride to several saloons. Ricer stated that Keegan sat between him and Hawkins in the back seat of the car and exchanged kisses with both.[137] Before the jury retired, Hawkins's attorney tried to have the case thrown out of court because the prosecution "failed to substantially offer proof to show the chastity of this woman."[138] He based his claim on "her [Keegan's] actions upon the first acquaintance with the defendant and certain other men, she freely kissing them, and in their company went automobiling, and frequented places where liquor was dispensed, and which she drank."[139] The judge refused to throw out the case, but the jury acquitted Hawkins after deliberating for half an hour. By 1920, Hawkins had married a woman named Olive and was working as a sales manager in a machinery manufacturing company.[140]

Men defending themselves against seduction charges attacked the evidence of the victims' chastity by raising doubts about their sexual morality. Legally, chastity referred to a physical condition signifying a woman's lack of penetrative sexual experience, but defense attorneys tried to argue that personal reputation was more important than bloodstained clothing. As in rape trials, the seduction victim who pressed charges exposed herself to a full range of insults regarding her behavior, morality, and virtue.

Although the history of acquaintance rape as a named social problem is relatively new, nineteenth-century feminists made significant strides to strengthen rape laws.[141] Legal scholar Jane Larson argues that reformers crafted laws that protected women from sexual violence and helped place gender inequality on the public political agenda.[142] In particular, Larson contends that the 1885–1900 campaign by the Woman's Christian Temperance Union (WCTU) to raise the age of consent functioned as a "back door" strategy that effectively attacked a range of sex crimes, including rape and incest. She contends that "the scope of rape reform aspired to by these early reformers was almost as sweeping as that eventually accomplished by the modern rape reform movement almost a century later."[143]

Criminal seduction statutes embodied a conservative strand of nineteenth-century feminism, yet these laws must be viewed in their historical context. Despite the gains women made during the first sexual revolution, male sexual assault and the sexual double standard flourished. In a historical era where personal familiarity with the perpetrator foreclosed any chance of seeking redress for sexual assault *as* sexual assault, seduction laws provided a needed legal resource. Seduction laws acted as a substitute for acquaintance rape legislation, and one can reasonably speculate that they acted as an instrument of social justice for vulnerable working-class and immigrant women.[144]

New York's seduction law acted as a vehicle for the prosecution of date rape, but the very concept of "seduction" impaired the law's guarantee of justice. Seduction trials resurrected an image of feminine submissiveness during an era when women were asserting new public and private roles. Seduction prosecutions staved off ruination and a marked reputation, but the complainants needed to be oriented toward matrimony. The requirements of the seduction law and the gender ideology underlying the law compelled seduction victims to deny their sexual passion outside of its marital purposes. In the performance-oriented space of the criminal courtroom, the cultural concept of seduction blurred consent and coercion. Seduction laws formally recognized coercion could take many forms; men might intimidate and manipulate their partners in the context of an ostensibly romantic relationship. Successful prosecutions, however, depended upon the victims' willingness to yield to both the restrictive criteria of the law and the risk of public humiliation during the trial.

Although the transcripts show how New York's seduction law was used to prosecute sexual assault, the law also foregrounds the cultural notion of "seduction" as an enduring obstacle to gender equality and social justice. A nineteenth-century gender ideology encoded in the seduction law, coupled with defense attorneys' strategies activating that ideology, limited the justice-producing aspects of the statute. Seduction trials exemplify Deniz Kandiyoti's idea of a "patriarchal bargain," or a situation where women can improve their social standing only by surrendering to some degree of male power.[145] The formal requirements of the law coupled with discursive strategies of defense attorneys worked to shore up the sexual double standard, to sanction women's nonmarital sexual expression, and to mitigate the law's ability to punish sexual violence.

The legal concept of seduction, describing a situation that is not quite consensual and not quite coercive, reveals the revolutionary and repressive quality of the early twentieth-century sexual revolution. Given their short-lived status in the twentieth century, many regard seduction laws as emblematic of America's sexually repressive past. Some scholars have characterized the push for seduction laws as a strategy of sexual social control aimed at working-class women and racial minorities.[146] From this perspective, moral reform efforts that led to the passage of seduction laws represent politically invidious projects designed to strengthen the power of middle- and upper-class Anglo-Saxons. Some have described these campaigns as "moral panics" or "sex panics" motivated by a combination of widespread social anxiety and Victorian sexual prudery.[147]

The moral panic scholarship has rightly highlighted the nativism, racism, and class bias of nineteenth-century moral reform, but the laws that reformers championed had unintended consequences, and people used the laws in ways that reformers did not foresee. Solely focusing on the repressive impulses of sex reform overlooks the extent to which these campaigns created legal tools to fight sexual violence. Seduction laws were "legal weapons of the weak," a way to address the gaps that left women vulnerable in Progressive Era marriage and sex law.[148] They acted as a prod for marriage in situations where seduction complainants were faced with single motherhood, social stigma, and no source of financial support.

Successful rape prosecutions in the early twentieth century faced a high burden of proof. Winnable rape prosecutions required corroborating third-party evidence of the attack, testimony of extreme violence, proof that the victim fought against her attacker, and verification of the victim's chastity (defined as both a physical and moral condition). By contrast, testimony about physical force was a common but nonessential element in early twentieth-century seduction trials. These prosecutions covered scenarios where men coerced women into sexual intercourse but fell below the early twentieth-century legal and cultural threshold of rape. Early twentieth-century seduction prosecutions addressed acquaintance rape decades before the 1970s anti-rape movement drew attention to the crime.[149]

Beginning in the 1930s, about one-third of the states enacted "anti–heart balm" statutes to abolish seduction laws and similar laws governing sexual fraud.[150] In 1935, New York abolished its laws criminalizing seduction, breach of promise to marry, alienation of affection, and criminal conversation. Anti–heart balm legislation gained ground in the Progressive Era alongside a growing recognition of women's active sexuality and an increase in effective birth control methods. The stereotype of the "gold digger" was popularized during this time to describe women who either married wealthy men purely for economic reasons or lured them into sex in order to extort money from them.[151] Dozens of Hollywood movies produced in the interwar years depicted devious women who blackmailed their suitors using heart balm statutes.[152] With an image of scheming women in mind, many lawmakers argued that seduction laws encouraged women to engage in extortion or blackmail. The repeal of seduction laws reflected an ironic merger between feminist efforts to acknowledge female sexual autonomy and men's suspicions about conniving women.

Chapter 3

Rape and the Double Bind of Progressive-Era Femininity

Estelle Freedman, in her landmark study *Redefining Rape*, observes, "At its core, *rape* is a legal term that encompasses a malleable and culturally determined perception of the act."[1] The meaning of rape changes over time and its definition fluctuates in response to social and political circumstances. The popular understanding and legal status of rape has worked to protect the presumed privileges of white men, including the sexual rights of slave owners and marital exceptions to rape law. Rape law has changed in response to the mobilization of women's movements. From the Woman's Christian Temperance Union effort to raise the age of consent to gains by second-wave feminists to highlight acquaintance rape, activism has shaped the legal response to rape. Rape trials, therefore, expose the complicated relationship between law, social movements, and sexual violence. As Dawn Flood has stated, "Rape trials expose the messy ways in which gender, race, class, and sexuality cannot be regarded without overlap."[2]

The first degree rape trials in the Transcript Collection give voice to some of the most disturbing and atrocious accounts of sexual violence considered in this study. The stories of rape recounted in the criminal courtroom include male employers assaulting their women workers, strangers attacking strangers, and what we now think of as date rape. In many of these narratives, victims were assaulted until they were wounded, bleeding, and unconscious. The savagery of the attacks, especially accounts about the victims' unconsciousness, placed these women in an untenable position at trial. On one hand, following a Victorian notion of women as inherently pure and passionless, testimony about their unconsciousness worked to secure their respectability and their status as women needing protection. On the other

71

hand, defense attorneys defending their clients of rape charges exploited
testimony about the unconsciousness of the victims to cast doubt on their
stories. The tensions between understanding women as sexual agents and
understanding women as sexually passive—the clash between older notions
of femininity and emergent understandings of women's sexuality characteristic of the first sexual revolution—shaped the types of narratives told in
the criminal courtroom.

In 1892, New York created two categories of rape: forcible rape and
statutory rape. New York's law against forcible rape defined it as, "A person
who perpetrates an act of sexual intercourse with a female not his wife, against
her will or without her consent."[3] The statute recognized conditions where
the woman was unable to give consent, due to her "idiocy" or "imbecility." It
acknowledged other scenarios as rape, where the woman would be unable to
give consent due to her immaturity or a mental or physical weakness. New
York's rape law applied to a wide variety of circumstances, but rape convictions were exceedingly rare in early twentieth-century New York City. Estelle
Freedman's research shows how New York courts were focused on victims of
sexual assault below the age of consent, which was set at eighteen years old
in 1895.[4] Between 1890 and 1910, the New York Supreme Court ruled on
thirty rape cases, and only one-third of the cases involved complainants over
eighteen years old. Convictions for forcible, or first degree, rape were rare. In
Stephen Robertson's sample of sexual assault cases from 1896 to 1932, only
30 percent of men charged with raping an adult woman were convicted. By
contrast, men accused of other felonies (like larceny or robbery) were convicted
at a rate that never dropped below 75 percent during those thirty-six years.[5]
Successful rape prosecutions typically involved situations where the defendant
subjected the victim to serious physical injury. As Robertson notes, "When a
woman had not such wounds, a rape prosecution rarely produced an indictment, let alone a conviction."[6] Due to these exacting requirements, most of
the trials considered in this study concern aggravated rape involving physical
violence, several assailants, and no prior relationship between the victim and
offender.[7] There are only sixteen adult complainants in rape trials represented
in the Trial Transcript Collection.

The low conviction rate can be partly explained by the strict requirements of the rape law. In 1886, New York became one of two states that
imposed a corroboration requirement in its state rape statute, and the state
higher courts interpreted the corroboration requirement in a way that over-
turned many convictions. Courts demanded that the evidence had to cor-
roborate every material fact of the crime. Also, the law defined rape as

occurring when the complainant's "resistance is forcibly overcome," creating and reflecting an expectation that women will fight back against the men who attack them.[8]

The resistance requirement of the New York rape law also accounts for the low conviction rate for men accused of raping adult women. Fear, as a reason for not forcibly resisting, was an acceptable reason only if the resistance is "prevented by fear of immediate and great bodily harm."[9] In 1838, *People v. Abbot* made the resistance test part of New York case law by insisting that victims display "utmost reluctance and utmost resistance."[10] The "resistance test" is a long-standing feature of rape law and a key target of anti-rape reform in the twentieth century. In the 1970s, feminist writer and activist Susan Brownmiller observed that "rape is the only crime of violence in which the victim is expected or required to resist." In a similar vein, Plummer notes, "Rape laws emerged as the only major laws where the victim was assumed guilty until proven innocent."[11] From the early nineteenth century until the 1970s, New York courts required rape victims to prove that they exhibited extreme resistance against their attackers.

The formal legal requirements of New York's rape law combined with the informal, but nonetheless significant, standards of respectable femininity created a double bind for the victims of rape. In rape trials, female victims were expected to resist their attackers but were deemed unfeminine for so doing. Jurors and judges expected women to have a mental trauma during the attack (manifesting as unconsciousness, nervousness, or hysteria), but evidence of those mental states also undermined the reliability of the women as witnesses. Courts held women accountable for their victimization for failing to physically resist their attackers yet required them to disavow the power that would make resistance possible. These trials show how enduring ideas about feminine respectability sabotaged the justice-producing capacities of the criminal justice system. Also, at the micro-level of courtroom verbal exchanges, trial participants deployed linguistic strategies that heightened or mitigated women's perceived sexual agency.

The stories of sexual danger examined in this chapter reflect two important arenas of sexual revolution: work and leisure. The two are linked insofar as profits gained in emergent employment fields allowed women extraordinary opportunities to participate in new city amusements. The first degree rape cases considered on the following pages encompass a range of situations: a dentist assaulting a patient, a supervisor attacking a coworker, a woman exploited seeking employment, and two instances of acquaintance rape. Despite these different scenarios, the trials share specific qualities that highlight the tensions between older and newer gender ideologies, and the battles over sexual respectability embedded in that ideological clash. The defendants were on trial, but the victims were as well. Defense attorneys challenged the victims' morality, and judged their prior sexual experience, as a way to assess their consent. Moreover, attorneys' rhetoric focused on the victims' unconsciousness, "hysteria," and "weakness of mind." For prosecutors, testimony about the women's states of mind underscored the severity of the crime. Defense attorneys took advantage of testimony about victims' mental states to undermine their accounts of sexual violence. The focus—from both sides of the aisle—on the complainants' consciousness and mental conditions (instead of the defendants' thoughts and actions) created an untenable situation for alleged rape victims.

"You can't believe hysterical women"

Martha Poulaillon, a French immigrant, went into Albert Roy's office for dental work in April 1913. The prosecutor's opening statement described how Roy pushed up her dress and attempted to rape her after he had filled some of her teeth. He told the jury in his introductory remarks, "She sat there with her mouth open and her head back when, he suddenly came forward. I will not repeat all that he did. I would rather have you hear that from her mouth and then you will understand it exactly as it happened."[12] Yet, very few, if any, jurors understood the crime through the voice of Poulaillon, who spoke through a court-appointed interpreter.

Martha Poulaillon trusted Albert Roy because he was a fellow French immigrant. At trial, she described how he lowered her in the dentist chair and started to undress. She said, "I kicked as much as I could to prevent him from doing that to me, he tried and tried for a long time and I thought he was going to choke me."[13] He pulled up her dress, but he backed away after he saw a sanitary belt over her underwear. Roy placed a dollar bill on her coat and told her to buy flowers with it, but she threw the dollar in his face.

Martha Poulaillon directly made a complaint at a police station. A detective, accompanied by Martha Poulaillon, her father, and a French interpreter, arrested Roy at his place of work. Albert Roy and the detective conversed through the interpreter. "You know, Officer, you can't believe hysterical women," Roy said.[14] The detective "asked him if he noticed anything in the lady's behavior, if she was hysterical." Albert Roy denied it. Detective Ditsch asked him if Poulaillon was under the influence of any anesthetics, and the defendant said that he used cocaine as a local numbing agent, but not laughing gas. Perhaps in anticipation of the defendant's courtroom strategy, the officer asked "if that would produce hysteria in a person."[15] The dentist said Poulaillon was conscious during the procedure and that the local application of cocaine would not create hysteria. Roy pleaded with the detective, "Now this woman is going to ruin me. What shall I do?"[16] The detective allowed Roy to speak to Poulaillon in front of the interpreter, and he implored her to not press charges.

The defense argued that Poulaillon's mental state made her an unreliable narrator of the events. They pointed to two sources of her alleged unreliability and mental instability: menstruation and anesthesia. Defense Attorney Levy asked, "When you have your monthlies are you more nervous than you are at other times?" to which she replied: "I was on that day especially."[17] His follow-up questions attempted to track a specifically mental source of "nervousness":

Defense Attorney Levy: You will excuse me asking you these questions. When you get your monthly courses, when you do get them do you get more nervous than at other times?

Martha Poulaillon: No, sir; I am just as usual.

Q: Don't it affect you that way at all?

A: No, sir; don't affect me at all.

Q: Did you ever have any hysterical attacks?

A: No, sir; I never was sick at all; in perfect health.

Q: I don't mean sick, bodily sick, but I mean nervously sick.

A: No, sir; I never have them.[18]

By introducing the idea of "hysterical attacks" before the jury, Levy's distinction between physical health and nervous health made women's menstruation more than a normal bodily condition. The idea that women are prone to bouts of hysteria was a staple of nineteenth-century thought, one used to deny them social roles. The questions interjected nervousness and hysteria as possible states that eroded the victim's capacity for rational thought, action, and memory. Doctors and other authorities saw nervousness as a unique condition besetting women. Women's nervous systems were seen as fragile and easily disrupted, and some physicians assumed that women had naturally thin blood, causing instability in their neural system.[19] Other physicians viewed women's reproductive system as a primary source of hysteria, and vaginal infections, irregular menstruation, and uterine disorders were all deemed direct causes of this ailment. As historian Carroll Smith-Rosenberg notes, "Hysteria was perceived by physician and patient as a disease both peculiarly female and peculiarly sexual."[20] However obvious, it is worth mentioning that no one on the all-male jury had personal experiences of menstruation, and, therefore, attorneys could sketch a link between women's physiological processes and forms of mental sickness without any experiential evidence on behalf of the jurors to contradict it.

The idea of menstrual-induced hysteria had rhetorical force, and Levy returned to the issue later in his cross-examination:

Levy: You don't think you were hysterical, do you?

Poulaillon: No, sir.

Q: Do you know what hysterical means, do you?

A: Yes, sir.

Q: Did you ever see anybody who was hysterical?

A: No, sir; I did not.

Q: You have never been hysterical yourself?

A: No, sir; I have never been.[21]

The final three questions of this exchange forced Poulaillon in a double bind. In this moment in the cross-examination, Levy's question, "You have never been hysterical yourself?" forced equally damning choices. She faced admitting to prior hysteria or (in the context of the other questions) admitting to having no basis to ascertain whether she was hysterical or not.

Albert Roy's use of anesthetics formed another source of Poulaillon's alleged mental instability. Both the court interpreter and the arresting officer testified that Roy admitted to putting cocaine on Poulaillon's teeth as a local anesthetic, but she denied this.[22] She said, "I never allow anyone to put any kind of medicine or anesthetic as you describe, in my teeth. I have courage enough to have them drilled without it."[23] Both Roy and his assistant testified that Poulaillon was under the influence of nitrous oxide and ethyl chloride while he treated her. His assistant testified that she saw the gas hood over Poulaillon's head and heard the sound of the nitrous oxide machine.[24] When Roy acted as a witness in his own defense, talk of anesthetics formed an important point of his early testimony under direct examination. He said that he routinely used cocaine, nitrous oxide, and ethyl chloride in his dental practice, but only when the patient was unable to endure the pain. Roy said he was "compelled to use" anesthetics with Martha Poulaillon: "I don't use them if the patient is able to stand it, because time is money."[25] His callous description had the rhetorical effect of affixing another layer of weakness on the complainant. Her weak constitution and low pain threshold required the doctor to use anesthesia he otherwise would have forgone and, under its influence, she became hysterical. This claim formed an important part of the description of her mental, emotional, and physical weakness.

Next, a neurologist testified for the defense that anesthetics could make a woman prone to nervousness and hysteria. He testified that the gas puts people in a series of "dreamy conditions" or "dreamy states" where the patients assemble recent memories or ideas in a mental fog.[26] He said that "in women I find very often they are of an erotic nature, and they usually have erotic dreams in a great many cases that I have observed."[27] Charles Colligan, the prosecuting attorney, declined the opportunity to cross-examine the witness. The testimony of the neurologist, nonetheless, worked to sexualize the victim by insinuating that she was prone to erotic imaginings while under the anesthetic gas.

Albert Roy's attorney also raised an apparent contraction that called into question Poulaillon's capacity to recognize the crime. She said that she was a virgin with a limited understanding of sex. The defense attorney asked her, "Did you know what an act of sexual intercourse was?" to which she responded, "No, sir; I did not." Levy followed up with, "You did not know at that time what it meant, how it was done?" Poulaillon said, "I was imagining what he was about to do."[28] While these responses worked to build an image of her innocence, they also worked to undermine her perceived reliability as a judge of the situation, allowing him to later challenge Poulaillon on a contradiction between her capacity to evaluate Roy's intentions and her professed virginity.[29] Yet, if she had not established her innocence, he could then portray her as sexually experienced and undeserving of the law's protection. The demands of feminine respectability placed her in a double bind. She was considered unreliable if she was not fully conscious of the violation but was deemed as unfeminine if she was aware of what happened to her.

In the micro-linguistic realm, the defense attorney's diction and use of repetition reinscribed Martha Poulaillon's double bind. The defense attorney's cross-examination of Martha Poulaillon challenged both her claims to virginity and her respectability. The defense attorney suggested to the jurors that she was in the grip sexual excitement. During his questioning, he depicted her hysteria and nervousness to show she was not coerced. To displace the image of Poulaillon immobilized by the dentist chair and vulnerable to Roy's attack, Levy tried on several occasions to have Poulaillon state that Roy had approached her in a passionate and sexually excited way:

> *Defense Attorney Levy*: In the meantime he tried to excite you, didn't he?
>
> *Poulaillon*: No, sir.
>
> *Q*: Didn't he try to excite you?
>
> *A*: No, sir.
>
> *Q*: He tried to—you may put this, if you please, in French—did he try to make you passionate?[30]

The side comment to the court translator to put the phrase in French reminded the jurors of the nationality of the witness, and it opened the possibility to the jurors that the French have a special term for, or different understanding of, arousal. He raised the issue of excitement a second time by referring to Roy's state of undress after she kicked him away. During the attack, Roy allegedly stood before her, exposing his penis. Levy asked about this incident during cross-examination:

> *Levy*: When was it that you had an opportunity to see that he had exposed his person?

Poulaillon: When I was fighting hard and defending myself, I happened to glance and saw his private parts.

Q: Were you very much excited then?

[objection—overruled]

Poulaillon: Certainly I was excited. I was defending myself.[31]

The defense attorney exploited the double meaning of "excitement" to refer to both the term's positive and negative valence. Poulaillon's answer shows the dilemma inherent in the question; by only addressing the negative emotions of excitement, she allowed the audience to read her answer as something else. Her prior confusion about Levy's meaning of "excited"—and his instruction to the interpreter to translate it as "passion"—threw into question the meaning of the word. Through these micro-linguistic moves, the defense attorney threw doubt on her narration of events. The sequence of questions allowed the attorney to challenge her morality.

During the trial, the prosecution and defense described Martha Poulaillon's body as registering nonconsent through its revulsion of the defendant. The prosecution portrayed her hysteria as the natural reaction of a woman under attack, but the defense pointed to the same details to suggest her unreliability as a witness. The defense also exploited the language barrier between the witnesses and the jurors and suggested that Poulaillon's reports of being "excited" were instances of passion. Both sides offered a reading of the complainant's bodily clues as a sign of respectability or complicity. Both worked under the taken-for-granted assumption that dental offices were inappropriate places for sexual relations among strangers. The other rape trials considered here reference the main domains of early twentieth-century sexual revolution: work and amusement.

Sexual Violence in the Workplace

Women entered the workforce in record numbers during the early twentieth century, and private employment centers emerged to fulfill the needs of both job seekers and business owners. New York City employment centers, not governed by any effective oversight or regulation, exploited job seekers by demanding fees for inefficient or malicious services. On some occasions, employment agencies would send men and women to jobs where they were fired without pay within a matter of days, and then the agency would send another unsuspecting person to the worksite for the same treatment. These financial incentives led employers and employment agencies to act dishonestly as a matter of routine. Frances Kellor investigated employment agencies by interviewing workers and sending investigators to examine agencies' practices. Her 1915 book *Out of Work* reported that the vast majority of employment agencies in New York City did not verify the legitimacy of the employer to which they were sending workers. She estimated that between 40 and 60 percent of women who used private employment agencies were exploited for nonconsensual sex work.[32]

In the 1915 trial *People v. Costanis*, Josephine Lesczinska, an immigrant from Warsaw, Poland, testified that she was raped by a Greek immigrant whom she met through the Schlesinger's Employment Agency on the Lower East Side. Lesczinska had been in the United States since 1912 working as a domestic servant at different times for a family, as well as for the Astor and Biltmore hotels. According to her testimony, John Costanis approached a woman from the agency, Yetta Whitehouse, asking for a waitress for his restaurant on Washington Street. Whitehouse arranged for Lesczinska to work for Costanis, and he assured Lesczinska that it would be light work and that she would receive many tips. They left for the restaurant with a member of the employment agency, but Costanis convinced the agency representative to turn back after they had walked a little way. According to Lesczinska's testimony, Costanis did not ask her to waitress but, instead, handed her a tambourine and told her to join musicians in the corner of the establishment.[33] Another woman danced while three men played the zither, violin, and harp. They stayed at the restaurant past midnight, and Lesczinska eventually asked to return home to her brother. According to her account, Costanis told her he had a room for her in a different tenement and, after taking her to the room, lit the room light and told her to undress. She said, "I held my clothes tight to me with both hands."[34] In her account, the employment agency was a ruse used to place her in an illegitimate line of work.

The prosecutor searched for details about the event that evinced coercion, focusing on the condition of Lesczinska's clothes:

Assistant District Attorney DuVivier: Now, when the defendant started to undress you, what did you do?

Lesczinska: I tried with all my might to prevent him.

Q: Well, what did you do?

A: I couldn't hold the defendant's hands, but I held my clothes tight to me with both hands (illustrating).

Q: Did you do anything else?

A: I tried the best I could, but I was undressed, and then the defendant took my clothes and he hung them up somewhere.

Q: Now, before you did that, did you do anything else, before he got all your clothes off?

A: Yes, I tried to do the best I could to get away from this defendant, or to run away from there, but it was impossible.

Q: Now, how much clothes—did he take off all your clothes?

Judge Crain: I think that savors a little of the conclusion of the witness. I think I would rather have her describe what she did, rather than say that she did her best.

DuVivier: Yes, sir; I thank you for your Honor's suggestion.[35]

Lesczinska's account portrayed Costanis as doubly betraying her, first when he promised her a job that turned out to be something that it was not, and again when he promised her a room and then insisted that she undress. The late hour and the unfamiliar surroundings put Lesczinska at a severe disadvantage, yet none of those factors gave evidence of her physical resistance required by law and expected by jurors. The complainant's vague description did not satisfy the resistance test requiring she fight back against her attacker. DuVivier persisted, asking, "Well, did you do anything else?" to which she replied, "I prevented—I tried to do the best I could, and he wanted to take off my shoes, and I was kicking, I wouldn't let him take off my shoes." The prosecutor seized the detail of her kicking and included it in the next series of questions:

DuVivier: Well, did you kick him or try to kick him?

Lesczinska: Yes, sir.

Judge Crain: Did you go to the door to open it?

A: Yes, sir.

DuVivier: And is this the skirt that you had on at that time? (indicating a skirt).

A: Yes, sir.

Q: And you say you tried to kick him?

A: Yes, sir.

Q: And in kicking him did you tear your skirt?

[objection sustained][36]

The prosecutor's repetition of the verb "to kick" acts as a poetic device that creates the image of Lesczinska's resistance. Repeating the idea that she fought the defendant in successive questions makes the action seem like a process instead of a one-time event. Matoesian refers to attorneys' creative use of repetition as giving an "incantatory force" to their questions.[37] The prosecutor's micro-linguistic tactics were used to meet the resistance standard required by New York's rape law.

Following the exchange about her kicking the defendant, Lesczinska described how the defendant entered into the bed with her. She said, "He put his hand on my private parts, and then put his knee between my two knees, and then he put it into me."[38] DuVivier then asked, "And how many times did he have intercourse with you?" "Three times," she said.[39] Similar to the questioning of Margaret Peters, the judge encouraged Lesczinska to relive the details of her attack in front of the men in the courtroom. The judge, at that point, intervened and encouraged her to "tell us every little thing you did" following the rape. She described how she took a handkerchief out and wiped between her legs and then washed herself. The prosecutor asked her to identify the handkerchief that she used, and then he offered it into evidence. According to Lesczinska's testimony, the defendant and the complainant slept in the same bed together and, the next morning, he said that "he wanted me to live with him, all the time, but I didn't want to." Their conversation continued as they walked out onto the street. He wanted her to return to the restaurant, but she refused, saying on the stand, "I objected to the way he acted" on the night of the attack.[40] As a police officer walked up the street and noticed the two of them arguing, she turned away from the defendant and the officer followed after her. She reported what happened and he took her to the station to make a formal complaint.

The defense attorney questioned the complainant about the bloody handkerchief and how and why she saved it. These questions placed Lesczinska in an untenable position. If she did not save the clothing, she would have no evidence of the attack. If she saved the clothing, however, it would appear to the jurors that she was trying to frame the defendant. Next, the attorney asked her about the act of intercourse and whether or not she removed her clothes:

Rosenthal: Now, did you have sexual intercourse with men before that time?

A: No, I was always a good girl.

Q: You were always a good girl?

A: Yes, sir.

Q: Now, did you take your stockings off?

A: Yes, I had them off at that time.

Q: You took them off yourself?

A: Yes.

Q: And your shoes?

A: Yes.

Q: And at that time he wasn't holding your feet and hands, was he?

A: Why, he was just standing near me.

Q: He was just standing near you?

A: Yes, sir.[41]

Questions about her stockings and shoes established her sexual agency and willingness to disrobe. The questions about her disrobing, paired with the question about whether or not she was a "good girl," shifted the blame back to the complainant and implied that the defendant did not coerce Lesczinska.

The attorney's questions regarding the moment before the alleged rape produced three different accounts of the attack. In the first version, the defendant slept in the same bed as Lesczinska, but recognizing that she was a "good girl" he left her alone, unmolested. His question to Lesczinska insinuated that his client acted with honorable intent:

> Now don't you know that you told this defendant that you were a good girl, after you got into bed, and after you undressed yourself and lied down in bed yourself, up close to the wall, that you told him you were a good girl, and don't you know that this defendant then told you, "Well, if you are a good girl, I don't want to touch you. God bless you. Go to sleep." And isn't that what happened?[42]

Lesczinska offered a second rendering of what happened: "Well, the defendant said to me at that time that he will be my sweetheart, and I am going to stay with him, and so, of course, for the time I consented."[43] She consented based on the understanding that they were a couple. This act aligned with a nascent Progressive-Era sensibility that premarital sex was acceptable as long as the couple were seriously committed to one another. Yet, this was a contested notion, and women were consistently judged by older ideas that upheld premarital chastity as the cornerstone of respectability.

At this point in the trial, the judge intervened on behalf of the prosecution, and he offered a third account of the crime. The judge, noting the contradiction between this statement and her previous testimony, asked a lengthy question to realign her narrative with the standards of force and resistance expected of successful rape prosecutions. In contrast to an image of the defendant acting virtuously upon hearing of the woman's chastity, and an image of the woman relying upon his good will, the judge offered a third story:

Judge Crain: One moment. Now, as I understand it, after you went into the room with the defendant and he began to take off your clothing the way you have described, you went out, and that you held your hands over your clothing, and that you kicked at the defendant; now, is that so? Now, yes or no to that.

A: Yes, sir.

Q: And I understand that you then went out into the hall with the defendant to go to the toilet, and that while you were going to the toilet in the hall, and while you were in the toilet and while you were coming back through the hallway to the room, you didn't call out? Now, yes or no to that.

A: When he didn't bother me, of course, I didn't holler. When he bothered me, that's the time I holler.[44]

Judge Crain raised critical details about the way she held her clothing as a way to rescue the case for the prosecutor, the timing of her exit from the toilet, her verbal outcry, and her kicking the defendant to align her testimony to the legal and cultural standards of nonconsent. Despite gains made by women in the Progressive Era, jurors expected to hear evidence that rape victims were "good girls," and defense attorneys used those expectations to undermine complainants and to shield their clients from judgment.

Similar questions about whether or not a complainant was morally respectable emerged in the trial of Julius Bloch, a supervisor in a cigar factory. New York was the center of cigar manufacturing in the country and, in the late nineteenth century, most cigar makers worked in the Lower East Side of Manhattan. Manhattan was home to approximately ten to twelve thousand cigar makers by 1920.[45] Cigar factories were primarily owned and operated by German and Bohemian immigrants, and they employed many women.[46] The growth of cigar manufacturing in New York City gave immigrant women opportunities for trade union activism. It also generated new sites of sexual violence.

Julius Bloch, in *People v. Bloch*, was accused of assaulting his coworker in a small cigar factory. Like the trial of Albert Roy, testimony from both the prosecution and the defense pivoted on claims about the victim's lack of consciousness during the attack and, as in *People v. Roy*, created difficulties for the complainant's narrative. Additionally, witnesses claimed that the

complainant, Margaret Peters, had a friendly and, perhaps, romantic relationship with the defendant. Julius Bloch's defense attorney seized testimony
about their relationship in order to assail Peters's sexual respectability and
to challenge her story of sexual assault.

Margaret Peters testified during direct examination that her married
supervisor called her to his office after work and raped her. The defendant,
a cigar factory foreman named Julius Bloch, argued that Peters incessantly
flirted with him and charged him with rape because of her malice and
jealousy. During *voir dire* (the process of juror questioning and selection)
Julius Bloch's defense attorney asked potential jurors if Bloch's status as a
married man made the crime more brutal. He asked one man, "Would the
question of the defendant's marriage, or non-marriage, in any way affect you
in the determination of the facts in this case?" The man responded: "If he
is a married man, it is more serious, I think, because he broke his marriage
vows."[47] This question and answer reflects the perceived severity of the crime
and the ways in which men in the early twentieth century thought about
sexual violence. This understanding made the betrayal of one's marriage vows
something that augmented the crime, making the punishment turn on the
man's violation of his marital vows rather than the violence perpetrated on
the complainant. The focus on Bloch's betrayal of his vows made the crime
about sex, commitment, and marital fidelity, instead of one about violence
and power, and the questioning placed the crime of rape on a similar scale
of harm as marital infidelity.[48]

Margaret Peters was the first witness in the trial to testify. She claimed
that Bloch told her to return to work after five o'clock because he needed
her to do something, but when she returned to the office he attacked her
by grabbing her left arm and dragging her across the room. He threw her
over a cigar box and, with her head over the box, he raped her as she told
him to stop: "I begged and cried, and implored him to let me go, and at
last I lost my mind. I couldn't do anything."[49] He handed her an apron after
the attack and told her not to tell her mother. But she told her family what
had happened when she returned home, and they took her to the police
station in the evening and to a doctor a few days later.

In cross-examining Peters, Julius Bloch's defense attorney reviewed
the details of the assault and the terms of her resistance. When asked
why she did not kick the defendant or push him away, she replied, "I was
unconscious, I lost my mind. I couldn't control myself."[50] He mistrusted
her account of pain and terror, given that she did not scream during the
attack, variously asking, "Didn't it hurt?" "Was it painful?" "And you never

cried out?"[51] The attorney's final question in this series—"You just said, 'Please let me go'?"—highlighted the centrality of physical resistance in early twentieth-century rape trials. The law regarded her verbal demand to be set free as an insufficient signal of her nonconsent, and the question conveyed suspicion about women's true desire and trustworthiness. The very mental state caused by the attack accounts for her relative lack of physical resistance; when the defense attorney asserted that Peters did not kick, push, or otherwise pull away from the defendant, she said, "I was unconscious, I lost my mind. I couldn't control myself."[52] Peters's claim that she was unconscious signified her lack of consent, but it also undermined her ability to recall accurately the attack. Peters's testimony epitomizes the double bind faced by Progressive-Era complainants in rape trials. The narrative required to establish one's respectability and lack of consent—lack of control and consciousness—can be used by defense attorneys to challenge the victim's memory of the attack.

As in *People v. Roy*, the complainant's testimony that she "lost her mind" and was unconscious provided fodder for the defense. The defense attorney used her police court testimony to suggest a contradiction between her lack of consciousness and her ability to describe the attack accurately:

Defense Attorney Schaap: Then you don't know what he did to you, except that, when you got up, and recovered consciousness, you saw your drawers all covered in blood?

Peters: No; the blood come [*sic*] pouring from me, and I said, "Look what you done."

Q: But you don't know what he did? You were unconscious all this time?

A: I was unconscious.

Q: You didn't feel what was going on?

A: Oh, yes; I felt the pain.

Q: After you got up?

A: While he had intercourse with me, I felt the pain.

Q: Well, how do you know that he had intercourse with you?

A: Well, I felt the pain.

Q: You say that, from the fact that he threw you down, and the fact that you had pain, and you saw the bloody drawers afterwards; is that it?

A: I don't understand how you mean.

Q: You didn't know that he was having intercourse with you? You were unconscious during that time; weren't you?

A: I was unconscious, but I felt the pain.[53]

Her description expressed anger and shock incompatible with consent, and she used the active voice to ascribe the entire series of events to the actions of Bloch. But her statement, "Look what you done," and the level of awareness implied by it, stood in tension with her claim to have lost consciousness. She recognized the situation from her pain but was in a mental state that disallowed her consent. Schaap probed the extent of her awareness by asking if she had a conversation with the defendant after the attack or incident, and she maintained that she had "no conversation at all."[54] The attorney followed up with, "You didn't ask him what he had done, or why he did it?"—a question that presumed she had no knowledge of the crime.[55]

The defense attorney asked questions to evaluate the complainant's resistance and consciousness, and then he attacked her morality. The defense attorney asked if Peters ever used obscene language or told "smutty stories" at work, leading the prosecutor to object and the judge to respond: "No; that will do. You have not any right to go into that kind of matter. If you desire to prove the girl's unchastity, you may do so in the proper way. If she were a prostitute, it is no excuse for rape upon her." The defense attorney agreed, but only conditionally: "None. But it may be offered in mitigation."[56] In the early twentieth century, the "proper way" to attack the complainant's character and to prove her unchastity involved discrediting her character witnesses and using witnesses for the defense to portray her as promiscuous. Julius Bloch's defense attorney pursued both of these approaches.

The defense called a series of witnesses who testified that Peters had low morals. The first witness testified that he heard no sounds during the time of the alleged crime. The next witness, Albert Barkman, testified that he remained on the shop floor during the time when the incident occurred but did not see Margaret Peters. Barkman seemed ready to cast doubt on both the incident and the complaint's respectability and moral status. When asked if Barkman witnessed any conversations between the defendant and the complainant, he testified that "they used to fool around a bit."[57] Pressed by the prosecutor to elaborate what he meant, Barkman said, "They used to try to box with one another."[58] During his cross-examination, the prosecutor latched on to the image of boxing and, presumably, attributed a degree of absurdity to Barkman's description by asking if they had boxing gloves or if he boxed with any other workers. Barkman said no.

Next, the defense attorney called the Gail sisters, who worked at the factory with Peters. Frida Gail testified that Peters told her that she needed to return to the factory after closing to "run an errand."[59] When asked about the complainant's behavior, she said that Peters and Bloch "fooled quite a little bit together." On the witness stand, she also stated that Peters used profane language, but she refused to elaborate what Peters said, only to say, "she talked very smutty in my presence . . . about men's privates, and about ladies' privates."[60] The politics of respectability meant that Gail would sully herself by repeating the profane things Peters allegedly uttered, and she expressed these standards, saying, "Well, she talked things that were not fit for girls to hear, and that some girls wouldn't dare to say."[61] After the judge assured her, "It is not anything against you, whatever you are going to say, if it is anything at all," Gail elaborated: "Well, she tried to make a girl believe there that she was in the family way, and she used to ask the girl who the father was of the child."[62] The witness described a sexually assertive woman who joked about racy topics and joshed with her boss and coworkers, and this defied a standard of innocence that the all-male jury expected of rape victims. The witnesses' testimony underscores the tension between gender ideologies during the first sexual revolution. Women experienced new freedom to express their sexuality and to be assertive, but they were judged by older standards of feminine propriety and modesty.

The defendant, Julius Bloch, took the stand and testified about his experiences from when he joined the company in 1900. He described a comfortable friendship with Margaret Peters where they talked about work and family affairs. He eventually fashioned Peters into an assistant. When Bloch broke a knife working on a machine, she gave him a replacement along with some "fancy pencils" as a gift.[63] He insisted on giving her money for the gift, but she refused. As their friendship grew, Peters allegedly became more intimate with Bloch. He testified that, every time she passed him, "she will either put her arms around my neck and kiss me, or so on, or sit down on my lap and start to fool around."[64] On the day before the incident, she sat on Bloch's lap and "started to hug and kiss me, and she put her hand in my pants."[65]

The defendant's description of the events maintained that they had consensual sexual intercourse and she was only pursuing the rape charge because she was jealous of his wife. In his telling of the story, Peters played an active role in setting the scene and propelling the events. She kicked the cigar case in order to make a "bed" and then pulled Bloch toward her. On cross-examination, Bloch said, "She had me around the neck," and she told him to "hurry up" because she had to return home before six.[66] The following day, Bloch and Peters spoke cordially to one another, and Peters told him that she had tickets to a social event and asked him if he would take her. He told her that he was taking his wife and, shortly afterward, a man arrived and charged him with rape.

Just as defense opened with witnesses attacking the integrity of the complainant, they closed with witnesses hailing the goodness of the defendant. Jennifer Bloch, the defendant's wife, stood as the final witness for the defense, which prompted the judge to remind the jury during her direct examination that the marriage condition of the defendant "has no bearing whatever upon this case."[67] She testified that in their seven-year marriage he always brought home his salary and came home on time. When asked if she had forgiven him, she said, "Yes, sir; I have forgiven him in all ways."[68] For Bloch's wife, and surely for others in the early twentieth century, his status as the breadwinner established his manhood.

After the opposing sides rested, but before the closing statements, jurors raised a number of questions. Judge O'Sullivan appeared to welcome the questions of clarification from the jurors and he said, "I think it is entirely proper that they should ask any questions that they desire to ask, so long as it is within the trial and its issues."[69] Unlike the relatively passive role played by jurors later in the twentieth century, jurors in early twentieth-century criminal trials were part of the storytelling process, and their questions during direct and cross-examination shaped attorneys' strategies.[70]

Two of the jurors asked about menstruation. The second juror asked if intercourse would produce blood if the woman was not a virgin, a question that led the court to call a doctor as an expert witness:

> *Dr. Lahane*: If the first intercourse had ruptured the hymen, it would remain permanently ruptured.

Second juror: And when reproduced, in any intercourse again—

A: No, sir.

Q: Blood again?

A: No, sir.[71]

Responding to questions from the defense attorney and the eleventh juror, the doctor explained that it was impossible to tell whether the blood stains were from menstruation or assault, and that the menstrual flow could last several days.[72] The tenth juror asked to recall Margaret Peters, the complaining witness, to ask her the date of her last menstruation and if she changed clothes after the incident. She replied that the date of her last menstruation was December 5th, and that she kept the same undershirt on but removed her underwear after the alleged crime.[73] These jurors searched for bodily signs of sexual consent and thereby added to the mortification and humiliation likely experienced by Margaret Peters as she recounted her ordeal.

After the jurors' questions were answered, the judge summarized the case for the prosecution and the defense. He noted that "there may be a distinction between consent and submission," and that the man "may have yielded to the allurements of the woman."[74] The judge explained that, legally, the complaining witness must show resistance in order to meet the criteria of first degree rape but, "That she was not unconscious is no sign that she gave her consent, at all."[75] Ultimately, Margaret Peters's story of sexual trauma failed to persuade the jurors. Caught between having to prove both her lack of control and her accurate memory of the rape, she was trapped in the double bind characteristic of early twentieth-century rape trials. The jury acquitted Bloch after deliberating for thirty minutes.

Urban Amusements and Sexual Violence

The 1907 trial *People v. Schonland* produced three stories about the day Jennie Toelberg met Frederick Schonland. These accounts drew on clashing gender ideologies in circulation during the first sexual revolution: an understanding of women as sexual agents who could partake in the delights of early urban

American and, conversely, an understanding of women as sexually passive and inherently pure. Schonland's defense attorney claimed that Schonland met Toelberg at a vaudeville house. She appeared distressed and, having run away from home, needed a place to stay. Toelberg, according to Schonland, was sexually aggressive, but he did not have sex with her. The prosecutor, Arthur C. Train, claimed that Schonland lured the sixteen-year-old girl from school and coerced her to attend a vaudeville show. Schonland took her to a hotel in the Tenderloin, raped her, and kept her there for the night. A police officer saw Toelberg and Schonland the following morning having breakfast, noticed Toelberg looked distraught, and arrested Schonland. The judge, Otto Rosalsky, voiced a third account of the crime. Angered by the deadlocked jury, the judge suggested that Schonland was likely a pimp who intended to turn Toelberg into a prostitute.

In *Schonland*, sixteen-year-old Jennie Toelberg testified that Fred Schonland approached her at school and coerced her into coming to a movie theater with him. According to her testimony, the defendant waited outside her school, met her as she was walking home, and threatened her and forced her to accompany him to Keith and Proctor's vaudeville theater, where they stayed from five o'clock in the afternoon until eleven. Afterward, she demanded that he take her home, but he insisted on taking her to dinner. While she was in the restaurant, he tried to find a room for both of them, but his landlord forbade him from allowing her into his room. A man named Jacob Freeman offered his room and, as soon as he left to find a place for himself to stay, Schonland attacked Toelberg. In direct examination, she described what happened:

> *Toelberg*: Well, he told me to go to bed with him; I told him no, I wanted to go home. So I started to cry and he kept on pulling the things off me and took me in his bed with him.
>
> *Q*: Did he pull your clothes off?
>
> *A*: Yes, sir.
>
> *Q*: Did you get into bed there?
>
> *A*: Yes, sir.
>
> *Q*: Did he take his clothes off?

A: Yes, sir.

Q: Did he have sexual intercourse with you?

A: Yes, sir.[76]

The following morning, they had breakfast at a restaurant and Toelberg looked visibly upset. A nearby police officer approached the two of them and the defendant assured him, "I am taking care of her, I am going to send her home."[77] While Toelberg remained silent, he told the officer that she encountered trouble at home and that she was at his "boarding house" all night. The officer turned to Toelberg and said, "Now, little girl, I don't believe this fellow. I am here to protect you and . . . after you get a little older you will understand it."[78] The officer took her home and to a doctor before she later made a complaint at police court.

The defendant, Frederick Schonland, claimed that he was far from Toelberg's school on the afternoon of the alleged abduction, and that he found her already at the theater. In his account, he thought that "she was a good girl and that she just had some argument at home," and so he held fast to the claim that he refused intercourse with her because he did not want to harm or injure her.[79] When asked "Did you make any effort to determine, from her conversation or actions in the room, whether she was a pure girl or not?" he said, "Well, I tell you that her actions was that she was not a pure girl." When the attorney prompted him to elaborate, he said, "From the way she went about it; the way she walked, the way she went from place to place."[80] She went right in the bed and removed her hat and cloak "just as though she had known me and was familiar with me."[81]

During the prosecutor's case, the first juror asked several questions about the times when Toelberg and Schonland walked along specific streets, and he also asked about her books and if the defendant took them from her.[82] Later, as the defense opened its case, the first juror interjected again. The first two witnesses for the defense were an usher at the moving-picture theater and a clerk at the Mills Hotel. The usher testified that he saw Schonland alone in the theater at about seven in the evening, and the clerk testified that Schonland was at the hotel during the time that he was said to have abducted Toelberg.[83] Clara Rosenschweig, who boarded Schonland, acted as the third witness. Rosenschweig recounted that Schonland told her that Toelberg had problems at home and he asked if she could stay in his room. The first juror asked, "When you noticed the girl did you notice that she had anything with her when she came to your store?" She said that Toelberg had a long coat and a nice hat, but "she didn't have anything with her; she played with my little cat."[84] He next asked, "Did you see the books in the girl's hand?"[85] She said she did not and that Toelberg continued to play with the cat.

The prosecutor recalled the police officer who found Schonland and Toelberg in the restaurant the morning after the incident, and the first juror asked him about the complaining witness. The juror wanted to know what she said in response to the questions the officer asked:

> *First juror*: Where was it that she told you, not using the words sexual intercourse, but at what point in the history of the story was it that the girl told you that, in point of fact, the man did have sexual intercourse with her in that room?
>
> *Officer Reardon*: In the Station House.
>
> *Q*: What did she say in the presence of the defendant in the station house?
>
> *A*: She said that he had done something to her, and that he hurt her, got on top of her and done something to her; she said he got on top of her and done something to her and had hurt her.[86]

Next, the prosecutor recalled Jennie Toelberg, the complaining witness. The prosecutor had her recall the rape, urging her to be as explicit as possible. He said, "Tell us what happened, everything, don't be afraid, you have heard these things so many times now, tell us what he did?"[87] After she recounted the crime, the first juror asked where she first saw the defendant. She reiterated her previous testimony that he waited for her outside her school. When the defense recalled Schonland soon thereafter, the juror asked about the complainant: "Did the girl cry when you got on top of her?" And the defendant responded, "I was not on top of the girl at all; I can swear I was not on top of the girl at all."[88] The juror's loaded question implied that the juror rejected Schonland's story that he kept his distance from her upon learning that she was a "good girl." The question, however, cannot be seen as entirely allied with the prosecution because it directed attention toward the complainant in an evaluation of her behavior, and it reveals that the juror regarded her crying as a measure of her nonconsent.

On the third day of the trial, Train delivered the closing arguments on behalf of the People. He said that some of the witnesses—"if not all"—

showed weaknesses of recollection and character, but that the main issue was whether or not the defendant had sexual intercourse with the complaining witness. Train told the jurors that their approach to the case should begin with a consideration of the complaining witness's modesty. He argued that it was "inconceivable that a girl with the ordinary aspirations of womankind would publicly announce that she was no longer a virgin unless it were fact."[89] He said:

> Now, you state this case is a very simple proposition. This young girl, or young woman, comes here and tells you all, and she tells the world, and she tells her schoolmates, her schoolfellows, that she is no longer a pure woman. Now, that is the fundamental rock on which this case rests. Now that is a horrible thing for any woman to announce to the world. It is tantamount to saying, "I am ruined." Now, your first consideration should be, what possible reason could a young girl, just entering womanhood, hoping for a home of her own, hoping for a good opinion of her fellows and of her family, what possible reason would such a child have for coming into this court in standing up before a lot of strange men in saying, "I am no longer a good girl," to use the ordinary parlance of the time, "I am ruined?"[90]

Train contended that the natural sexual modesty of women discouraged them from talking about their sexual experience. No one would voluntarily announce they were "ruined," Train reasoned, but he also conceded some ground to the defense, suggesting that Toelberg was more complicit than she indicated on the stand. The prosecutor undercut the story of his own witness by suggesting, "The same shame, the same womanly instinct which would lead her to deny that she had been violated, unless it were true, led her on the stand to endeavor to make you believe that she resisted."[91] The prosecutor argued that Toelberg, "like all women, she naturally is not going to admit that she willfully surrendered herself to the lust of the defendant."[92] He used a similar phrase later in his closing remarks, noting that the complaining witness has an instinct "not to appear to have willingly surrendered herself to the desires of a stronger man."[93] Train said that her actions would lead "anybody of any ordinary common sense to conclude that the girl at least went half way."[94] During the first sexual revolution, virginity was no longer considered the central criterion of moral worth, especially among the working class. Yet, Train's comments during the trial suggest that judgments of sexual virtue and sexual sin carried a powerful cultural force.

Train conceded to the defense a degree of consent on behalf of Toelberg and Schonland, but one that implicated the defendant a charge of rape all the same. Train outlined what he considered to be a truthful rendition of the key events:

> If Jennie Toelberg had come down here and said: "I did meet the defendant uptown, and he said, 'Come on to the theatre,' and I said, 'Well, I perhaps better not,' and he said, 'Oh, do come,' and finally I went with him, and that then after the theater we went to a restaurant and then went to a room and we had sexual intercourse," which is probably the truth, coupled with a certain amount of reluctance on the part of the girl, but she is not entirely unwilling, you would have had a case where the girl would appeal to you as telling a story which was entirely true.[95]

Train said it cannot be true that the defendant "forced her to go anywhere," and he noted that she could have sought help from a police officer or someone else to make an escape. Nonetheless, Schonland's age and influence exerted a powerful force on Toelberg. According to Train, the defendant "found her a comparatively easy mark" because she was "not a particularly bright girl," and it was "entirely possibly that her physical side had been developed at the expense of her mental side."[96]

> [T]here is not a man in the room I will venture to say that would not arise and laugh, and laugh heartily, if he were asked to believe that this defendant picked a girl up in Keith's Theater or anywhere else, called her with him to the Sans Souci, spent the evening with her, took her to a restaurant and then took her to a room in East Broadway and slept in the same bed with her, under the same sheets with her all night, and then, although he was able to have sexual intercourse, knew what it was, who would have had sexual intercourse with her under other circumstances, was so pure and noble and good that he did not.

Train raised questions about New York City's entertainment culture and the forms of intimacy it fostered. The attorney maintained that the defendant's self-serving account was unbelievable, and anyone who did believe it was highly gullible. "Now, what kind of children does Colonel Townsend think you are?" he asked.[97] Train continued to attack the defendant's integrity,

mockingly referring to him as "Sir Galahad of the Tenderloin."[98] The prosecutor argued that taking her to the Sans Souci restaurant (named after
the French phrase for "carefree") raised suspicions about his intentions and
moral character. Train said, "Now, there seemed to be some question in the
mind of the jury and possibly the Court, whether or not a man who thought
a girl was a good woman would take her to that place."[99]

Although Train depicted the complainant as partially at fault, he
introduced a characterization of the defendant that allowed the jury to
consider his possible involvement in a more serious crime. Train told the
jury that it was their duty, before they "acquit this defendant on his tale
of purity," to consider whether or not Schonland acted as a pimp trying
to entrap a naïve girl.[100] He raised the familiar story of white slavery as a
frame through which to view the defendant's actions. He asked, "Now, if
the defendant were seeking to secure a girl for the purpose of prostitution,
how would he go about it?"[101] Train supplied the answer: "The process would
be to get hold of some girl who was sufficiently young to be worthwhile,
and to compromise her so that she would be afraid to return home and
if possible make her the willing instrument of his lust or a willing worker
for his support."[102] Not only was Schonland a pimp who tried to ensnare
Toelberg, but Clara Rosenschweig, the woman who boarded Schonland,
was also part of the conspiracy: "If the defendant is a pimp, she may be a
madam for all I know."[103]

During the final moments of his closing statement to the jury, Train
argued that they must find the defendant guilty for the sake of Jennie
Toelberg's father. The prosecutor described Jennie Toelberg's complicity in
the crime, but he said that she was basically a good girl, and he reminded
the jury of the father's testimony claiming that she "has only been to the
theatre three or four times and then with him or his wife."[104] This case,
the prosecutor maintained, was "precisely the kind of a case which the law
intended to meet" because she was at heart a "good girl, who has been
protected by her family."[105] Train said, "Wasn't the law made to protect
Neils Toelberg just as much as any other man whose daughter may be
wronged? The law doesn't stop at 100th Street. This law was passed for the
purpose of protecting young women against themselves as well as against
the blandishments of outside parties."[106] Here, the attorney implied that the
law against rape protects not only the middle- and upper-class women of
mid-Manhattan and the Upper East Side but women who lived in poorer
neighborhoods as well. Train also forged identification between the jurors
and the complainant's father and, during this revealing moment, repackaged

rape as a property crime instead of a crime of violence. Train ended his closing statement with an image of a father's outrage to which he invited the jurors to commiserate.

The judge gave instructions to the jury and described the role of reasonable doubt and good character evidence. At the foreman's request, the stenographer read aloud to the jury the testimony of Jacob Freeman—the man who offered his room to Toelberg and Schonland on the night of the incident. The jury retired thereafter but returned to the courtroom with a note for the judge penned by the foreman: "Your Honor: You will let me know whether, if we find the defendant guilty, and recommending clemency, will the penalty be lessened to one or two years, as we won't give him more than two years."[107] The judge admonished the jury and told them that the note "is little short of impudence" and that it is not within their province to consider the punishment. Again, the jury entered the deliberation room and then returned without reaching an agreement.

The judge excoriated them after the foreman announced the deadlock, stating that he personally has "prosecuted as many cases of rape and defended as many as any man ever did in this county" and that "if there ever was a prosecutrix who told a story which a mind open to conviction would accept, it was this girl."[108] In his criticism of the jurors the judge said that he assumed that, because he reprimanded them for their "highly improper conduct" in making their judgment contingent on his sentence, the jurors "deliberately go out and say that they cannot agree."[109] The judge said that he considered making an unusual move of discharging the men "from further considering any criminal case."[110] The judge adopted Train's characterization of the crime as an instance of compulsory prostitution and, using a term synonymous with "pimp," the judge described the defendant as a "cadet" who "would have taken this girl and sold her as a vehicle to whomsoever would pay."[111] In this instance of jury nullification, the jurors acted outside of their appointed roles, created or forced a deadlock, and allowed the defendant to go free.

The Schonland trial occurred during the early years of the "white slavery" scare that swept the United States. Segments of the public raised concerns about young white women abducted and sold into forced prostitution. The judge referenced the white slavery narrative as a way to add weight to the account of coercion, but he could not overcome the doubts of at least one juror. The first juror appeared hesitant to punish Frederick Schonland given Toelberg's lack of sexual innocence and, perhaps, contributed to the deadlock. Given the questions that he raised during the trial, it is reasonable to conclude that the decision in the trial turned on Toelberg's alleged lack of respectability instead of Schonland's alleged coercion and perfidy. Similar to the other first degree rape trials considered in this chapter, the complainant's behavior and attitude was in the spotlight as much as the defendant's, if not more so.

Like the trial of Schonland, testimony in *People v. Morrick* uncovered allegations of staggering brutality. The 1918 trial of Samuel Morrick revolved around charges that he raped May Davis, a twenty-three-year-old bookbinder from Birmingham, England, after seducing her in the Riviera theater. The couple had gone on three dates. Davis testified that following their last outing together, Morrick forced himself on her and strangled her until she was bleeding from her ears. Morrick's attorney painted Davis as a sexual instigator and implied that she consented to having intercourse with the defendant.

May Davis was the first witness for the prosecution, and she described how she met the defendant, Samuel Morrick, through the acquaintance of a mutual friend named Frank Torak. Davis knew Torak as a friend for over a year and as someone to whom she gave informal English lessons. In May 1917, Davis and Morrick made plans to meet, and Morrick visited her at her apartment. On their first date, Davis and her girlfriend met with Morrick and Torak to play pinochle. She lost the game and, as a penalty, the group decided that she should kiss Morrick as a joke. At trial, the defense attorney made an issue of the kiss, although the complainant described it as "just a bit of fun."[112]

After the game, Morrick took her to the Riviera movie theater on the Upper West Side, one of the most opulent theaters in the country.[113] At first, they had to stand through of the show because all of the seats were occupied. They sat down when seats became available and, at this point, their stories about that evening diverged. According to Morrick, May Davis acted as a sexual aggressor. Morrick's defense attorney accused May of coming up to him and rubbing her cheek against his face.[114] When seats became vacant, the couple had an opportunity to sit in the front row, but Davis allegedly pulled him toward the back and said, "Let's sit here."[115] Cloistered in the rear the theater, Morrick complained about his line of sight, and so Davis suggested that he sit on her chair. Morrick said that in "the picture there was a couple of suggestive scenes, and she got hold of my hand and twined her fingers in between mine."[116] His courtroom account described the intimacy between them: "I was stroking her limbs both upper and lower, and she turned around and she bit—no, she just kind of nibbled at my cheek, and several times she rubbed her cheek up against mine, and I could feel her flesh how hot it was through her clothes."[117] The testimony echoed concerns social reformers voiced about new forms of entertainment, like dark movie theaters, which allowed immorality to flourish.

When May Davis took the witness stand, the defense attorney pursued the narrative that she was promiscuous and knew that Morrick was interested in sex. The defense attorney suggested that Davis knew that Morrick had sexual ambitions based on his behavior during their first date, and so she should not have been surprised by his advances on their second date. The attorney hit her with a cascade of questions to convey his incredulousness: "You thought all he wanted was companionship?"; "You didn't know anything he wants?"; "You accepted his invitation, went to a show with him, took a taxicab with him and he took you home, and was in your company and still you did not ask him about anything, what he wants of you?"; You try to make us believe, this Court and jury that at no time you never knew what this man wanted with you, is that right?"[118] These questions depicted May Davis as a sexual agent who knew where the evening would eventually lead. The defense attorney's approach created a framework for the jurors to understand the alleged assault that transpired on their third date.

On their next date, Morrick met her on the stoop with a bundle of flowers for her birthday later in the week. She said that the flowers needed water, and so he followed her inside the apartment. During the conversation that followed, Morrick told her that he was going away to Boston to look after his sick mother. Davis said on the witness stand that Morrick began "changing the conversation."[119] Samuel Morrick told May Davis that he came to "get his satisfaction" and when she asked him what he meant, he replied, "You know what I mean, every New York girl does."[120] She informed him that she "was not that kind of girl. I am surprised at you. I was introduced to you through a gentleman. Why don't you leave."[121] According to her testimony, he grabbed her tight with his arms. She tried to talk to him more but did not scream because she "didn't want to ruin my reputation in the house."[122] This placed Davis in a double bind created by patriarchal Progressive-Era gender ideologies. She resisted screaming because it would damage her reputation in the house. Yet, by not screaming, jurors could interpret her lack of resistance as a sign of consent.

Morrick allegedly threw her on the floor and put his hips on her chest. Having immobilized her, he strangled Davis until she passed out and began bleeding from the ears. She scrambled across the floor and caught an image of him grabbing his overcoat and running down the hallway of the building. At this point, she set aside concerns about her reputation and called for help. The second witness for the prosecution, Harry Rains, lived in the building, and he described hearing a scream and saw "Miss Davis coming from her room, shrieking as loudly as she could."[123] He caught hold of her as she appeared "almost collapsing," placed her on the stairs, and yelled for the police out of the front door.[124] A police officer came to the scene and found May Davis in a terrible state. At trial, the officer described her as having swollen eyes, with her right eye discolored and completely closed, and blood was all over her face and oozing from one of her ears.

The police officer arrested Morrick. The conversation between the officer and Morrick reveal the attitudinal barriers facing women who made charges of first degree rape. Their exchange shows how the legal system, personified by the patrolling officer, embodied and created rape myths that prevented law enforcement from taking action against rapists.[125] This is consistent with the research of gender historian Dawn Flood. Flood identified and analyzed the role of rape myths in Chicago sexual assault prosecutions, including the idea that women habitually lie about rape charges, that women were "asking for it" by acting or dressing in a way that the assailant used to rationalize the violence he inflicted. The officer, Charles Strubell, approached the scene of the crime where a crowd had gathered following Davis's screams. The defendant assured him that "it is nothing but a family affair."[126] The officer encouraged the suspect to talk about the crime, but he did so by supplying the suspect with the proper cultural responses that mitigate his responsibility for the assault.[127] In the patrol car, the police officer noticed that the defendant had seminal discharge on his pants, and, according to the officer, Morrick said, "I must have gone off when I attacked her."[128] The officer asked him, "Did she give you any encouragement?" and Morrick said that he "must have been crazy or insane when I attacked her."[129] The police officer told him, "If I were you, before I would do anything, I would consult counsel." Police officers typically try to encourage crime suspects to talk as much as possible. Morrick's assault on Davis occurred about fifty years before the Supreme Court's decision in *Miranda v. Arizona*, which compelled police officers to inform criminal suspects that "anything you say can and will be held against you in a court of law."[130] In this instance, the officer who arrested Morrick gave him unsolicited advice to seek legal counsel. This was a remarkable departure from the ways that police typically conduct an arrest. Catharine MacKinnon's analysis of US case law demonstrates that laws practically collaborate with rapists with regard to the standards required to distinguish between consent and coercion, but it is important to note that the alliance between the legal sphere and the rapist occurs at different levels of the criminal justice system.[131] In arresting Morrick, the police officer acted as a collaborator in the crime when he dispensed valuable legal advice to the suspected criminal.

Although Morrick practically confessed his guilt to the police officer, the defense attorney portrayed the physical harm to May Davis as an accident stemming from their intimate embrace. Davis's testimony placed her in a double bind similar to what we have seen in previous rape cases considered in this chapter. On one hand, she said that she passed out at the moment when Morrick assaulted her. She was unable to give consent because she was unconscious. On the other hand, her unconsciousness hurt her reliability as a narrator of the attack. She stated during direct examination, after he started strangling her, "I was unconscious after a while when I started to regain consciousness I was in awful agony from the blood, bleeding from the ears and I just went to scramble off the floor."[132] The defense countered by asking a string of questions designed to counter the narrative of coercion and to cultivate an image of mutual affection:

> *Davis*: As soon as he knew I refused his offer he forced me to the floor, put his knees on me, overpowering me, strangling me around the neck so I could not scream.
>
> *Defense Attorney Feldman*: He didn't say anything any more?
>
> *A*: When he pleaded with me to yield to him I refused.
>
> *Q*: Did he embrace you?
>
> *A*: Yes, sir, he did, I couldn't get away from him.
>
> *Q*: Did he kiss you?
>
> *A*: Yes, sir, he did, but I resented it.
>
> *Q*: He kissed you?
>
> *A*: By force.
>
> *Q*: How many times?
>
> *A*: About twice.

Q: Did you count them?

A: No, sir, I can remember.

Q: What is that?

A: I can remember.

Q: Is it not a fact that you fell to the floor yourself?

A: He threw me to the floor.[133]

According to the defense attorney's narrative, he hugged her and she accidentally slipped, fell, and "became a little in a dazed condition."[134] Also, the fact that her skirts were pulled up became a point of contention for the defense attorney. Due to her unconsciousness, Davis was unable to say how her clothing came to be in that condition. During cross-examination, Morrick's attorney questioned her about her clothing in order to show her sexual consent:

> *Defense Attorney Feldman*: The only blood you found was on the collar?
>
> *Davis*: On the white collar and on this collar (indicating).
>
> *Q*: Otherwise everything was in good order, is that right?
>
> *Prosecutor*: I object to the form of the question.
>
> *Q*: There was no tears or blood or anything?
>
> *A*: There was no tears on my clothes.
>
> *Q*: All you know was that the skirts were up, is that right?
>
> *A*: Yes, sir.
>
> *Q*: How they got up you don't know, yes or no?
>
> *A*: I don't know. I was unconscious.[135]

The trial of Samuel Morrick exposes the twisted logic whereby the severity of his attack on May Davis functioned to undermine the charge of rape. Her lack of consciousness during the assault was used by the attorney to call into question her reliability.

~

These trials are important to consider because they indicate the extent to which the US legal system has made progress in addressing sexual violence, but they show the enduring continuities between rape trials past and present. Early twentieth-century rape trials provide a close look at an era before rape shield laws when defense attorneys and their witnesses mounted attacks on the chastity and reputation of sexual assault victims, effectively putting the complainant on trial and forcing her to endure questioning about her private life. Although a woman's risk of rape by an acquaintance is several times more likely than stranger rape, date rape remains a drastically under-reported and under-prosecuted crime.[136]

Legal criteria that reflect culturally approved notions of masculine and feminine sexuality shackle mechanisms for prosecuting rape. Throughout the twentieth century, prosecutors drew on mainstream assumptions about heterosexual romance to consider how jurors will assess victims' accounts of sexual assault.[137] Prosecutors abandoned rape cases where the victim falls short of middle-class norms of feminine propriety, lives in an impoverished neighborhood, or engages in illegal activities.[138] Also, prosecutors tended to regard victims' accounts of stranger rape as more credible and convictable than instances of date rape, despite the overwhelming prevalence of the latter crime.[139] Once a case is selected for prosecution, the complainant often finds similar legal and cultural barriers inside the courtroom. Male-centered gender ideologies order and shape the linguistic and rhetorical strategies of defense attorneys, leaving many women feeling traumatized by their courtroom experiences.[140] As the trial transcripts demonstrate, ideologies of feminine passivity hamper the successful prosecution of rape, from the initial screening of a given rape case to the verbal tactics used by defense attorneys to blame the victim.

Chapter 4

White Slaves and Ordinary Prostitutes

By the end of the nineteenth century, prostitution was ingrained in New York City's social fabric and the city had effectively created a *de facto* system of licensed prostitution.[1] New York's Raines Law of 1896 was intended to attack vice and immorality by requiring saloon owners to pay high fees. The law stipulated that hotels could only serve alcohol on Sunday if they had ten or more beds, and this prompted saloon owners to add rooms creatively so that they could serve liquor. Within a week of the law's passage over one thousand saloons changed in order to meet the new requirement, and so-called "Raines Law hotels" became hotbeds of prostitution. These hotels, as well as privately owned brothels, afforded New York City prostitutes considerable freedom and protection in the management of their business.[2] In a similar fashion, working-class tenements allowed women to engage in sex work on a relatively casual and unsupervised basis.[3] Prostitution permeated the city at the close of the nineteenth century, annually generating millions of dollars for profit for those involved in vice trade.[4]

Although New York City did not have a formal, segregated vice district, prostitution was prevalent throughout the city. Perhaps the most popular images of prostitution are of the brothel habitué and the streetwalker, but much of the sex-for-money exchanges in New York City fell somewhere between the highly private and highly public worlds of the brothel and street. Prostitution flourished in what vice investigator George Kneeland grouped together as vice resorts: tenement houses, furnished rooms, and massage parlors. The vast majority of instances of prostitution examined in this study took place in furnished rooms or tenements. In his 1913 report on prostitution in New York City, Kneeland's investigators found over 1,100 vice resorts in 575 tenement houses.[5]

In the early twentieth century, the growth of prostitution received an unprecedented amount of attention from the US public. Popular cultural representations of early twentieth-century prostitution revolved around the image of the "white slave." Reformers and journalists represented the problem of forced prostitution through the narrative of "white slavery," wherein immigrant white slave procurers lured naïve native-born white women into prostitution by deceit or force. White slavery stories emphasized the innocence of the abducted woman and the depravity of the procurer. Reformers authored white slavery stories that depicted Southern and Eastern European immigrants violently trapping white girls into a life of prostitution by drugging, beatings, and threats. Many white slavery narratives described how men lured women into white slavery through false promises of employment. Prominent anti-vice reformer Ernest Bell described a typical case: "One of the best known department stores in this city was at that time running a Labor Bureau; the girl went there and in due time was presented to a pleasant-faced ladylike woman, who offered her employment as a 'parlor-maid.' The poor girl, with glad heart and bright hopes, set off for her new home; but before night fell she found that she had been sold into a slavery worse than death."[6] White slavery narratives stressed that appearances could deceive. Work opportunities could be dangerous, and friendly faces can trap an unsuspecting woman into a life of vice.

The reform literature also depicted false promises of marriage as a fast route to white slavery. Bell discussed this scenario in *Fighting the Traffic in Young Girls*, a widely popular book about white slavery: "The White Slaver haunts the excursion boat, makes love to the girl whose head is turned with silly notions about romantic courtships and marriages; he takes her to a Justice of the Peace or a 'marrying person' of the excursion resort type, and a ceremony is performed. They go to the big city and she is sold into a slavery worse than death!"[7] Accounts of white slavery suffused popular culture with melodramatic representations of sex work. White slavery narratives—represented in books, magazine articles, silent films, and newspaper exposés—tended to simplify the reasons women entered the vice trade, and they routinely distorted the roles of its participants. Gilfoyle notes the mismatch in the early twentieth century between the image and reality of New York City prostitutes: "Individual prostitutes increasingly worked out of concert saloons and Raines Law hotels, thereby gaining a measure of independence from brothels. Ironically, in the very same years when the white slave controversy focused attention on the brothel and the coercive practices of some proprietors, female prostitutes probably felt less institutional coercion in their work."[8] The mismatch between the lived experience of early twentieth-century prostitutes and the white slave trope shows how moral panics arise from perceived social problems instead of real evidence of harm.

The white slavery issue received extraordinary attention from the US public in the opening decades of the twentieth century, especially from 1907 to 1917. In 1913, for instance, approximately fifteen hundred people viewed the white slavery film *Traffic in Souls* every week during its run in New York City theaters.[9] US officials arrested over two thousand people from 1910 to 1918 for violating a federal law against forced prostitution.[10] During those years, over thirty cities launched vice investigations, over forty states passed laws to prevent forced prostitution, and a variety of social movement organizations—ranging from the Ku Klux Klan to the Immigrant Protective League—circulated stories about white slavery to bolster various political projects.[11] White slavery stories suffused popular culture with representations of prostitution that emphasized the innocence of the abducted woman and the depravity of the procurer.

Evaluating the extent of coercive prostitution in the Progressive Era is difficult for a number of reasons. Assessments based on reformers' accounts, arrest records, or reports from sex workers pose distinctive limitations. While acknowledging the prevalence of coercion and sexual violence facing working-class women, scholars have argued that the disproportionate public attention to white slavery constituted a scare or panic.[12] The abundance of melodramatic white slavery stories and the tendency of reformers to focus on abductions have generated difficulty for historians documenting the extent of coercive prostitution in the Progressive Era. While most scholars characterize the response to prostitution in the Progressive Era as a panic or scare, historian Ruth Rosen cautions that melodramatic representations of the sex trade obscure real evidence of violence and coercion. Rosen compiled vice report data to conclude that as many as 9 percent of prostitutes from 1900 to 1920 entered prostitution in the way depicted in white slavery novels (violent abduction and imprisonment).[13] The true percentage is possibly higher due to the fact that women abducted in the way described by the white slavery narratives were less likely to appear in state- or city-level vice reports. Dismissing reformers' concerns as hyperbole underestimates the extent of violence in the commercial sex trade and distorts the long and brutal history of human trafficking. Taking reformers' accounts at face value, on the other hand, leads to a misleading account of women's agency and self-direction.

In 1907, at the height of the white slavery scare, New York lawmakers created Section 2460 of the state penal code to address instances of "compulsory prostitution" where pimps and procurers conspired to "induce, entice, or procure" women into the sex trade. The statute made it a crime for individuals "knowingly receiving money for and on account of procuring and placing women in the custody of another person for immoral purposes."[14] Despite the growing prevalence of intermediaries who earned money from the sex work of others, few faced felony convictions for their involvement in the vice trade under the new law. Women bore the brunt of anti-vice policing in New York City, and police charged most women apprehended for prostitution with "disorderly conduct," a misdemeanor.[15] In 1907, the New York City police court processed approximately nine hundred cases of disorderly conduct per month. Prosecutors reserved the charge of "compulsory prostitution" for cases involving blatant use of force.[16] The trial transcripts considered in this chapter suggest that many members of New York City's criminal justice system regarded Section 2460 as a "white slavery" law. For instance, in *People v. Drenka*, the first compulsory prostitution case in the Trial Transcript Collection, the defense attorney argued during sentencing that "the intention of the legislation, if it was anything, was to prevent this barter of women. In fact this whole white slave legislation was responsible for this additional section enacted in 1907 called compulsory prostitution. What the legislature intended by this is evidently to prevent men trading with women."[17] In *People v. Spano*, police allegedly told the defendant upon his arrest that he was being charged with "white slavery."[18] In *People v. Dix*, the prosecutor referred to the charges against the defendant as charges of "white slavery."[19] Newspapers referred to the trials using similar language.[20] Reserved for the most egregious and violent cases of abuse by pimps and procurers, Section 2460 legally covered scenarios that most closely approximated popular representations of "white slavery" at a time when the image of the "white slave" had strong cultural resonance.[21]

New York's law against compulsory prostitution in 1907 foreshadowed the passage of the Mann Act in 1910. Also known as the White Slave Traffic Act, the Mann Act made it a federal crime for any person to transport across state lines "any woman or girl for the purpose of prostitution or debauchery, or for any other immoral purpose."[22] The law was supposedly aimed at forced prostitution, but federal prosecutors used the Mann Act against consensual couples. In 1913, for instance, prosecutors charged heavyweight boxing champion Jack Johnson with violating the Mann Act by consorting with a white prostitute named Belle Schreiber. The *Johnson* case shows the willingness of prosecutors to use the White Slave Traffic Act in cases that widely departed from the stories of white slavery in popular culture. It also illustrates how sex crime laws, and the narratives of sexual danger that underwrote them, worked to enforce racial and ethnic boundaries. There was no evidence that Johnson enslaved or tricked Schreiber, but his perceived desire for white women prompted authorities to scrutinize Johnson for possible Mann Act violations shortly after the law was introduced.[23]

Prosecutors in the 1910s successfully applied the law to unmarried couples engaged in consensual sexual intercourse outside of their state of residence, and courts upheld this application of the law due to flexibility of the law's phrase "or for any other immoral purpose."[24] The 1917 *Caminetti* case applied a wide interpretation of the Mann Act, and hundreds of women faced Mann Act prosecutions after 1917.[25] New York compulsory prostitution prosecutions were similarly flexible, and compulsory prostitution trials often revealed instances of "ordinary" prostitution that brought compulsory prostitution charges.

White slavery had strong cultural resonance in New York City because of the precarious position of working-class respectability. Upper- and middle-class social activists saw little difference between prostitutes and so-called "charity girls." Meanwhile, working-class men and women in early twentieth-century New York increasingly rejected the view of virginity as the ultimate sign of moral worth and the notion of premarital intercourse as akin to prostitution.[26] Many working-class women cultivated relationships with men with whom they traded sexual favors for gifts or an evening's entertainment. The practice of "treating" changed the working-class sexual economy. According to historian Elizabeth Clement, "Treating emerged as an intermediate category, a line somewhere between the morally gray area between prostitution and the premarital intercourse that often occurred in courtship."[27] Working-class women in New York City refashioned the economics of courtship, and, within the constraints imposed by their unequal sex status, class location, and immigrant statuses, they challenged traditional codes of sexual morality. Compulsory prostitution trials exposed the tensions between representation of women as sexual agents and as white slaves.

Thirty-one compulsory prostitution trials were archived in the Trial Transcript Collection for the years 1907 to 1915, dating from the enactment of the law until the white slavery issue began to ebb. Many complainants in compulsory prostitution prosecutions differ in some important respects from those depicted in white slavery narratives. For instance, although white slavery narratives typically emphasized the threats posed to native-born white women, only 19 percent of the complainants fit that racial and ethnic category. Eighteen (45 percent) of the complainants in the thirty-one trials were from Southern and Eastern Europe. Also, while white slave narratives often infantilized the victims of coercive prostitution, 67 percent of the complainants in the trials were eighteen years of age or older. Approximately 20 percent of the alleged victims were younger than eighteen years old, and the ages of four complainants are unknown (representing 13 percent of the trials). Finally, although white slavery stories often described women ensnared into the vice trade after leaving home to seek work in the city, most of the complainants in the trials were already employed. In fact, two-thirds of the women represented in the trials were employed, or had been at one time, and most worked as domestic servants or factory workers.

Trial accounts differed from white slavery stories in many ways, but many complainants' accounts of violence strongly echoed the white slavery narratives in popular culture. Alleged victims of compulsory prostitution described a range of brutal and deceptive methods that pimps used to entrap and hold them in sexual slavery. In approximately 39 percent of the trials considered in this study, complainants testified that the defendants assaulted them. About 21 percent of complainants testified that the defendant imprisoned them, 27 percent testified that the defendant raped them, and others recalled that the defendant threatened them with knives (24 percent) and guns (15 percent). In addition to physical coercion and threats, complainants also testified that they were deceived by a white slavery procurer. In many cases, the accused pimp or white slaver made false promises of marriage (36 percent) or employment (12 percent) to steer the victim into prostitution. Approximately 73 percent of the compulsory prostitution trials include testimony about how the defendant promised the complainant money or clothing.

Judges helped jurors negotiate the differences between white slavery narratives and the testimony aired in the New York City Court of General Sessions. In some of the examined trials, judges emphasized the simple clarity of the decision facing the jurors and they openly advocated on behalf of a particular outcome. In *People v. Cilento* a woman named Ella Matthews accused Joseph Cilento of forcing her to prostitute herself in order to earn money for his food and clothes. The trial involved clashing stories that respectively described Cilento as a brutal pimp and Matthews as a common prostitute. Approximately a half-hour after the jury retired for deliberation, the tenth juror told the judge that some jurors felt that there was insufficient evidence to prosecute the defendant. In response, the judge reduced the fact-finding in the case to its bare essence: "The question is did she give to him, without consideration, moneys which she had made as a prostitute."[28] The jury returned fifteen minutes later still unable to reach a verdict, and the judge chastised them before dismissing the case. He said that "this is about as clear a case that you could get" and added "if you find a man who has been living on the prostitution of a woman do you want a photograph or a moving picture of that particular five dollars?"[29] Jury nullification occurs when a jury disregards the rule of law and instead votes their conscience. The outcome in *Cilento* appears to be a case of jury nullification, given that they voted to acquit despite it being "about as clear a case that you could get."[30]

Judges helped direct jurors' interpretation of courtroom narratives by giving instructions to them before deliberation, typically by explaining the concept of reasonable doubt and articulating their specific fact-finding roles. While attorneys and jurors referenced a scenario of abduction and forced prostitution through supposedly pertinent testimony and questions about locked doors and barred windows, judges tried to shear the cases of those legally extraneous details. As commonly explained in their jury instructions, the facts of the trial did not need to fit the white slavery narrative in order for jurors to arrive at a guilty verdict. In these trials, judges instructed jurors on how to evaluate the sexual behavior and moral status of the complainant, typically telling them that the complainant's sexual activity or immorality did not exonerate the defendant. According to the law and the judges, the statute protected virgins and ordinary prostitutes alike.[31] The distinction between virgins and prostitutes, however, animated many of the compulsory prostitution trials.

Belle Moore and the White Slavery Narrative

The trial of Belle Moore was the most publicized compulsory case in New York City. Unlike other compulsory prostitution trials in the Transcript Collection, *People v. Moore* received extensive coverage in the local papers. Assistant District Attorney James Bronson Reynolds accused Belle Moore, a twenty-nine-year-old mixed-race woman, of serious crimes including running a white slave racket on the West Side, selling teenage girls into forced prostitution, and being responsible for the abduction and death of an eleven-year-old girl named Helen Hastings. The trial of Belle Moore is an important event in New York City history because it exposed the connection between anti-prostitution efforts and racial tensions. The African American community in New York City increased nearly threefold from 1890 to 1920, and an African American woman accused of enslaving white girls crystal-lized the fear and racism harbored by white city residents. The Belle Moore trial, according to historian Barbara Antoniazzi, was a kind of public per-formance that laid bare the gender and racial tensions of Progressive-Era New York City.[32]

The case against Belle Moore started with a chain of events initiated by journalist George Kibbe Turner. Turner was a quintessential muckraker, exposing urban corruption in a series of articles in *McClure's Magazine*. A 1909 article titled "Daughters of the Poor" accused Tammany Hall of coor-dinating a vast white slavery conspiracy. His article contained the hallmarks of the Progressive-Era white slavery narrative. According to the article, white slave procurers (called "cadets") traveled to the industrial towns of New England to look for poorly paid factory girls to lure to New York City. One procurer, Turner noted, dressed as a priest to gain the confidence of his victims. As the city's vice industry expanded, white slave procurers heavily recruited from the slums and tenement houses, and Italians and Eastern European Jews haunted the city's dance halls to look for women to ensnare into prostitution. Turner observed, "The amusement of the poor girl of New York—especially the very poor girl—is dancing."[33] Therefore, the dance hall became the "chief recruiting grounds" for new white slaves.[34] Turner directly blamed Tammany Hall Democrats for the city's vice problem and declared that the only way to address New York City's prostitution problem was to defeat Tammany Hall at the ballot box.

Tammany Hall politicians responded to Turner's charges by initiating a grand jury investigation into white slavery. At the time, many believed that the grand jury effort was a way for Tammany Hall to whitewash or downplay the extent of prostitution; the investigation was designed to produce no evi-dence of white slavery and Tammany corruption. Judge Thomas O'Sullivan, a strong Tammany supporter, commissioned the grand jury and appointed an inexperienced and young foreman, John Rockefeller Jr. Rockefeller's family name gave the investigative effort a gloss of respectability, and it became known as the Rockefeller Grand Jury in the press. Tammany Hall did not expect, however, for Rockefeller to pursue his investigative work to the extent that he did. The grand jury studied the city's prostitution trade for over six months, long past the time they were required to meet. When they ran out of money, Rockefeller used a quarter-million dollars of his personal wealth to keep the investigation afloat. Some of the money was used for undercover investigators.

Frances Foster and George Miller were hired by the Rockefeller Grand Jury to pose as brothel owners seeking white slaves. Frances Foster, a Radcliffe graduate and social service worker, pretended to be "Frankie Fuller," the manager of a Seattle brothel. George Miller, an investigator for the National Immigration Commission, assumed the name "Dick Morris" and pretended to be a rich bachelor looking for young, white prostitutes. Miller frequented Baron Wilkin's saloon, a "black and tan" establishment that catered to African Americans and whites.[35] From the 1890s into the 1920s, white middle- and upper-class New Yorkers went on "slumming" excursions into predominantly African American establishments in the Tenderloin district.[36] The potential for interracial contact in black and tans made them wide targets for municipal reforms, and it is no surprise that the Rockefeller-sponsored investigators found useful contacts in the Tenderloin. According to an assistant district attorney, investigators made arrangements with a twenty-nine-year-old women named Belle Moore to purchase two teenage girls. Moore was arrested and charged with compulsory prostitution.

The 1910 white slavery prosecution of Belle Moore received thorough press coverage owing to the interracial nature of the case and sensationalist claims made by the prosecutor to the New York City press. The assistant district attorney accused Belle Moore of selling two girls into sexual slavery, and he also suggested to reporters that Moore abducted, prostituted, and possibly killed a white blue-eyed girl named Helen Hastings. The prosecuting attorney boasted that police had captured one of the leaders of the city's white slave racket, and New York City newspapers followed up with spirited reporting about Belle Moore, the "notorious procuress."[37]

The Moore trial exemplified many facets of the early twentieth-century outcry against the sex traffic. The press reports, for instance, were wildly sensationalistic, and the trial disproved many of the dramatic allegations leveled against the defendant. The "young girls" (twenty-five-year-old Belle Woods and twenty-three-year-old Alice Milton) revealed themselves to be experienced prostitutes, and the district attorney failed to substantiate the abduction (or existence) of the blue-eyed eleven-year-old girl. The alleged white slaves testified that they had full knowledge of the transaction and were going to "Frankie Fuller's" brothel on their own free will. The trial illustrated how Progressive-Era concerns about sexuality conjoined and amplified fears about racial intermixing.[38] The criminal prosecution targeted someone who fell outside the narrow category of early twentieth-century whiteness, and the trial exposed white racial anxiety about interracial contact. Investigators

George Miller and Frances Foster insisted that Moore provide them with white as opposed to "colored" girls. They also testified that Moore threw late-night parties with guitar music and lascivious dancing.[39]

While Moore fascinated reporters as an "extremely light mulatto" purportedly leading a West Side vice racket, the investigators drew scrutiny for their willingness to consort with underworld informers in interracial saloons and cafés.[40] A central strategy of Belle Moore's defense attorney was to accuse the investigators with taking too much pleasure in their excursions into New York City's interracial underworld. Moore's attorney, Alexander Karlin, repeatedly questioning Frances Foster about whether she thought it was proper "for a college woman to go about among negro sporting joints."[41] Belle Moore represented the supposed threat against white womanhood posed by sexually dangerous immigrants and African Americans, while Frances Foster represented the supposed perils of a "New Woman" whose sexual autonomy risked white "race suicide" by attracting them to miscegenation.[42] Karlin used the same approach with investigator George Miller. He insinuated that Miller, posing as bachelor "Dick Morris," indulged in the vices he was trusted to investigate. Karlin accused Miller of sharing a bed with Belle Moore after one of her late-night parties. He also insinuated that Miller slept with the prostitutes, drank heavily, and that he occupied "the same bed" as an African American named Alex Anderson.[43]

Judge Thomas C.T. Crain delivered extensive instructions to the jurors before they retired for deliberation. Crain was born near the Tammany Hall building on 14th Street and worked with the Tammany organization his entire life. In 1911, he was the presiding judge over the trial of the owners of the Triangle Shirtwaist Factory, the factory where nearly 150 garment workers died in a massive fire.[44] Crain was fifty years old at the time of the Moore trial and had been a judge in the Court of General Sessions for four years. He reminded jurors of the plain language of Section 2460 and told them that they were not to consider whether "this law is a wise law or an unwise law."[45] Crain also instructed jurors that it is irrelevant whether they "approve or do not approve of the general investigation."[46] Counter to the typical white slavery story, including the scandalous account of Moore abducting little girls, Crain emphasized that it was immaterial whether or not the "white slaves" consented to work for Frankie Fuller. Likewise, it did not matter that Alice Milton and Belle Woods were not "chaste" because, as the judge noted, "[t]his law safeguards the prostitute as well as the pure virgin in this respect."[47] The jurors retired for fifteen minutes, were taken to dinner for an hour, and returned to begin deliberations at 7:35 in the evening. Seventy minutes later, the jurors returned and delivered a guilty verdict.

During sentencing, attorney Alexander Karlin made several unsuccessful demands for a new trial. When his final motion was denied, he appealed to the judge to show mercy. Judge Crain should be lenient toward Moore, Karlin reasoned, because she was not a stereotypical white slave procurer and her supposed victims had sexual agency and were not true "white slaves." He said, "There is not any person that can point the finger of scorn at this defendant and say that she lured any women of purity and innocence from their homes and led them to the path of destruction and ruin."[48] Karlin conceded that "her morals have been rather loose, and that she has not lived that pure life that we would like any of our women to live," but he urged the judge to consider her lack of prior convictions and evil intent.[49] Judge Crain was not persuaded. He sentenced Belle Moore to the maximum punishment allowable by the statute, no less than two years and six months and no more than five years in the Auburn Prison for women.[50]

The Moore trial was unique because the trial received a tremendous amount of attention in the local newspapers and it involved an African American female defendant (the majority of prosecutions targeted men, including an overrepresentation of Italian and Eastern European immigrants). The Moore trial, however, was typical insofar as the pivotal testimony revolved around the question of the sexual respectability of the defendant and victims. Moore's attorney, like others defending their clients against charges of compulsory prostitution, underscored the differences between the stock white slavery narrative and the realities of New York City's vice trade. Compulsory prostitution trials show how courtroom participants, including jurors and judges, wrestled with the expectations generated by cultural narratives of urban sexual danger.

Charles Dix, the English White Slaver

Sixteen-year-old Katie Howboto arrived in New York City from Austria in 1911. Howboto later recounted, first to an assistant district attorney in police court and then to jurors in two separate criminal trials, that she worked as a domestic servant in Manhattan for a number of households and typically earned about sixteen dollars a month. Howboto met Charles Dix in the summer of 1913 and rented a furnished room in Harlem for $2 dollars a week. Months later, Dix offered her a room for a small weekly rent with the mutual understanding that she would do routine housework. Howboto lived at the place for a week before Dix sexually propositioned her while alone in her bedroom. Alone, Dix became violent when she rebuffed his advances; he threw her on the bed and raped her. She tried to cry out, but he restrained her and told her "don't holler."[51] Howboto testified that Dix kept her as practically a slave, prevented her from leaving the premises, and daily sent upward of a dozen men to have sex with her for money.

Charles Henry Dix, a forty-three-year-old Englishman, lived with his wife Bertha and their son Albert in Harlem for at least four years before he met Katie Howboto.[52] He first met Howboto when she and an Italian man sought to rent a room from him.[53] Dix said he refused them because they were unmarried. He said, "I told her she ought to be ashamed, a servant girl like her, monkeying around with Italian fellows of that kind."[54] According to Dix, she told him that she lived with "some Jew fellow I picked up on the street" and that she had been staying with the Italian for only a few days.[55] Dix portrayed Katie as a common prostitute, and he depicted himself as her savior in retrieving her clothes from her former pimp and giving her a place to stay. Police arrested Dix, Howboto, and two other women after raiding his house.

The earliest version of the crime is found in the "Statement of Katy Howboto" given to the district attorney before the trial. Transcribed and translated from a verbal report given to court authorities, it offers a first-person chronicle of her troubles with Dix. Although it reads like the spontaneous disclosure of her experiences, its perspective hides the role of the questioner and obscures the artificiality of the interview situation. The district attorney elicited her story with a particular legal purpose in mind, and he matched the essentials of her account against specific legal criteria. Her pretrial statement represents the first telling of her plight, which differed in some details from future versions she gave at trial.

According to her courtroom testimony, Katie Howboto arrived in the United States in 1911 with her aunt Natka Dyssu on the *Augusta Victoria*, which originated from the port of Hamburg.[56] She worked as a domestic for three families before seeking a furnished room from Charles Dix.[57] One night, after she had lived with him for a week, he went up to her room. "Wake up. I want to talk to you," he said.[58] Howboto awoke to find him standing near her bed in his underwear. Dix asked her where she was from and where she had previously worked, and then the conversation took a different turn. Charles told Katie that he planned to divorce his wife, wanted to marry her, and wanted to sleep with her right then. She rejected his advances and he said, "Now, listen, don't talk so foolish, I want to have connection with you."[59] She said, "Nothing like that. If you want a girl like that you can get a girl, and I can get a different job, and I want to go away."[60] According to Katie Howboto, Dix hit her in the face, knocked her over the bed, and told her, "You can't get away. If you try to get away, I'll pull your hair off."[61] Dix said, "I'll hit you so hard you won't know where you are."[62] He walked downstairs, leaving her alone and terrified. He allegedly unfastened his trousers and raped her. Howboto told jurors at Dix's first trial, "I wasn't so strong, and I was afraid of him, the way he was speaking."[63]

After Dix's assault, Howboto overheard a conversation between Dix and an unknown man. Dix told the man, "I have a little girl upstairs, and you could go upstairs and she will take you because she listens to me everything I say."[64] Thereafter, the stranger appeared in her room, with the intention of having sex with her for a dollar. She drove him away, but Dix insisted that she pay for the profits he lost in the failed transaction. He warned her that she had to have sex with whatever man showed up at her door. Fifteen men came to the furnished-room house to have intercourse with her on the first day. Police described it as a "regular dollar house," but she or Dix occasionally had the men pay $2 or $3.[65]

Sadie Smith was a twenty-six-year-old woman who went to live with Charles Dix a few weeks after Katie moved into the house. She referenced a work history as a domestic servant and as an employee of Woolworth's five and ten cent store and Callan's dry goods. She said she first met Dix while doing housework for someone who lived near his residence. After he spotted her wearing a blue calico dress commonly worn by domestics, he approached her and asked her to work at his place. Once there, Dix allegedly declared Sadie Smith "was no better than Katie Howboto" and would have to take men.[66] In a statement given to an assistant district attorney, Smith said, "He said that if I didn't do what the other girl was doing he would make me do it, or I would never leave the house alive."[67] Sadie Smith recalled that she and Howboto stayed the night at a friend's place and returned the next day for their things. She said that Katie "seemed to be afraid to be left alone in the house."[68] While Sadie packed Katie's bag, Dix entered the room, punched her, and grabbed her until "she was blue in the face and out of breath."[69]

A month after the physical altercation between Sadie, Katie, and Charles, police went to his place. They had heard reports that he had an illegal gun and that prostitution was practiced on the premises, and testimony in Dix's second trial also intimated that the officers were looking for heroin and cocaine as well.[70] A police officer testified at Dix's trial that a prostitute named Rose Ryan told him that Dix had a gun downstairs and that "he says whenever this place was raided he would shoot the officers, that he would kill them."[71] When a police officer confronted Dix, the defendant admitted that he had a gun but told the officer, "It is up to you to find it . . . I have some old army relics down there."[72] The police failed to find a gun. Later, an officer knocked on the door of the residence and pretended to be a customer looking for paid sex. Officer McGuirk told Rose, "I want to have a good time."[73] Rose, who used Dix's house for prostitution, led him into the back room and began to disrobe. She told him, "There's a nice little girl for your friend. She's downstairs, but Dix has her here all the while."[74] The police officer placed her under arrest and signaled for his colleagues to arrest the others.

Katie Howboto told Officer McGuirk that she worked for Charles Dix as a domestic servant earning $10 a month. Testifying at Dix's second trial, McGuirk recalled the exchange: "He [Dix] says 'Why, I get her here cleaning house for me.' I says to Katie Howboto, 'Is that a fact?' And she laughed and she said 'yes.' She was in a kimono."[75] The officer's testimony suggested that Howboto was a prostitute. He told Howboto to dress and then he followed her upstairs into her room. There, he found approximately twenty used towels on the sofa. "I said to her, 'what are they doing there?' And she says, 'I use that for myself.' I then said, 'You use them for the men, don't you?' And Katie smiled."[76] Although he testified for the prosecution, the officer's details about Howboto laughing, presumably at the absurdity of claiming to be a domestic worker while attired as a prostitute, undercut the image of her as a victim of compulsory prostitution. In fact, compulsory prostitution was not the original charge. Prosecutors first charged Dix with keeping a disorderly house, but the prosecutor changed the charge to compulsory prostitution three days later. In the words of the officer, "The White Slavery charge was made against Dix when Katie Howboto made her statement which she failed to make previous."[77]

According to Dix's defense attorney, Katie Howboto was an irrepressible flirt who routinely led men into her room for sex. The defense attorney called several individuals to attest to that claim. Howboto was not an imprisoned prostitute, had full freedom of movement. A chauffer named Edward Coulton was the first witness for Charles Dix's defense. Coulton testified that Katie and Sadie left the apartment unescorted two or three times a day. He recounted one incident when Katie was up at the window. "She was flirting with me or I was flirting with her, either one," he said. Edward Coulton exchanged mischievous glances with Katie Howboto, and then he held up six fingers to suggest a time to meet. Katie waved him off and pointed to a spot near the basement door. At the basement doorway, she handed Edward a note that said that she would like him at ten o'clock in the evening. According to Coulton, the note also told him to bring a friend.

The image of Katie Howboto as irresponsible and lustful was amplified by Bertha Borden, the second witness for the defense. Borden rented a furnished room to Katie before she went to live with Dix. Borden testified that she had to kick her out after a week because Katie allegedly stayed with a man named Happy and she routinely tossed her room key out the window to different men. Neighbors warned her "to be careful of that 'Happy.'"[78] Borden compelled Katie to leave a few days after an incident where a man approached the apartment and told her, "Happy gave me the key to come up and tell his wife something."[79] During cross-examination, Dix's defense attorney tried to impugn Borden's credibility by questioning her about her husband's arrest and imprisonment for selling cocaine from his candy store on 18th Avenue.[80]

Next, the defense called Dix's next door neighbor as a witness, an Englishwoman named Mrs. Annie Shepard, followed by Dix's wife Bertha. Both women painted an image of Katie as a sexually licentious liar. Katie told Mrs. Shepard that she was on the Titanic when it went down.[81] Bertha Dix later added, "The first time I ever saw her she told me she came off the Titanic that got sunk. That is how I knew. She said she came off the Titanic and she had a funny hat on, and I said, 'That hat looks like the Titanic,' and she took a room."[82] Later, Katie told her that she thought she was pregnant but could not identify the father. Bertha told her, "Now, look here, Katie, if you are going to have a baby, you better find out about it, and find out who the father is."[83] She told her that the father was possibly an Italian barber she had been seeing. After detailing Katie's affairs with men, Bertha testified that Katie went out nearly every night; she was hardly an imprisoned white slave.

Like his approach with Annie Shepard, the prosecutor tried to impeach the credibility of Dix's wife. On cross-examination the topic quickly changed from Katie's behavior to how Charles and Bertha lost custody of their child Albert after police caught him stealing. Next, Dix's defense attorney questioned Sadie Smith about her first meeting with Dix:

Defense Attorney Sol Hyman: You never lived at Dix's house before?

Sadie Smith: No, sir.

Q: How did you come to go there?

A: I was looking for a room so it would be near my place of business, so as to save carfares. I met a friend of mine and he told me there was plenty of furnished rooms in that district that would save me carfare.

Q: Were you a respectable girl at that time?

A: At what time?

Q: On the 23rd of February, 1914.

A: Respectable?

Q: Had you been going with men before that?

A: I made no business of it, no, sir.

Q: But you did go with men?

A: Yes, sir.

Q: Without compensation, without being paid for it?

A: Yes, sir.

Q: How many men?

A: Only one.[84]

The prevailing middle-class code of propriety held that upright women do not have sex before marriage, and a woman could be considered to be "going with men" even if they had an exclusive relationship with a single man. The attorney invoked an understanding of respectability that made chastity central to proper femininity, a definition that, by 1914, was under considerable strain.

Sadie made a hard distinction between premarital sex and prostitution in response to the attorney's question, but his follow-up question ("But you did go with men") indicated that her answer failed to satisfy his adopted definition of "respectability." The exchange shows overlapping understandings of respectability as they converge in the institutional setting of a criminal courthouse. The organization and structure of meaning outside the courtroom endowed the term "respectability" with different valences, and so Sadie's clarifying question ("Respectable?") illustrates more than a casual misunderstanding; the question underscores conflicting perspectives on sexual and social respectability.

Florence Baker and the Movie Theater

The prosecution's case against Charles Dix echoed elements of seduction stories reformers recounted during the nineteenth century: an upper-class man preyed on the economic insecurity of an impoverished immigrant. Prosecutors in *People v. DiMattio*, *People v. Brown*, and *People v. Orlick* hewed closer to the white slavery narrative by describing Florence Baker's descent into white slavery after she pursued a false assurance of employment. Florence Baker's mother died when she was fifteen, forcing her to quit school and find work as a chambermaid and domestic servant. She worked steadily in Germantown, Pennsylvania, for four years, earning $15 dollars a month. In 1914, she left for New York City with little money when the family she worked for could no longer pay her. Baker arrived at New York City's Penn Station in the afternoon and walked to a picture show in East Harlem. She stayed there until seven in the evening, during which time she struck up a conversation with an Italian barber named Prospro DiMattio. While in the theater, DiMattio assured her that he could find her housework.

Prospro DiMattio's method of entrapment of Baker corresponded to a common variant of the white slavery narrative. Reformers depicted darkened movie theaters as fertile hunting grounds for white slavers looking for women to ensnare. Cheap theaters formed a central part of the tapestry of commercial amusements that proliferated in early twentieth-century New York City. They caused concerned among civic activists and reformers because of the private space that movie houses afforded unwed couples.

The majority of movie attendees in the early twentieth century were foreign-born and working class.[85] Movie houses and nickelodeons quickly became an important source of information about urban existence, and by watching realistic images of city life on the movie screen immigrants recognized that their hardships were shared. Movies, "the poor man's amusement," spoke to working-class concerns about labor conditions, the fairness of the judicial system, and political corruption.[86] From these immigrant and working-class origins, movie audiences became more diverse, such that by 1910 twenty-six million Americans, nearly a third of the population, attended movie theaters on a weekly basis.[87] By 1920, half of the population went to the movie theaters weekly.

Women's attendance at movie theaters helped reshape gender relations during these years by giving women an acceptable public space and form of sociality. Film historian Shelley Stamp argues that the cinema "rede-fined the ground upon which women might participate in urban life."[88] Sharon Ullman similarly notes how "film contributed significantly to the renegotiation of public sexuality."[89] Theaters provided a space for women to congregate in the city outside the home and factory. Movie theaters also expanded the opportunities for men and women to meet and conspire. By 1910, women formed a substantial part of movie audiences. The presence of women in neighborhood movie theaters troubled middle- and upper-class reformers. Stamp noted, "Cinemas were described by many observers as arenas of particular carnal license, where women were alternately preyed upon by salacious men who gathered around entranceways, and themselves tempted to engage in untoward conduct."[90] In particular, reformers worried about depictions of prostitution enticing women into the life. Mrs. Barclay Hazard, in a 1914 article for *Current Opinion*, noted the danger movies posed for certain women: "The girl of the border-line type, the type first named, goes to see these films. To her untrained, unbalanced and extremely susceptible mentality the only appeal made by such pictures is one of allure-ment."[91] Jurors in New York City criminal trials carried assumptions about movie theaters as possible sites of immorality and moral danger.

Visiting a movie theater in the 1910s was a very different experience compared to later in the century. Attending a movie in the early twenti-eth century entailed sociability that would be considered rude in modern theaters. Theaters played the same short films continuously throughout the day and customers could come into the theater and stay for as long as they liked, so it was not uncommon for someone to drop in for a few minutes, nor was it odd to spend all day in the theater. Compared to cramped tenements, movie theaters functioned as community living rooms for New York City's working class.[92] Theaters bustled with neighborhood activity, and audience members routinely talked back to the screen and conferred among compatriots about the plots and the printed dialogue on screen.

Ironically, many films shown in early movie theaters trumpeted the dangers of white slavery.[93] The year Baker met DiMattio in the theater, 1914, was a highpoint in the production of white slavery films. Films shown in New York City theaters that year—*The Exposure of the White Slave Traffic*, *Smashing the Vice Trust*, *The House of Bondage*, *A Soul in Peril*, and *The Traffic in Girls*—drew enormous crowds.[94]

According to the prosecutor, DiMattio and Baker left the theater and traveled to a nearby barber shop owned by DiMattio's friend, Louis Orza. Baker said that DiMattio threw her on the bed in the backroom, tore off her clothes, raped her, and then locked the room. She testified: "[T]he next morning I wanted to get out and he told me if I didn't stay here he would kill me."[95] She spent three days in the back room of the barber shop, where her captors told customers that her cries were merely the sounds of a quarrelling couple. Thereafter, DiMattio compelled her to stay at the apartment of Louis and Josephine Baroni. She testified to spending three sleepless nights, fully clothed, wedged between the couple on the bed. Florence said that the Baronis "told me I had to stay where I was; that I wouldn't dare move out of the house.[96] She stayed with the couple for three days before another white slaver, Sam Orlick, brought her to a furnished-room apartment on 105th Street. Orlick paid two dollars for the first week's rent and assured Dora Waible, the keeper of the three-story flat, that he and Florence were married. The following day Waible found Florence locked in the room and called the police to have Orlick arrested. The inn keeper testified before the jury that she knocked on the door and demanded that Baker open it. "Well, I have no key," Baker responded. When Waible opened the door, she found Baker undressed. "She wanted to be taken out," said the inn keeper at DiMattio's trial.[97] Police arrested five individuals for forcing Florence Baker into prostitution: Prospro DiMattio, Louis Orza, Sam Orlick, Max Drexler, and Joseph Anthony.

The strictures of the white slavery story helped the defense strategies in *People v. DiMattio* and *People v. Orlick*. In those trials, the defense attorneys used Florence Baker's testimony about coercion to underscore its difference from accounts of sexual slavery dominant in white slavery narratives. Baker, the defense attorneys maintained, willingly consorted with DiMattio, the Baronis, and Orlick. The defense attorneys defined consent and willingness with reference to white slavery narratives; she was either enslaved in each of the three apartments or she lived there on her own accord. Sam Orlick's defense attorney, for instance, asserted Baker's willingness to go to the furnished room with the defendant by defining free will as the absence of extreme physical coercion:

Defense Attorney Neustadter: Was it on Sunday that you left the flat with Orlick?

Baker: Yes, sir.

Q: And he didn't threaten to kill you there?

A: In the room he threatened me.

Q: Did he threaten you in the house?

A: No, sir.

Q: You went with him voluntarily?

A: I do not know what you mean.

Q: You went with him of your own free will?

A: No, sir, I did not.

Q: Do you know what free will means?

A: Yes, sir.

Q: Did you leave the house of that Italian barber's workingmen of your own free will?

A: No, sir.

Q: Did he threaten to kill you if you didn't leave?

A: No sir.[98]

The attorneys conferred agency to Baker by linguistically positioning her as the subject of the action and by describing her movement with the active voice ("you left"; "you leave"; "you didn't leave"). The attorney sandwiched his questions about her free will within questions about death threats, suggesting that death threats were the only acceptable impediment to the exercise of her will. He raised questions about severe forms of duress she allegedly faced and the physical constraints on the doors and windows that prevented her escape. By summoning some hallmarks of the standard white slavery narrative the attorneys invited the jurors to compare the stock scenarios of abduction and forced prostitution with the contradictory evidence presented in the complainant's testimony. The structure of the questioning was homologous with the attorney's story. Through this question sequence, the attorney invoked the binary logic of the white slavery narrative: she was either imprisoned or acted with unfettered will.

Sam Orlick told jurors that Florence willingly went with him to the furnished-room house but, finding it not yet ready, they went to a restaurant and a movie theater beforehand.[99] Florence Baker, not Sam Orlick, was the sexual aggressor once they paid for the room. Orlick testified that Florence was perturbed by his lack of affection: "She was hugging me and kissing me, and she is asking me why she has to do all the work; why I don't hug her."[100] After having sex with her, he left and locked the door behind him because "she asked me to lock the door, so I shouldn't disturb her."[101] Orlick went to the movies for four hours and found the police waiting for him upon his return home.

The defense strategies in *Orlick* and *DiMattio* used the white slavery narrative to define the parameters of their defendants' criminality and culpability, and the judges in both trials actively opposed this rhetorical move. In *People v. DiMattio*, the complainant revealed some confusion about the location of the railway station.[102] Raising the image of a naïve country girl whose thirst for city life led to her downfall, the defense attorney asked:

Neustadter: You consider yourself a country girl or a city girl?

Baker: Well, I didn't live in Philadelphia all my life. I was born in the country.

Judge Wadams: What difference does that make? There is not one law for a country girl and one for a city girl.

A: I consider myself a country girl.[103]

DiMattio's defense attorney persisted in this line of questioning by asking her if the attractions of Broadway and the burgeoning entertainment district drew her to the city. He referenced Broadway's reputation because of its copious electrical lights as "the great white way." This rhetorical tact prompted the judge to clarify the scope of the statute:

Neustadter: When you came to New York, before you came to New York, did you ever hear of Broadway and the White Lights?

Baker: No.

Q: You never did?

A: No sir.

Q: You never heard the saying, "Life in New York"?

A: No.

Q: You never heard of Broadway in New York when you were in Philadelphia?

A: No sir.

Judge Wadams: I don't see what bearing that has.

Neustadter: I will connect it.

Judge: The law is that if she came here to be a prostitute, anyone who took her in to achieve that object would be guilty of a crime, and whether she is good or bad. The only question is, you may prove any vicious or immoral acts on the question of her credibility. Now, you have not shown any vicious or immoral act. You have shown, if you please, that she is stupid and foolish but the law is to protect just such people.[104]

In *People v. Orlick*, Judge Wadams also expressed impatience with the defense attorney's suggestion that a successful prosecution required proof that Orlick held Florence Baker as an archetypal white slave. Neustadter persisted in underlining the elements of coercion that helped construct Florence as a white slave while the judge attempted to contain the scope of the defense attorney's questioning. Neustadter challenged the suggestion that the Baronis deprived Florence of decent food, and his questions provoked the judge to intercede:

Neustadter: Did you give her something to eat?

Florence Baker: Yes, sir.

Q: Did you ill treat her at all?

Judge Wadams: There is no claim she was. It is entirely immaterial.

Neustadter: If you Honor please, the complaining witness claims that she was kept by duress in that house.

Judge Wadams: The jury will determine that, and how much force was necessary to keep her there, [and] take her story in connection with her own appearance and character, as indicated to them by her manner on the stand.[105]

In his cross-examination of Josephine Baroni on her alleged imprisonment of Baker, the attorney tried to underscore her mobility:

Neustadter: Did you keep her [Baker] there by force?

Josephine Baroni: No, she told me if I kindly let her stay there until she have [sic] a job.

Q: Did she go out with you in the day time?

A: She went out with me to buy some underwear.

Q: Did she buy some?

A: Yes, sir.

Q: Did she go out alone?

A: No, sir.

Q: Did you permit her to go out alone?

Judge Wadams: There is no claim that this woman exercised any duress.[106]

The final pages of the trial transcripts suggest that juror discussions centered on whether or not coerced noncommercial sex fell under the statute. When jurors asked about the scope of the statute, Judge Wadams replied that coercion did not define the crime, but that her status as a commercial object bought by other men made the law applicable. The judge said that the crux of the case was not the locked door, but the wide range of nonphysical forms of compulsion: "The evidence with respect to the locking of the door should be considered by you with relation to the definition of compelling, but, as you recall, if the girl was not locked, if he enticed, or induced or procured Florence Baker for the purpose of prostitution by her, he would be guilty, whether he locked the door or not."[107]

Abraham Belkin and False Promises of Marriage

The complainant's testimony in *People v. Belkin* described how sixteen-year-old Annie Jacobs emigrated from Minsk, Russia, with her brother and sister, arriving in New York City in early October 1911. Less than a year later, she met Abraham Belkin at a picnic in Liberty Park and a few months thereafter left her home unannounced. Jacobs testified that she was lured away from home upon Belkin's promise of marriage. Belkin kept her imprisoned for several days before selling her to Annie Brown, a woman who also faced white slavery charges upon Jacob's complaint.

According to prosecutors, Belkin held Annie Jacobs captive after she followed him into his room and he locked the door behind him. He told her, "I don't want my aunt to know that I have a girl in the room."[108] At that point, Jacobs had never been alone with a man in a room, and fearing that "he wanted to deprive me of my virginity," she threw herself against the door.[109] Finding it unmovable, she attempted to open the window latch, but it was locked. She testified that he restrained both of her wrists with one hand and put the other hand over her mouth: "he wouldn't let me cry out loud."[110] The next morning, after he had taken her virginity, he brought breakfast up to the room but she refused to eat and remained there the entire day "sitting and crying all the time."[111] In fact, Belkin forbade Jacobs from leaving the room even to use the bathroom; he brought in a large chamber pot for her to use.[112]

The prosecutor called Marion Goldman, the chief inspector of the New York Probation Association and overseer of the Waverly House women's detention center, to support the account of enslavement. She testified that she visited the apartment the previous day and entered through the kitchen alone after finding the door unlocked. She located a small five-by-six-foot room where Belkin allegedly held Jacobs. Goldman testified that the door was secured with a bolt and that a chair was wedged into the door knob. She said that the "perfectly new" bolt stood in contrast to the dilapidated surrounding.[113] The door looked old, and the bolt was the only new piece of hardware that she saw.[114]

As in *DiMattio* and *Orlick*, the defense attorney in *Belkin* imported the criteria of nonconsent from the white slavery narrative and argued that the prosecutor failed to show that Abraham Belkin coerced Annie Jacobs under the standard implied in the white slavery narrative. For example, the attorney drew jurors' attention to the window in the room where Jacobs was captive. Authors of white slavery narratives often situated the brothel window as the white slave's key means of escape, and Belkin's attorney mirrored that narrative element in his questioning.[115]

Defense Attorney Sarasohn: Well, when you tried to lift that window, and you found it was locked, and you were alone with a man in the room, and he was threatening to rob you of your virginity, why didn't you strike at that window, break it?

Annie Jacobs: He was holding my hands, I couldn't do it.

Q: Was he holding both hands?

A: Yes, sir.

Q: Why didn't you shriek? Now, tell that jury.

A: To whom should I have made an outcry?

Q: Looking from that window, didn't you see people on the street?

A: No.[116]

The attorney interpolated her consent from her lack of desire to scream or break through the window. The attorney suggested that fiercely resisting rape was the only way a woman in such a situation could preserve her honor. The "resistance test" was an informal standard in seduction prosecutions and a formal standard in rape trials that used the ferocity of the victim's resistance as the measure of her nonconsent.[117] This corresponded to a gender ideology that made women's premarital virginity more important than their lives, aligning with a common refrain in the anti-vice reform literature that rape and forced prostitution were fates worse than death.[118] The idea that a woman would naturally risk her life to preserve her virginity also fit a prevailing gender ideology that viewed premarital sex in terms of "ruination."[119]

Belkin's defense attorney also used the white slavery narrative against the prosecution by comparing the complainant's freedom of movement with that of the archetypal white slave. On the Sunday prior to Belkin's arrest, the complainant Jacobs and the defendant Belkin went to the moving pictures. Belkin's defense attorney asked Annie Jacobs about the weekend excursion to question why she did not act on her opportunity to escape and return home. She said that she "was green and I didn't know where to turn and I didn't know where to go."[120] She saw people in the street, "but I didn't know to whom to apply and I was afraid."[121] The attorney pressed her on the issue: "Pardon me, you say you were afraid. Were there any chains on you?"[122] After a brief verbal skirmish among the attorneys, Jacobs threw the challenge back at Sarasohn: "Was it necessary even to have chains on me?"[123]

Jacobs' counter-question during her cross-examination broke with the white slave story in two ways. The very act of putting a question to the attorney revealed an assertiveness that defied the stereotype of the meek white slave whose will had been shattered by cruel captivity. Talking back to the attorney contradicted her professed naïvety. Also, Jacobs's question undermined the centrality of abduction and imprisonment in the white slavery narrative. She suggested that the power Belkin had over her, and her compulsion to stay in the sex trade, did not stem from locked doors, chains, and physical beatings. Jacobs's moment of resistance implicitly referenced coercion that fell outside the melodramatic parameters of the white slave story, including the complex psychosocial dynamics between pimps and prostitutes and the economic realities that structured women's participation in the vice trade. The white slavery narrative subverted this socioeconomic understanding of prostitution by emphasizing physical entrapment over and above other, equally relevant, narratives of coercion.

In *People v. Belkin*, the prosecutor contended that Annie Jacobs was a seduced virgin held by force and compelled to have sex with men. The defense used different witnesses to suggest Jacob's sexual agency and her eagerness to leave the confines of her parents' home for excitement in the city. An employee at the Grand Palace Hall dance academy told the courtroom that Annie Jacobs frequently visited the establishment and had attended dances there soon after her arrival in New York City. He said that Annie caused trouble at the dance academy by "fooling around" with the boys and sitting on their side of the room. When the judge asked him what he meant by "fooling around," he said, "You know, the boys throw jokes and she listens to it, and sitting on the boys' side."[124] When she "started to dance around with some girls," the instructor told her to behave and threatened to eject her.

Abe's cousin, Jacob Cohen, also testified for the defense and elaborated Annie Jacobs's sexual experience. Jacob Cohen testified that Abe Belkin did not lead Annie into prostitution; rather, Annie corrupted Abe. Cohen testified that Annie Jacobs introduced Abe and his cousin to a prostitute named Annie Brown and the four of them had sex in the apartment. Jacob Cohen said that he and his cousin waited outside Brown's apartment until Annie Jacobs called to them: "You don't have to be bashful, come upstairs."[125] The men asked Jacobs and Brown if they were ready to leave for a picnic when another woman named Annie (Eisenstock) said, "Boys, if you want, let us have a picnic here."[16] Cohen said, "I asked her what kind of picnic, so she took me in her bedroom and asked me for a half dollar."[127]

Assenta Bruno, Physical Violence, and Womanly Honor

The trial of Antonio Russo offers yet another example of how the defense used the details of the white slavery narrative to support the defendant. In *People v. Russo*, a twenty-two-year-old woman named Assenta Bruno testified that a man named Antonio Russo forced her into prostitution. She and her husband arrived in New York City in 1905 and met a fellow country-man who helped them find housing and employment. She testified that her husband worked as a photographer and she worked as a confectioner, yet the defense attorney insisted that she worked as a prostitute immediately upon her arrival to the United States. In April 1908, she left her apartment with a woman named Maria Elvira. According to Bruno, Elvira told her that they were meeting up with another countrywoman to find new employment, but she deceived Bruno by taking her to Russo's home and leaving her after five minutes. Bruno testified that she tried to escape the apartment, but that the defendant "kept [her] there by force," threatened to cut her face, and raped her.[128]

Bruno's testimony through an interpreter created confusion that the defense attorney readily exploited. He used her misunderstanding of English to linguistically blur romantic intimacy and rape:

Defense Attorney James Brande: And you didn't shout, you didn't scream?

Assenta Bruno: I couldn't shout, because he had threatened me, and he was threatening me.

Q: About the cut in the face?

A: Yes.

Q: And did you finally take your clothes off?

A: He undressed me, the defendant.

Q: Then what happened? Did you sit around the room, or start to clean up the room?

A: He had the first sexual intercourse with me, then.

Q: You went into the bedroom; did you?

A: Yes.

Q: Did you walk in?

A: No; he took me by force.

Q: What did he do?

A: He caught hold of my hands (illustrating).

Q: Certainly. He embraced you? Is that what he done [*sic*]?

A: Yes.

Q: And you walked in with him, in an embracing manner?

A: Yes; by force I went.[129]

Russo's defense attorney tried to build an image of a consensual sexual relationship between Assenta Bruno and Antonio Russo, both his alleged rape and the agreement that she give her body to other men for money. After offering her account of how the defendant sexually assaulted her, Bruno said, "And that very same night he made me a prostitute."[130] Again, Russo's defense attorney exploited the gap between his question and Bruno's evident misunderstanding of the translator's translation. The attorney rephrased her statement: "In other words, the defendant in his persuasive way, persuaded you to stay there, and live with him; is that right?"[131] Although her response indicated that she did not comprehend the question, in the process of answering it she asserted the guilt of the white slave procurer and a watchman named Francesco. "Yes," she replied, "this defendant and this Francesco were both of them the persons who kept me there."[132]

Assenta Bruno stayed at his apartment for eight days and had sex with four or five men a day. Francesco guarded Bruno and compelled her to give him all the money she earned. When asked if she demanded to be let out of the apartment, she responded, "Every five minutes I used to ask him that."[133] The defense attorney pressed her on her willingness to sleep with the defendant and asked her a string of questions designed to challenge the boundaries of her honorability. He suggested that a true woman would not debauch herself, even if faced with a grave physical threat:

Defense Attorney James Brande: Did the defendant say that he would cut your face?

Assenta Bruno: Yes.

Q: And you were an honorable woman up to the time that you got to this defendant's home, weren't you?

A: Yes, sir.

Q: And you had never resided in a house of prostitution before that?

A: No.

Q: And you had had no sexual intercourse with any man?

A: No.

Q: And yet, on the threat of a man, who threatened to cut your face, you debauched yourself as a prostitute; is that right?

A: Yes. Through threats and through revolvers, I had to obey.

Q: Well, what did you do to save your honor?

A: How could I scream when he threatened to cut my face? And he told me if I notified the police, or put him in trouble, he would cut my face.

Q: But you thought more of your face than you did of your Honor?

A: I was thinking of all these witnesses that are here in court, and all these people, and my life was in danger and I couldn't do anything.[134]

Brande again asked, "At the time you were in the house of the defendant, when you say he forced you, were you in fear of losing your honor, or were you in fear of having your face cut?"[135] A question asked moments later also tried to convey an either/or choice between physical violence and honor, and between complete freedom and absolute compulsion. Brande asked, "Well, which do you value most, a cut on your face or your honor?"[136] Moments later he pressed her again: "Did you prefer to have sexual intercourse with this man, of your own free will and accord, rather than to get your face cut?"[137] The judge sustained objections to both questions.

The supposed choice between physical mutilation and womanly honor is only intelligible under a cultural schema that views prostitution and premarital sex as fates worse than death. The attorney imposed a resistance test, suggesting that an honorable woman would submit to having her face slashed before submitting to sexual debauchery. This strategy put Bruno in a double bind. She affirmatively signaled her consent by not resisting her attacker as much as she could. On the other hand, by pushing back against both the attacker and the attorney's questions, she broke from the script of feminine submissiveness that the questioning presupposed.

Giuseppe Spano and Claims of Heroism

In *People v. Spano*, defendant Giuseppe Spano argued that he tried to rescue the complainant, Mary Hynes, from a life of poverty and prostitution. According to his story, he and a friend met Hynes and two other women at a café, and the men arranged with the women to exchange money for sex. He testified, "They were street women and we had connection, every one of us. They make $7 that night."[138] A month after Spano had sex with Mary, she got into a fight with her pimp Joe Fay and, according to Spano, "If it was not for me she sure get killed that night."[139] In this account, Mary begged Giuseppe not only to save her from a violent pimp but to turn her into an honest woman:

> One night she come to the barber shop and says to me that she was put out, that the child was dying of consumption and they had been dispossessed in the house and she was tired of this past life. She said, "You have saved my life two times and I want you to help me. I promise you I will stop this business," she says, "I am tired of it. I have been doing this for the last seven or eight years, but I see it does no good to me. I done away with one child one time while I was residing with a fellow." She told me a whole lot of lie.[140]

He offered his apartment to her and claimed that he gave her eight dollars a week for her living expenses. According to Spano, she told him, "I can't control myself, I want somebody to control me because it seems to me very hard, because I met a friend and they always get me in the same life, in the same line, I cannot control myself, I want somebody to control me."[141] When asked in cross-examination about his motivation in taking Hynes, he responded, "to make a noble life out of her and to show her friends or her enemies how bad girls became to be good girls. I tried the best I could in my power and I want she should stop all those kinds—going out and getting drunk, going out for soliciting and all that. That was my only interest."[142] In Spano's courtroom story, Mary's moral weakness and susceptibility to others' influence required a firm hand; she wanted someone to control her.

Giuseppe Spano's father, a shoemaker named Francesco, supported his son's story. He testified that Giuseppe begged him to allow Mary Hynes to live in their apartment. He framed his son's motives in the best possible light. According to Francesco, he said, "'She is a girl that had nowheres to go and I found her in the street,' and then I said to my son 'What are you to do with her? There is no room for her.'"[143] Ultimately, Spano's narrative of the heroic rescuer failed to convince the jury. They found him guilty, and the judge sentenced him to five to nineteen years in prison. His father, who various witnesses insinuated was a member of the Italian mafia, or the "Black Hand," was deported shortly after the trial.[144]

Annie Jacobs, the White Slave from Minsk

The trial of Abraham Belkin illustrates the active role of jurors and judges in white slavery cases. The prosecution contended in *People v. Belkin* that Annie Jacobs was an innocent, naïve girl who was twice betrayed by Abe Belkin: first, when he took her virginity and kept her captive in Brownsville, and again when he compelled her to become an inmate of Annie Brown's house of prostitution. The defense maintained that Annie Jacob's prostitution began in Minsk; she was not innocent as she claimed, had considerable sexual experience, and lived and practiced prostitution with Annie Brown and Annie Eisenstock on her own volition. Although we will never know the precise issues of contestation that led to two deadlocked jury deliberations, the questions the jurors raised during the trial provide acute insight into the narrative fidelity of the competing stories.

After the jury reached a deadlock in his first trial, Belkin was taken to trial a second time, but that jury was similarly unable to reach a consensus about his culpability. The outcome did not stem from jurors' lack of interest in the case. Judge Crain remarked that "very pertinent questions put, from time to time, by different jurors" augmented the trial's integrity.[145] The difficulty the jurors evidently had in assessing Belkin's guilt or innocence mirrored the problems the prosecution faced in portraying the complainant as a victim of white slavery. During Belkin's second trial, the jury retired four times. The final time before the insurmountable deadlock prompted their excusal and the defendant's release, jurors asked the judge for guidance in evaluating Annie Jacob's sexual past with the defendant. Did it matter if the complainant had sex with the defendant before selling her body to other men? If he brought her to the tenement house for his own lascivious purposes and not necessarily for profit, does that constitute compulsory prostitution? For both questions, the judged answered in the negative.[146]

The *Belkin* transcripts suggest a mismatch between jurors' expectations about white slavery and the details uncovered through various testimonies. Ultimately, this led them to an inconclusive assessment of Annie Jacobs's morality, sexual experience, and relationship with Abraham Belkin. During Belkin's second trial, the judge admonished Brown for speaking in too soft a voice on the witness stand. At that time, the fifth juror asked the court if it would be acceptable for him to "request the witness take off her hat, so that we can see how she looks."[147] The prosecutor bolstered the request, noting that "the question of her age may become very important."[148] Apart from visual cues from which to read Annie's innocence or experience, jurors questioned witnesses about the room where she was allegedly held against her will. The eleventh juror asked about the bolted room, desiring to know "upon which side of that door the bolt was."[149] The witness, Abe's brother, denied that the door was bolted. He said that it was secured by "a plain lock" that "was never locked."[150] The tenth juror raised a similar question about Annie Brown's Mangin Street apartment. He asked the defendant if any furniture was propped up against the door. Belkin denied that there was. He responded in the negative to the juror's follow-up question ("Nothing blocking that door?").[151]

Jurors in *People v. Brown* voiced similar concerns about Annie Jacobs's imprisonment. During Annie Jacob's direct examination, the ninth juror asked if Annie had "clothes enough to go out?"[152] The theft of the white slave's respectable clothing was a common element in white slavery narratives. For example, in *Panders and Their White Slaves*—one of the many semi-fictional books about white slavery published during the Progressive Era—anti-vice reformer Clifford Roe tells of a typical instance: "As in nearly every case when girls are procured, her street clothes were locked up, and she was not allowed to communicate with the outside world."[153] In an essay about white slavery, Roe wrote, "After the girls are once within the resort, the stories are about the same. Their street clothes are seized and parlor dresses varying in length are put upon them."[154] Chicago district attorney Edwin Sims discussed an example of white slavery and noted, "[A]s is the case with all new white slaves she was not allowed to have any clothing which she could wear upon the street."[155] Placing the testimony in *People v. Brown* in a wider context suggests that popular culture—at the very least—provided the conditions of possibility for the question to arise in the juror's understanding of the case. Judges gave jurors explicit instruction and guidance in how to evaluate the evidence before them, but jurors drew from popular culture as well as formal legal instruction.

In these cases, jurors carried concerns about locked doors and coercion into the deliberation room. Often impatient with testimony that dwelled on locks, keys, and barred windows, judges frequently reminded attorneys and jurors of the minimal requirements of Section 2460 captured in terms like "entice" and "induce." However, the questions jurors asked witnesses during the trial, and the questions jurors posed to judges during their deliberations, demonstrate that many jurors expected to hear about locked doors, barred windows, deprivations of food, and stolen clothing. The white slavery narrative shaped expectations as to how legal actors should tell and hear stories of forced prostitution in the courtroom.

≈

Examining the trials individually shows how the generic white slavery story shaped jurors' assessment of compulsory prostitution cases. Expectations about the stock white slavery scenario of abduction and imprisonment and of innocence and villainy guided attorneys' courtroom strategies. For prosecutors, the white slavery scenario proved to be more of a hindrance than a help. While the stories told in court matched, and sometimes exceeded, the violence represented in popular white slavery narratives, the archetypal white slave's lack of sexual agency clashed with the realities of New York City's prostitution trade. As a result, prosecutors emphasized the case elements that matched the stock white slavery story, but they emphasized the legal scope of the white slavery law and how the defendant could be guilty whether the complaint consented to sex or not.

Defense attorneys employed time-worn strategies for proving their clients' innocence, including challenging the credibility of the prosecutors' witnesses and disputing their chronology of events. Beyond the standard tool-kit of criminal defense strategies, attorneys defending their clients against white slavery charges sometimes used the criteria and dichotomous logic of the white slavery story to their own advantage by highlighting gaps between the core elements of the white slavery narrative and testimony about the complainant's alleged freedom. The defense used the narrative structure of white slavery stories against the prosecution.

The white slave story was a narrative touchstone for legal actors in early twentieth-century compulsory prostitution cases, but it was a story that served both sides of the case. Prosecutors emphasized the dimensions of compulsory prostitution cases that fit with a larger narrative of white slavery, but they did not have the final say in how those courtroom stories were told or interpreted. Judges, oriented toward the formal legal parameters of Section 2460, tried to ensure that the trial argumentation centered on the proper legal topics. Jurors, oriented toward the facts of the case in their role as fact-finders, asked questions of witnesses and judges that revealed the strong cultural assumptions guiding their interpretation of those facts. Defense attorneys leveraged these assumptions by contrasting the stock elements of white slavery stories with case details that glaringly failed to fit the overarching narrative of abduction and forced prostitution. Taken together, all four parties created the stories of compulsory prostitution ultimately evaluated by the jurors.

Although discursive activity in compulsory prostitution cases did not exclusively revolve around the white slavery narrative, trial testimony shows the handprint of that story in the early twentieth-century courtroom. White slavery narratives shored up female domesticity by depicting city amusements and urban employment as dangerous for young women. The contrast the white slavery narrative made between the country and the city implored young women to remain in the protective space of the home. Socio-legal scholars Patricia Ewick and Susan Silbey argue that hegemonic narratives can function to "colonize" the consciousness of their audiences, pushing other stories and explanations out of consideration.[156] The white slavery narrative worked in this way by offering simplistic, yet morally resonant, explanations for why women engage in prostitution.

Chapter 5

Sodomy, Manhood, and Consent

For most of the twentieth century, "sodomy" has been understood as an act of sexual connection among individuals who share the same perceived biological sex.[1] The link between sodomy and same-sex desire has been generally taken for granted in legal, popular, and political culture. In 1993, for instance, former US senator Strom Thurmond shouted on the Senate floor during a debate about gays in the military, "Heterosexuals do not practice sodomy!"[2] But the idea of sodomy as "gay sex" is remarkably new. From the colonial period through most of the nineteenth century, sodomy laws criminalized a wide range of sexual conduct, including bestiality, pedophilia, and public masturbation. Colonial religious authorities considered sodomy a capital offense, but they did not conceive of sexuality as a source of personhood that drove sexual action.[3] Their concerns about sodomy centered on the idea that the crime wasted sexual energy in violation of cultural and religious mandates to procreate.[4] No one viewed sodomy laws as pointed toward a gay status group or subculture, if only because the modern notion of sodomy as a group-defining practice was not yet in place and the term "gay" as a term for a man who has sex with other men was decades from taking hold in public discourse.

Before the early twentieth century, sodomy arrests were extremely rare. New York City prosecutors, for example, pursued only twenty-two sodomy cases between 1796 and 1843.[5] From the 1880s to the early twentieth century, most sodomy prosecutions in New York City involved victims under the age of eighteen. These cases were primarily instances where older men raped boys.[6] The number of sodomy prosecutions increased in the 1880s and 1890s largely due to the efforts of the Society for the Prevention of Cruelty to Children (SPCC) and the Society for the Prevention of Crime. Their focus remained on men who sexually abused children.[7] Reflecting national trends, the historical pattern of sodomy arrests and prosecution in New York City shows that, until the early twentieth century, prosecutors reserved sodomy prosecutions for sexual predators and rarely sought prosecution when the crime involved consenting parties, even if they were same-sex couples.[8]

In the early twentieth century, law enforcement agencies and their proxies changed the scope and enforcement of the sodomy laws. From 1901 to 1905, New York City police arrested an average of sixty-five people for sodomy per year, which represents a threefold increase over prior years.[9] Whereas prosecutors' earlier use of sodomy statutes primarily addressed men's coercive sex with weaker or nonconsenting parties, the twentieth-century use of the law tied nonnormative sex to a homosexual status group. Jonathan Katz contends that the backlash against gays represented a "wedding of social disgust and state mobilization."[10] According to George Chauncey, "Federal, state, and local governments deployed a barrage of new techniques for the surveillance and control of homosexuals, and the number of arrests and dismissals escalated sharply."[11] The shift in the New York public's understanding and prosecution of sodomy was fueled by scandal.

The Oscar Wilde scandal in 1895 became a touchstone for understanding homosexuality and degeneracy into the twentieth century. By the 1890s, Wilde was an accomplished journalist, novelist, poet, orator, and playwright. His 1890 novel *The Picture of Dorian Gray* cemented his reputation as a literary force, but it also drew criticism for its supposed amoral aestheticism and references to same-sex desire. Wilde began an affair with Lord Alfred Douglas in 1893 that drew the attention of Douglas's father the Marquess de Queensberry. Hostilities escalated between Wilde and the marquess. The marquess accused Wilde of being a sodomite and Wilde, against the advice of his friends, brought a libel case against the Marquess de Queensberry. In return, the marquess gathered evidence against Wilde, and Wilde was charged with gross indecency and sodomy. He was eventually found guilty, sentenced to two years of hard labor, and died three years after his release.[12] His widely publicized trials for sodomy helped an Anglo-American middle- and upper-class public link sodomy and same-sex desire, instead of the common view of sodomy as a degenerate practice only engaged in by the lower classes, new immigrant groups, and racial minorities. The Wilde scandal was an important transitional episode that bridged older understandings of sodomy into a new paradigm that fused an individual's identity with their sexual object choice. The trials gave greater visibility to gay subcultures in Anglo-America.

At a local level, controversies surrounding Tammany Hall shaped the public's understanding of law and sexuality. Tammany Hall referred to a building where Democrats met, but "Tammany" was shorthand for a political machine. Controversies surrounding Tammany Hall that dominated New York City from the 1850s to the 1930s provide important context for sodomy prosecutions in the city. Anti-Tammany forces, including polarizing figures like Reverend Charles Parkhurst, Inspector Edward Walsh, and Captain Max Schmittberger organized raids against saloons, bathhouses, and brothels.

Charles Parkhurst was a pastor in Lenox, Massachusetts, from 1874 until 1880. He moved to New York City in 1880 and served as pastor in the Madison Square Presbyterian Church for almost three decades. Reverend Parkhurst's political clout grew, and he was elected president of the Society for the Prevention of Crime in 1891. The next year, Detective Charles Gardner and his friend John L. Erving went on several excursions into New York City's underworld. At the "Golden Rule Pleasure Club," Gardner pointed out to Parkhurst that the waiters were "fairies," men dressed as women who acted stereotypically effeminate.[13] During the same trip, Parkhurst saw "French circuses," where women performed cunnilingus on one another in front of an all-male audience.[14] Parkhurst was shocked by both the public displays of sexual deviance and the police malfeasance that allowed the explicit performances to continue.

Parkhurst successfully pressured New York politicians to investigate police corruption, prompting Senator Clarence Lexow to create the Lexow Committee in 1894. John W. Goff directed the investigation as its chief counsel. Although Goff was an Irish Catholic immigrant, a common constituency for the Democratic machine, he was "bitterly anti-Tammany."[15] By 1903, Goff was a New York City judge presiding over the trials of bathhouse attendees charged with sodomy.

Max Schmittberger worked for Tammany boss "Clubber" Williams until Lexow investigators confronted him for accepting an illegal bribe. Schmittberger turned on Tammany Hall and became a key witness for the Lexow Committee. With full legal immunity, Schmittberger testified to elaborate payoff schemes with gamblers, brothel owners, local politicians, and his fellow police officers. Schmittberger's police colleagues branded him a traitor, but he became "the pet of the reformers" after revealing his secrets in court.[16]

The Lexow Committee eventually produced a damning multivolume report of extensive police corruption. The cumulative pressure on

Tammany Hall led to their mayoral defeat in the 1894 election, and anti-Tammany reformers gained political power: Goff received a judgeship and Schmittberger was rapidly promoted to police captain.[17] Schmittberger "emerged as the reform administration's favorite 'broom,' assigned to precincts that were deemed to need a wholesale cleaning."[18]

Edward Walsh, a detective who organized raids on saloons, gambling dens, and bathhouses, was promoted to police inspector in 1903 by a newly hired and anti-Tammany police chief. The police chief, under the direction of the Republican mayor, sought to dampen Tammany's influence by enacting immediate and radical personnel changes on the police force. Although five police captains were fired from the force, Walsh received a promotion and was appointed to the police force in 1875. He became a captain in 1900 and was promoted by the new police commissioner to inspector in early 1903.[19] Nicknamed "Smiling Dick," Walsh was known for his tough tactics and for encouraging police to explore the legal limits of brutality.[20] The Ariston raid was one of a handful of large-scale undercover police operations Walsh and Schmittberger commanded, during a time when officers' methods of entrapment were coming under increasing scrutiny from the New York City public.

Opponents of Parkhurst criticized reformers' heavy-handed tactics and the aggressiveness with which the "reformed" police force attacked vice. In a *North American Review* article titled "Lawlessness of the Police in New York"—published just weeks before the first New York City bathhouse raid—Supreme Court justice, Tammany supporter, and future New York City mayor William Gaynor commented on "[s]everal typical instances of the lawless invasion of houses by the police in the City of New York."[21] He noted the general disregard New York City police had of search warrants and procedural limits on their ability to arrest, and he called attention to the particular practice of mass arrests conducted on behalf of political bosses. Gaynor concluded that the lawlessness of the New York City police force created a profound crisis in its public legitimacy. Sodomy prosecutions in the early 1900s occurred in a context where the police were viewed with as much suspicion as the defendants.

Given the controversial status of New York City police, jurors in sodomy trials weighed their distrust of the police against individuals accused of sodomy. The crime of sodomy, once understood as a predatory act, was something seen as emanating from a particular group of men with "inverted" sexual desire and identity. Once seen as a serious, but rare, crime, the spread of sodomy and homosexuality was described by prosecutors as a threat to Anglo-American civilization. For example, a prosecutor in a 1901 sodomy case told jurors, "Under other forms of civilization, this had been permitted, but the history of the world has shown that some of the most magnificent of human civilizations have been wiped out, at the very summit of their refinement, by the prevalence of crimes of this character."[22] Four sets of sodomy cases in early twentieth-century New York City show how sodomy trials were referendums on historically specific notions of respectability and manliness. Two cases stem from police raids, one case was brought into the justice system through the New York Society for the Suppression of Vice, and the final case involved a police officer who noticed suspicious activity while on a late-night patrol of Harlem.

Raid at Tecumseh Hall

The raid of a "French circus" in 1904, and the sodomy trials that followed it, uncover the expansiveness of New York's sodomy law and the role of police in regulating New York City's underworld. The Tecumseh Hall and Hotel, located on 33rd Street between First and Second avenues, functioned as a meeting place for various German immigrant organizations. In the early years of the twentieth century, the backroom of the hall was used for a sex show. Prosecutors levied sodomy charges against the performers, but the testimony in the Tecumseh trial did not center on the identities of the offenders or, necessarily, the same-sex nature of their activities. The stories elicited and emphasized by the prosecutor unearthed general displays of debauchery, including interracial sexual coupling, seductive dancing, the potential desecration of an American flag, and an obscene poem.

In 1908, Vera Olcott, an important witness in the Tecumseh trial, attracted notice as a Salome dancer at Huber's 14th Street dime museum. One critic lauded her for giving a "more substantial conception" of the dance that was "Oriental, not Greek, in spirit."[23] Vera Olcott was an experienced dancer by the time she performed at Huber's in 1908. She was skilled in a similar dance called the "hoochie coochie" popularized in her hometown, Philadelphia, Pennsylvania. In 1904, a man named George Bundi offered Olcott and two women $7 each to travel from Philadelphia to New York City to sing and dance in a concert. One of the women, Cora Smith, later testified that she did not know the true nature of the performance until she was in the dressing room.

In the rear of Tecumseh Hall, Cora Smith, Birdie Smith, Flora Temple, and Vera Olcott sat in a small room behind the stage awaiting their scheduled performance. At about 8:30 in the evening, Detective John O'Shea approached the front of Tecumseh Hall dressed in normal attire, with the intent to buy a ticket for the backroom show. From its entrance on East 33rd Street, Tecumseh Hall appeared to be a regular German beer saloon. Five or six men sat around the bar when the detective arrived that Wednesday evening.

It is unclear how New York police knew about the Wednesday night performance in 1904, but they could have learned about it from a variety of sources. A tenement house occupied by laborers was located directly above the Tecumseh Hall and the saloon. The decision to target John Schaumloeffel, the owner of the establishment, was consistent with the strategy of anti-vice activism in the early twentieth century. In addition to focusing on individuals who participated in vice, prosecutors turned their attention to the owners of the establishment wherein the illegal acts occurred. John Schaumloeffel leased the premises for two hundred dollars a month. The hall functioned as a meeting place for lodges, Tammany Democrats, labor unions, and German singing societies. Police knowledge about the performance was not surprising given the extensive police surveillance of political radicalism in early twentieth-century New York City.[24]

Detective O'Shea walked across the saloon and reached the entrance of the meeting hall. John Schaumloeffel stood near the doors and asked O'Shea if he wanted to see the "circus." O'Shea paid $2.50 for a ticket—a fee much higher than the cost of admission to an average theater or performance. He approached two swinging doors in the back of the saloon, and the entrance led to a large hall with a four-foot stage, lit by a large electric light. An African American man guarding the back entrance met O'Shea and seated him about fifteen feet from the stage. Eventually, men filled all of the seats and some stood crowding in the back.

A man named John Sheppard walked onto the stage around 8:45 to announce the performance. Sheppard was allegedly paid five dollars by the owner of the hall to introduce the acts for the evening. The opening performance was the only one where the performer remained fully clothed: a woman sang a song and left the stage. Sheppard next introduced Birdie Smith as the second performer, a white woman he indelicately described as "the girl with diabetes of the asshole."[25] Birdie Smith danced for five minutes and disrobed except for her stockings and shoes.

Vera Olcott was the third performer, and John Sheppard announced her as "the girl with the tight asshole" as she walked onto the stage. Olcott said she was going to perform the "hoochee coochee," "the Spanish belly dance."[26] She removed all of her clothes except her shoes and stockings during her five-minute routine. A woman named Flora Temple followed Vera Olcott, performing a "Spanish dance," finishing with a contortion act.[27] The dances were followed by a pair called "The Cock Sucking Sisters," Helen Colson and a man named Arthur Ashton dressed in women's clothes. They climbed on stage, removed their clothing, and, according to the detective, "gave an exhibition of sexual intercourse."[28] John Sheppard announced an intermission.

The show returned thirty minutes later with much more explicit fare. After the intermission, the announcer called on stage two African American women who disrobed and performed cunnilingus on one another on the stage floor. According to the detective's testimony, John Schaefer, one of the event promoters, stopped them and "told them that they better do it on the table." He placed a table on the stage and "and told them to get on that so the audience would not have to stand."[29] Sheppard asked the audience to get close in order to see "that it was on the level, that they were doing the sucking all right."[30] An audience member known as Butcher Sam ascended the stage and declared that "they were doing it all right."[31] According to one witness, someone pulled an American flag from the wall and moved to use it to wipe the dust from the table, but men in the crowd jeered and they moved it away. He pulled one of the women from the other and had intercourse with her for about five minutes and then had intercourse with the other. The announcer called for "a little of the same thing in the same color," and then an African American man in the audience came upon the stage and had sex with one of the women. Interspersed between these acts were a piano and singing performance of "Goodbye Eliza Jane"—a 1903 Tin Pan Alley tune about a woman who took a man for all he was worth before leaving him for another—and the recitation of a speech (or poem) called "Stand Up Noble Prick."[32]

The show ended at 10:00 and Detective O'Shea called in about twelve to fourteen police who announced a raid. Men rushed to escape through the windows, fanlights, and other possible exits as the officers announced the raid and began their arrests. One detective testified that it "looked like a small-sized riot."[33] Amid the chaos, Detective Edward Reardon arrested the doorman and told him "he was under arrest on a charge of sodomy, which was about the filthiest crime on the statute book."[34] According to the detective's testimony, Schaefer seemed unusually calm and bragged to the officer about having "pulled those shows off" in Philadelphia. The detective allegedly found Birdie Smith, the first performer of the evening, in the coat room performing fellatio on a man named William Hargie.[35] Police arrested a total of forty-eight men, including Victor Watson, a journalist for the *New York American*. William Hargie, and several others, forfeited bail and were fugitives of justice at the time of the trial. John Schaumloeffel faced prosecution and the transcript of his trial is the only surviving document in the Trial Transcript Collection stemming from the raid.

John Sheppard was a vaudeville performer hired by Schaefer and Schaumloeffel to sing and dance in the performance. Schaumloeffel allegedly paid him five dollars extra to act as the announcer. Sheppard pleaded guilty, testified that he had participated in six or seven similar performances with the group, and told prosecutors that the performers engaged in oral sex in each performance. John Schaumloeffel testified on his own behalf and claimed that he had no idea that his hall was going to be used for an indecent performance. He rented the hall to Schaefer for free upon the assurance that a "good class of people" would attend and spend money on drinks.[36] Both the prosecutor and the judge questioned him about the high price of admission. "Didn't you think it was a pretty expensive performance, $2.50 and five dollars a ticket?" the prosecutor asked.[37] The judge also suggested that the price of admission should have provoked suspicion in his mind as to the character of the entertainment.[38] He professed ignorance. In response to his reply that he was "a little green," the prosecutor asked him about his former work as a bartender in a hotel that "was raided constantly."[39] The prosecutor also suggested that a group called the "Apollo Pleasure Club" met at the Tecumseh Hall, but Schaumloeffel denied knowing anything about it.[40]

At least one of the Tecumseh Hall performers was able to rebuild her life and career after the raid. In 1910, Vera Olcott, the hoochie coochie dancer from Philadelphia who performed in Tecumseh Hall, began her successful theater career performing alongside Fanny Brice in "The Follies of 1910."[41] By 1923, Olcott attained astronomical success as a Parisian show girl, appeared at the Palace Theater in London, and won a $100,000 contest for having the most beautiful legs in Paris.

The Schaumloeffel trial uncovered the visual pleasures found in the backrooms of New York City's legitimate establishments. Although histories of urban underworlds emphasize the woman-to-woman sexuality found in "French circuses," such acts were only a part of a larger tapestry of titillation. Echoing the vaudeville tradition, the show at the Tecumseh Hall involved dance, comedy, and audience participation in addition to, of course, public sex. Historian Chad Heap argues that the practice of "slumming," whereby members of dominant social groups experienced vicarious thrills by watching the performances of racial and sexual minorities, bolstered white middle-class identity. By 1900, German immigrants, like the organizers of the Tecumseh Hall sex show, participated in slumming to reinforce their white identity by defining themselves against African Americans and other immigrant groups. While the Tecumseh Hall performance hints at the role of "slumming" in New York City's racial and sexual politics, the prosecution of the show demonstrates the capacious role of sodomy law in regulating emerging spaces of sexual and interracial contact.

The Ariston Bathhouse Raid

Civic activists spearheaded the public bathhouse movement in the second half of the nineteenth century because they viewed them as bulwarks against communicable disease and vehicles of working-class uplift.[42] In 1901, temperance crusader Carrie Nation "declared her unequivocal approval of the Turkish bath as an institution" after visiting one in Chicago.[43] Along with ritual baths developed for the Jewish community, the baths in New York City catered to individuals at opposite ends of the class hierarchy. For poorer New Yorkers, public baths were developed in tenement districts as part of a larger campaign for public health.[44] By 1915, there were sixteen public baths in New York City. For wealthier New Yorkers, elegant Russian and Turkish baths opened in the basements of hotels and other patches of expensive real estate.

Bathhouses served functions other than public health and religious ritual. Historian George Chauncey referred to New York City's bathhouses as "the safest, most enduring, and one of the most affirmative of the setting in which gay men gathered in the first half of the twentieth century."[45] Bathhouses were rare spaces where gay men could be alone and where they did not have to share space with hostile outsiders. The bathhouses were perceived as protected places where men could meet other men for sexual encounters without fear of being blackmailed.[46] Bars serving an exclusively gay clientele did not emerge until the late 1930s, and so the bathhouses that were established at the turn of the century formed an important social role for urban gays. Chauncey writes, "Gay bathhouses had appeared in New York by the turn of the century, and by World War I several of them had become institutions in the city, their addresses and distinctive social and sexual character known to almost every gay New Yorker and to many gay Europeans as well."[47] For a time in 1903, men had sex with other men at the Ariston Bathhouse on Broadway and 55th Street.

A small glass sign illuminated by a red lamp marked the entrance of the Ariston baths. Patrons paid a dollar to enter, and the cashier gave them a sheet and assigned them a dressing room and valuables lock box. Depending on the day of the week, the Ariston baths housed an all-male or all-female clientele and employee roster. The bath had a swimming pool, steam room, hot room, and four cooling rooms with leather and wicker cots. Visitors could also find an exercise room with gym equipment, a place to purchase drinks and cigars, and a parlor wherein to socialize. The parlor was the largest room in the establishment, lit by a crystal chandelier with a dozen gas lights. This main room led to two separate cooling rooms, which were faintly lit by the parlor's glow. For at least some period of the bath-house's history, men routinely met one another in the cooling rooms and elsewhere to have oral and anal sex. Beginning in February 1903, police placed the venue under surveillance. At least one police officer, a tall man of Irish descent named Norman Fitzsimmons, visited the baths on two occasions prior to the raid.

On Saturday, February 21, 1903, at nine o'clock in the evening, police officers Thomas Phelan and Norman Fitzsimmons entered the Ariston baths, paid the entry fee, and began their undercover surveillance. Twenty minutes later, according to Phelan's courtroom testimony, a man named Walter Bennett placed his arm around the officer's waist and invited him into another room so that Bennett could give him "a very pleasant time."[48] Norman Fitzsimmons, another undercover officer, asked Bennett if he could join them, but he was rebuffed. "No, I like a fat boy," Bennett told the officer.[49] But Walter Bennett was very interested in Thomas Phelan, and the pair made arrangements to meet later in the evening at 2:30 a.m.

Into the early morning of February 22nd, other undercover police officers joined Phelan and Fitzsimmons to survey the premises. Police witnessed numerous instances of oral and anal sex among various bathhouse patrons. Most of these acts took place on or around the cots in the cooling rooms. In particular, many erotic encounters occurred in the cooling room in the southwesterly corner of the facility. The "southwesterly cooling room," as referenced in court documents, had seven cots arranged close to one another. Light from the adjacent parlor and from a ground glass window that looked out onto 55th Street offered the room little illumination.

At 1:45, a small party of police inspectors and captains entered the building and placed everyone under arrest. The officers searched the rooms of the establishment and herded about seventy-five half-naked men into the parlor. Police led the bathhouse patrons past a group of undercover police officers and they selected the individuals against whom they had complaints. Thirty-four men were arrested. The suspects were allowed to dress into their street clothes and were led away from the bathhouse and arraigned at the West Side police court. Police accused the proprietor of the baths, John Begley, with keeping a disorderly house, a charge commonly reserved for those involved in the prostitution trade, and held him in $2,000 bail.[50] Some of the men were charged with disorderly conduct and liquor law violations, but at least sixteen men were charged with sodomy. Of the sixteen held on sodomy charges, twelve eventually faced trial, and five of the transcripts survived and were stored in the Trial Transcript Collection. Of the five defendants represented in legal records, there were three verdicts of guilty, a guilty verdict with a recommendation of leniency, and a mistrial. Two of the guilty verdicts were appealed, and the different outcomes of those appeals had everything to do with the status and social class of the two defendants.

The Ariston sodomy defendants came from an economic and ethnic cross-section of New York. Some were members of the upper class, including an architect for a prominent New York architecture firm. As the *New York Times* noted, some of those caught in the raid were "men of professions and of high social standing."[51] Other defendants came from working-class backgrounds, including a tailor, a waiter, and a traveling salesperson. A few of the defendants were immigrants, including two Germans and a Swiss man.

The district attorney sought plea agreements with some of the men, including a forty-year-old man named John Rogers.[52] Avoiding the term "sodomy," the *New York Times* stated that Rogers faced "nine separate charges of serious crime."[53] The district attorney suspended the other eight counts in exchange for Rogers's pleading guilty to one count of the indictment, resulting in a twenty-year prison sentence. Commenting on the relative leniency on the other eight counts, the *Times* noted, "Should Judge Cowing so have wished, Rogers could have been sentenced to 180 years."[54]

At a time when city police drew as much public suspicion as bathhouse attendees, the trials had broad social stakes. The *New York Press* said that the Ariston raid "is the only case of the kind in the history of the New York police."[55] Historians regard the Ariston affair as one of the first bathhouse raids targeting men who had sex with other men, and it reflected to the expansion of queer subcultures in the opening decades of the twentieth century.[56]

The prosecutor's case against the Ariston men was strong. Although sodomy charges were relatively rare in the early twentieth century, many saw it as a grave crime, and those involved in the Ariston Bathhouse trials were no exception. Judge John Goff in *People v. Casson* said that the charge "brings to mind a species of horror to think that any person, any human being endowed with intelligence, with reason, would be guilty of such horrible practices."[57] In *People v. Galbert*, he said that the mere mention of the crime "is liable to carry with it a certain revulsion of feelings that may be reasonably entertained by every man who has a decent regard for the proprieties and manliness of his sex.[58] Even defense attorneys conceded to the seriousness of the charges their clients faced. In his closing arguments in *People v. Bennett*, Defense Attorney Greenthal called it "the most heinous crime on the calendar" and claimed that the "charge is more serious than a charge of murder in the first degree."[59] In Charles LeBarbier's opening statement for the defense in *People v. Galbert*, he referred to sodomy as a "monstrous crime" and declared that there was "nothing more dirty or more low or more bestial than this horrible crime."[60]

Despite the strident tone used to characterize the crime of sodomy, evidence from the Ariston trials indicate that the reputedly demonic nature of the crime did not saturate jurors' decision making. In fact, jurors weighed the credibility of the bathhouse defendants against the dubious reputation of the police force and its new investigative practices. In *People v. Casson*, for instance, at least some jurors felt that the defendant deserved mercy because of his immigrant status. Theodore Casson lived in Greenwich Village and earned about $15 dollars a week working for a confectioner on Broome Street. At trial, he was accused of walking up to John Rogers, leading with his erect penis, and offering it to Rogers to suck. Officer Robert J. Hibbard testified that Theodore Casson moved "his head backwards and forwards and this defendant moved his body backwards and forwards and he went through the indecent motions, and went through the motions of ejaculation."[61] Officer Hibbard saw at least twenty or so incidents of sodomy, but he could only identify twelve of the original thirty-four suspects.

On the witness stand, Theodore Casson spoke through a court interpreter and denied that he had any sexual connection with other men at the baths. He said, "I was only there to take a bath, nothing else."[62] The prosecutor asked him why, if he lived and worked in the Village, he was walking around Midtown after ten at night. Casson said that his foreman, who lived a few blocks from the Ariston, was sick and he was paying him a visit as a coworker. In response to a question by the third juror, Casson testified that he had been in the United States only eighteen months. During their deliberations, jurors sent a note to the judge: "Is it permissible to bring in a verdict with a recommendation for mercy in view of the fact that the defendant is a foreigner and possibly unfamiliar with the laws of this State?"[63] The judge answered yes and the jurors returned a guilty verdict with a recommendation for mercy. Casson appealed the ruling, but the State Supreme Court upheld the verdict.

The equivocation of the jurors reflected the precarious situation for the prosecutors. Jurors were undoubtedly aware of the scandals surrounding the New York City police force in 1902 and 1903, and prosecutors and judges expressed concern that jurors would disregard police testimony as the product of corruption. In *Casson*, Judge Goff warned against jury nullification, the practice where jurors ignore the law pertaining to the case and vote their conscience. The judge noted the "very serious criticism" mounted against the police force, but he implored the jury to carefully consider the testimony of the officers.[64] Speaking about the police, Goff said it would "be exceedingly unjust and beyond the power of a jury to simply condemn one or more men as perjurers because they belong to a class." In another Ariston trial, the judge told jurors: "Your verdict must not be delivered for the purpose of vindicating the police on the one hand, or of showing any resentment against the police on the other. You must render it as a matter of simple justice."[65] In general, judges warned jurors not to find the defendants guilty because of the odiousness of the crime, and not to distrust the police because of recent news of police corruption.

Their controversial status aside, the police had built a compelling case. They made at least two diagrams based on their firsthand observations of the bathhouse. Prosecutors used one of the two diagrams in each of the trials, and they questioned police about the diagram early in direct examination. Prosecutor Ely's frequent reference to the Ariston floor plan permitted the jurors to imagine a voyeuristic walk through the bathhouse. It allowed prosecutors to pinpoint the exact location of the alleged crimes and to establish supporting details that gave their accounts an added layer of veracity.[66] In sum, prosecutors had a strong case against the accused by most accepted criteria. The reported instances of sodomy occurred in full public view, sometimes in the presence of a dozen or more witnesses. Against this, defense attorneys had limited options.

Defense attorneys for the Ariston defendants challenged the eyesight and memory of the police officers due to the hustle and bustle of the bathhouse, the varied lighting, and the thick steam. Defense attorneys verbally fenced with prosecutors over the amount of light entering the cooling room, the height of the cots, and the chronology of events. Two broad lines of defense, however, engaged the sexual worldviews of the jurors. Ariston defense attorneys argued that the sex acts were physically impossible and socially impossible. The incidents were physically impossible because of the angles of the penis and buttock, and they were socially impossible owing to the moral rectitude of the defendants.

The argument for the physical impossibility of sodomy was most robust in *People v. Kregel,* a trial of a married Jewish tailor with five children. Andrew Kregel arrived at the bathhouse at about one o'clock in the morning and a man named Charles Chamberlain approached him soon thereafter. According to the prosecution, Chamberlain put his erect penis in Kregel's behind and reached around with his right hand to manipulate Kregel's penis. As this occurred, another bathhouse patron, John Rogers, approached the defendant and took his penis in his mouth. Police arrested all three of them approximately an hour later.

At trial, Kregel claimed that he had never before been to a Turkish bathhouse, and he denied all of the testimony about the alleged sex. He told jurors that a customer at his shop gave him a ticket for the bathhouse in exchange for repairing a coat. Kregel testified that he was smoking in the parlor when Chamberlain approached him and said, "Be kind and give me a cigarette and I will treat you to a little whiskey."[67] The man, later identified as Chamberlain, gave Kregel whiskey in exchange for a cigarette. Later, Kregel looked for a cooling room and passed Chamberlain, who "put his hand on my shoulder, one hand, and with the other hand he punched me in the side."[68] Kregel did not explain why Chamberlain punched him, only that he had decided to leave the bathhouse when the raid began.

Besides his plain denial and his attorney's challenge to the police officers' memory and ability to see in the poorly lit cooling room, Kregel's defense endeavored to show the physical impossibility of the alleged act. Kregel's defense attorney called Dr. Pierre A. Siegelstein, a thirty-four-year-old graduate of New York City Medical College, to the witness stand. He told the court that he had previously testified as an expert witness in two sodomy trials. Siegelstein's presence on the witness stand attests to the growing role of doctors as medical witnesses in sex crime trials. The authority of medical jurisprudence grew in nineteenth century and, although the legal system sometimes imposed limits on doctors' testimony, jurors increasingly conferred respect and legitimacy to their medical claims.[69] Kregel's defense attorney asked the doctor a series of questions to refute the idea that two men could have anal intercourse standing upright due to the angles of the penis and anus:

> *Defense Attorney Snitkin*: It has been testified to here in this Court before this jury that two men in an erect position committed an act of sexual intercourse through the anus; now I ask you from the relation of the anus, from the position and direction of the penis when it is erect, could such an act be perpetrated in a standing position?

> *Dr. Siegelstein*: Absolutely a physical impossibility.[70]

Citing the way muscles of the anus contract and the physiological response of the anus to external stimuli, he declared that "it would be more possible for the elephant to pass through the eye of a needle" than for the alleged act to have occurred.[71]

> *Snitkin*: I will repeat it; is it not an undeniable fact that in order to introduce the penis into the anus or any instrument, you must first separate the folds of the buttocks and then dilate the sphincter muscles before you can do so?

> *Judge*: The question is: is it not an undeniable fact?

> *Dr. Gibb*: The anus had to be dilated of course, by the object you are putting into it.

> *Snitkin*: Is it not a fact that in order to be able to separate the folds of the buttocks and dilate the sphincter muscles of the anus it is necessary to either place the person in the knee chest position or Sims position?

> *Dr. Gibb*: No, sir.[75]

People v. Kregel was the only case of the five where the defense lawyer aggressively argued the bodily unfeasibility of anal sex. In the trial, the conflict between the two medical authorities simultaneously addressed the physical mechanics of sex and "sodomites" as a class. Assistant District Attorney James Ely, on redirect examination of Dr. Gibb, brought out an explanation for how some men could have sex standing upright, yet it remained a difficult physical posture in general. Gibb testified, "Frequent dilation of the

anus causes the muscles to become more flapped and more easily dilatable."[76]
Ely prompted him to elaborate:

> *Ely*: In your experience have you ever known of cases in which
> the anus was in a constant state of dilation, in other words, not
> closed at all?
>
> *Gibb*: Yes, sir.
>
> *Q*: In what class of cases?
>
> [objection—overruled]
>
> *Gibb*: Sodomite.
>
> *Ely*: Have you had experience in treating people addicted to
> sodomy, in your professional career, to a certain extent?
>
> [objection—overruled]
>
> *A*: I have seen a number and treated them.
>
> *Q*: Your experience covers a period of how long in this class of
> cases.
>
> *A*: About 12 years.[77]

The medical witness backfired for the defense by allowing Ely to introduce
testimony about a "sodomite" class whose bodies depart from normalcy. The
exchange between the prosecutor and the doctor slipped between considering sodomy as one among a class of sexual crimes to considering sodomites
as a class. Ely's final question again referred to a "class of cases," though
it carried the referent of his prior question about "people addicted to sodomy." In the trial, the medical meaning of the term "cases" fortified its legal
meaning. The medical authority to speak of a class of men with perma-
nently dilated anuses reinforced the power of anti-vice and law enforcement
groups to police sexuality. In this case, the prosecutor failed to persuade the
jury and their indecision led to a mistrial. The New York Supreme Court
reduced Kregel's bail from $2,000 to $750. Kregel escaped after paying the

lower amount, leading Judge Goff to criticize sharply the justices who, he said, "unwittingly aid and abet in fraudulent defeat of criminal justice."[78]

Alongside claims about the physical impossibility of sodomy, some attorneys underscored the *social* impossibility of the scenes described by the police officers. The character-based defense of the Ariston defendants rested on claims to respectability, using wealth and social status as a positive indicator of normative sexuality. This is particularly apparent in the defense strategies for George Caldwell and Walter Bennett. By convincing jurors of the high social status of their clients, defense attorneys tried to secure their perceived respectability and, therefore, their innocence.

Social class played a large role in the defense strategy of George Caldwell, a thirty-eight-year-old architect who gave his name as "George Galbert" at his arrest. Caldwell was an architect for the firm Carrere and Hastings, leaders in the Beaux Arts movement in architecture and design. George Caldwell was accused of engaging in illegal sexual activity with Bennett in the northwesterly cooling room. During the raid, Caldwell hid in one of the rooms and locked the door behind him. As Inspector "Smiling Dick" Walsh walked through the premises with a team of police officers, he stopped at the locked door and instructed whoever was inside to leave. Caldwell asked, "What is the matter?" and Walsh yelled, "Well, come out here, Maude, and you will see what is the matter."[79] When Caldwell emerged, another officer said, "Oh, here is the indignant lady."[80] George Caldwell cursed at the officer and then ran across the couches toward the doorway until the police restrained him.

During his opening statement, Charles LeBarbier, Caldwell's defense attorney, promised jurors "a galaxy of weighty, prominent, important businessmen of New York on the question of character."[81] LeBarbier called architect John Carrère, along with four other character witnesses, to attest to Caldwell's moral health. He was best known as the designer of the New York Public Library but, by the time of the Ariston trials, John Carrère had gained considerable notoriety as the architect of the 1901 Pan American Exhibition. Shortly after his death in 1911, the *New York Times* stated that he "had for many years been one of the best known figures in the artistic circles of this city."[82]

In *People v. Galbert*, Caldwell's attorney implored jurors to remember the positive appraisal of Caldwell's character given by Carrère and others who testified on his behalf: "Now, gentlemen, I importune you, speaking to you as men, I importune you, before you reach a conclusion, not to treat lightly the testimony of those men."[83] He argued that good character "is a good name. It has been said, 'Good name in man or woman is the immediate jewel of their souls.' And we have built it up here, with all the force that we have been able to bring into this case."[84] Further, Charles LeBarbier tried to introduce into the judge's instructions to the jury the notion that good character can create reasonable doubt.[85] After Caldwell was found guilty and faced sentencing, LeBarbier again used Caldwell's character witnesses as the basis of his mercy plea: "no finer array of gentlemen could now come forward than those who took the stand in his behalf."[86]

George Caldwell stated that it was the first time he had been in the Ariston baths and claimed that he was asleep on a cot in one of the cooling rooms when the raid took place. According to his testimony, Officer Phelan walked toward the steam room and stopped by a scale. Caldwell put his arm around Phelan and offered to weigh him. Later in the evening, Thomas Phelan allegedly witnessed Caldwell walk over to Walter Bennett, who rested on a cooling room cot. Phelan witnessed Caldwell as he "raised Bennett's leg, and turned him around, and then he inserted his penis into the anus of the man Bennett."[87] The witness noted his close proximity to the two men ("I went over and stood right alongside of him, right alongside of the couch"[88]). The defense attorney used this detail to cast doubt on the entire scene depicted by Phelan. Assuming that most men would be too embarrassed to have public sex, Caldwell's attorney challenged the credibility of the officers:

> Yet, shameless to everything, shameless to the witnesses there, to the officers, to everybody in that room, the defendant walks in, and the sheet comes off of him, and not a word is said about him before, as to any act of any kind or character that would reflect upon him; and he stands before those officers, watching him, with his penis erect. Is it true? Is it credible? That is what I want to ask you.[89]

Men who had sex with other men constituted highly visible subcultures in early twentieth-century New York City. These men maintained strong social networks in the bachelor apartments, rooming houses, cafeterias, cafés, and restaurants. Despite this, the world of the bathhouse and the practices described by the officers were likely alien to the middle- and upper-class New Yorkers who served on Caldwell's jury, and defense attorneys appealed to this presumed ignorance. The men selected for the jury in *People v. Galbert* included a real estate agent, a company vice president, a Wall Street broker, and men who worked in insurance, publishing, and engineering. Caldwell's attorney highlighted his client's respectability and social class to show the social impossibility of him committing such a grave crime.

Charles LeBarbier's final line of defense, one that he briefly introduced during his closing remarks, raised the image of George Caldwell resisting arrest. After recalling the taunts the police threw at Caldwell while he hid in the bathhouse, LeBarbier asked, "Did he go out as a Maude, simpering and afraid? Was he coming out in a cringing way, knowing that he had been caught in a vile act? No, he came out of that room, ready to fight, and he was restrained from fighting by somebody getting hold of him."[90] Thereafter, LeBarbier read the part of the transcript that recalled how Caldwell cursed at the officers. With this, the attorney appealed to the new body-centered model of masculinity and, at least unintentionally, the Progressive Era's fascination with boxing and muscularity.[91] This gendered performance, both the alleged resistance against the police and the retelling of that resistance in the context of the trial, suggested Caldwell's fit with the early twentieth-century gender order and the dominant model of masculinity. Despite the attorney's best efforts, the jury found George Caldwell guilty and he was sentenced to over seven years in prison.

Walter Bennett was accused of wearing his sheet like a skirt and "trailing the sheet along three or four feet."[92] The prosecuting attorney asked one of the undercover officers to describe how the defendant walked around the bathhouse:

Officer McCutcheon: Well, on one occasion, he had a sheet arranged around his body in such a manner that it left a train behind.

Defense Attorney Greenthal: I object to that, "in such a manner."

Judge: Strike out those words. [To McCutcheon] Describe the condition of the sheet.

McCutcheon: Well there was a train behind, and he would lift it up, and show his legs and go through certain motions with his body. I could hardly describe the motions.

Ely: What?

McCutcheon: I could hardly describe the motions that he went through.

Ely: And were there other people about, as he was walking about, trailing this sheet after him, and showing his legs and making the motions?

McCutcheon: Yes, sir.[93]

This testimony suggests that the characteristically feminine way of wearing the sheet was a subcultural code and not simply a stylistic practice adopted exclusively by the defendant. Walter Bennett, the man accused of penetrating George Caldwell in the Ariston cooling room, worked in a number of fields, including the hotel business, the theatrical business, and as a steward, waiter, and caterer. He admitted that he frequently visited the Ariston baths, sometimes five or six times a month.[94] The night of the arrest, Bennett claimed he went into the steam room to find a "rubber," a bathhouse employee who would rub him down, but they were all busy. According to Bennett's testimony, he saw Detective Fitzsimmons in the steam room. Fitzsimmons said, "It's hot in here, ain't it?" and invited Bennett to sit down next to him. Bennett declined and walked away to bathe in the pool room and visit the in-house manicurist. Walter Bennett said that he was sitting at a table reading the *Evening Telegram* when the raid occurred. He flatly denied that he exposed himself in a provocative way or trailed his sheet behind him like a skirt. The sheet-as-skirt likely marked someone as a "fairy," a man who had sex with other men, adopted feminine mannerisms, and assumed the receptive position during sex.[95] Indeed, Bennett was accused of acting as the passive partner in a sexual exchange that occurred in the northwesterly cooling room. Caldwell reportedly approached Bennett, lifted his "skirt," and inserted his penis into Bennett's anus. Thereafter, the two men hugged and kissed one another.[96]

Like the other defense strategies in the Ariston trials, Bennett's attorney raised minor contradictions in the officer's testimony and argued that the alleged act was physically impossible. In *People v. Bennett*, the defense attorney also tried to prove his client's innocence by introducing evidence of Bennett's sexual desire for women. Against the police officers' descriptions of sodomy, Bennett's defense attorney called three character witnesses, two women and a minister, all of whom had known Bennett for many years. Catherine Bolton told the courtroom on direct examination that she had known Bennett since he was fourteen years old when he worked as a bellboy at the hotel where she resided. She intimated, but stopped short of confirming, that she and Bennett had been romantically involved. When the prosecutor asked, "Well, how have you known him?" She replied, "Well, I have known him in a rather peculiar way." The attorney instructed her to "tell us, don't characterize," to which she responded, "Well, I have known him—it had been partly in that way, and partly in a friendly way, not in a social way."[97] In his closing arguments, Greenthal emphasized his character-based defense: "I do not want you, gentlemen, to lose sight of the fact that this man has a good character, an excellent character, with good people behind him."[98] He said, "We produced other women, ladies, that also testified to the same effect."[99] His linguistic repair of "women" to a more class-based category of "ladies" worked to interpolate the defendant's morality from his respectable associates.

Just as the medical testimony about the impossibility of upright anal sex backfired for Andrew Kregel's defense by allowing the prosecutor to summon an image of physically distinct sodomites, the character evidence proved similarly problematic. In his closing remarks, the assistant district attorney asked:

> Do you not think it is amazing that this defendant is unable to produce a witness as good character, except a woman, barring the minister? Just think of it. There is not a single witness who testified to that man's character, except women. They think he is a very fine fellow. But, if he is the creature that the People claim they have proved him to be, do you suppose that any one of these women would know anything about it? Do you think that a man who has an unnatural taste, a carnal appetite for connection with his own sex, associates with women to any great extent, or shows the cloven foot to them?[100]

He finished his closing arguments by reminding the jurors of the character witnesses:

> Remember, too, the attempt that he has made to give himself a character, by these women. All his character witnesses are women, or so-called women, except the minister, who are—what shall I say?—who are all girls together. Gentlemen, on all the evidence and the circumstances in this case, I ask for a verdict of guilty of sodomy, as charged in this indictment.[101]

According to the prosecuting attorney, the feminine perspectives of the women and the minister could not provide any reliable gauge of Bennett's character. Moreover, the phrase that the witnesses "are all girls together" implicitly grouped Bennett with persons who present counter comparisons to hegemonic masculinity. Prosecutors portrayed Bennett as another girl who dressed, acted like, and kept company with other women. Jurors found Bennett guilty and he received the same sentence as George Caldwell, seven years of hard labor.

George Caldwell and Walter Bennett sat in Sing Sing as their attorneys prepared lengthy appeals. Bennett's appeal was unsuccessful, but Caldwell stayed in Sing Sing for only three months before his sentence was commuted by New York governor Benjamin Odell. Caldwell's legal victory stems almost entirely from his wealth and family connections. Unknown to most trial participants, the Caldwells were a prominent Kentucky family, and George Caldwell was the grandson of a former Kentucky governor. Moreover, Katherine Caldwell, George's sister, was close friends with Alice Roosevelt, the president's daughter. The dismissal of George Caldwell's conviction was the fourth time President Roosevelt intervened on behalf of the Caldwell family.

The bathhouse and sex raids demonstrate growing state surveillance and criminal action against persons deemed sexually deviant. The trials of the defendants show how that action pivoted on questions of respectability and manliness. Disreputable manhood was revealed and constructed in testimony about disgusting language, interracial and same-sex sexual relations, the wearing of sheets as skirts, having multiple sex partners, and the open casualness of it all. Respectable manhood was signified in testimony about wealth, refinement, expensive amusements, and interest in women. These trials were about more than the violation of a statute; they were contests about proper manliness and gender roles.

Anthony Comstock and the Male Lodger

The growth of gay subcultures in New York City mirrored the development of anti-vice activism. Organizations like the Committee of Fourteen and the New York Society for the Suppression of Vice targeted emerging spaces where men could have sex with other men. They had squads of undercover investigators and notepads filled with details about the city's urban amusements. These organizations exercised enormous power as law enforcement proxies, often working with police and detectives on raids and stings. The public roles of these organizations have been well documented, but the trial of *People v. Bushnell* suggests how moral reform campaigns reached inside the middle-class home.

Sunday afternoon in 1901, after May Bushnell returned to New York City from an out-of-town trip, she confronted the deep betrayal of her husband George. She suspected something was wrong during the first weeks of their marriage but hoped their move from Chicago to New York City would give them a fresh start. Soon after they moved, however, George Bushnell invited a seventeen-year-old male border to live with them in their small three-room apartment. The couple had little privacy, and May Bushnell complained that there was someone in their home "nearly all of the time" during their short marriage.[102] George and May Bushnell were married only two weeks when the first border left, and he was quickly replaced by another young man who stayed with the couple for three months.

Twenty-two-year-old Daniel Cole was born in College Point, New York. He divided his time between seeking a "classical education" at the Rectory School in New Milford, Connecticut, and working as a bellhop in New York City. He first met George Bushnell in September 1899 at the Hotel Imperial. Cole worked at the hotel and Bushnell came by to visit him on several occasions. Daniel Cole said Bushnell invited him to lodge with them "so that I might have a little social comforts and other amusements and enjoyments which I did not have then."[103] George Bushnell's desire to help young men might have stemmed from his Catholic charity work, his faith, and his desire to help the less fortunate, but prosecutors alleged his motives were predatory. Daniel Cole's testimony in court a year later suggested that he knew George Bushnell had same-sex desires when he asked him to move into the home. He said, "He told me that he desired to reform, and that he trusted that I would be very comfortable with himself and his wife."[104] Cole decided to live with May and George Bushnell in January 1901.

In March, May Bushnell traveled to southern Ontario to visit her uncle-in-law. While his wife was absent, George Bushnell entered Daniel Cole's room late at night, woke him from his sleep, and invited him to his room. Cole evidently suspected that some sexual activity would transpire between the two of them. He resisted the offer at first and told him that he was worried that May "might catch on."[105] Bushnell assured him of his proper motives, told him "nothing would happen," and that he "had thoroughly made up his mind to reform, and that I could go in with perfect safety."[106]

Daniel Cole entered Bushnell's room and the two of them talked. According to Cole, George Bushnell regaled him with a story about a priest he had sex with who "could suck a regiment of men."[107] The recitation of this

story excited Bushnell and, according to Cole, Bushnell moved to embrace
and kiss him. Cole recounted how "he seized me with his hands and forced
his penis into my rectum."[108] He testified that the alleged assault caused
him horrible pain, and bleeding from his rectum soiled his clothes. Daniel
Cole was awake most of the night, and when May Bushnell returned home
in the morning, he confronted her with a scandalous story. He told her, "If
you knew what happened last night you would not live with your husband
five minutes."[109] That morning, when George Bushnell learned that Daniel
Cole told his wife about their sexual encounter, he threatened to kill or jail
him. Cole, still in agonizing pain, went to a hospital, was diagnosed with
an anal fistula, and spent over a month in treatment.[110] From there, Cole
moved to Connecticut to live for eight months. Then, he returned to New
York City to testify against George Bushnell.

May Bushnell visited the office of the New York Society for the
Suppression of Vice and spoke with its president, Anthony Comstock.
Comstock was America's leading anti-vice crusader of the nineteenth century. Comstock served in the Union Army during the Civil War and moved to
New York City in 1865 to become a dry goods salesman. He made his first
fight against vice three years later in 1868. Comstock learned about a book-
seller peddling obscene books, purchased one of them, and made a formal
complaint to the police, which led to the book dealer's arrest.[111] Comstock's
tactics drew attention from the Young Men's Christian Association (YMCA).
The New York YMCA successfully petitioned the New York State legislature
to enact a law against the mailing of obscene materials through the mail
system, and the organization regarded Comstock as an important ally.[112]
The YMCA secretly funded Comstock's anti-obscenity efforts, and their
financial support allowed Comstock to create the New York Society for
the Suppression of Vice (NYSSV) in 1874. During its first two years, the
work of the NYSSV led to the arrest of 106 people.[113] Empowered by
an 1873 law that made it illegal to send obscene objects, contraceptives,
abortifacients, and pornography through the US mail, Comstock escalated
his anti-vice efforts and expanded his range of targets. By 1900, Comstock
and his organization took aim at fairy culture and cross-dressing men.[114]

Anthony Comstock was a nationally renowned figure, both reviled
and admired, by the time May Bushnell visited him in his New York City
office. Comstock convinced Bushnell to travel to New Milford, Connecticut,
in order to convince Daniel Cole to make an affidavit against her husband.
Cole agreed, and the two of them went to Comstock's office to formalize the
paperwork. He testified that when May Bushnell brought the situation to his

attention, he interviewed a number of people and gathered more evidence about the conduct of George Bushnell. Comstock allegedly developed a list of young men Bushnell lured from his Catholic mission and sodomized. He also found evidence of Bushnell's arrest on a vagrancy charge in New York City and Syracuse. Persuaded of his guilt, Comstock wrote to Bushnell and asked him to call at his office. There, on August 2, Bushnell talked with Comstock for about half an hour. The only record of the conversation comes from Comstock's memory as he recounted it in Bushnell's trial.

Comstock told George Bushnell that he had seen reports "in reference to your conduct with young men and the assaults that you have been making on young men." Comstock cited the incident with Daniel Cole and May Bushnell's discovery of "the bed all covered with filthy matter." Comstock told him he had a reputation as "a sodomer, a moral pervert," but Bushnell claimed he had lived an upstanding life since his marriage. Comstock threatened him with arrest if he continued to assault boys and young men. "You are to be pitied," Comstock said. "You have got into a condition that you can't break away from, that you can't control yourself under certain circumstances." Bushnell promised him: "I will give you a pledge that I will live hereafter a strictly moral life." Whether or not Bushnell lived up to his promise, Comstock had him arrested.

The trial commenced on April 24, 1901, and Daniel Cole was the first witness for the prosecution. Cole's active participation in the act raised important questions about the line between sexual consent and victimization in sodomy prosecutions. Bushnell's defense attorney first questioned Cole as to why he appeared in court at all. Cole knew, as a Connecticut resident, that a New York subpoena could not compel him to testify. Cole said that he promised Comstock he would testify and did not want to break that promise. Next, the defense attorney raised the issue of Daniel Cole's complicity in the act of sodomy, and Cole made a strong effort to dodge the question:

Defense Attorney Amos Evans: And do you think a man like this ought to be convicted?

Daniel Cole: I think he ought to be punished, yes.

Q: Yes. How about yourself?

A: Well, what do you mean?

Q: Eh?

A: What do you mean?

Q: Don't you think you ought to be punished too?

A: Well, I think we ought all to be punished for some things.

Q: For some things?

A: Yes.

Q: Don't you think that you ought to be punished for your part in this transaction?

A: What part?

Q: Didn't you submit to this?

A: No.

Q: You did not?

A: No.

Q: The matter occurred—the occurrence took place against your will, did it?

A: Yes.

Q: When he went in and asked you to come into the other room you objected, didn't you?

A: I told him I didn't want to.

Q: You didn't want to?

A: No.

Q: And you told the reason why, didn't you?

A: Yes.

Q: What was that reason?

A: Well, thought that—

Q: Don't you remember the reason that you gave to the District Attorney upon the direct examination?

A: This morning?

Q: Yes.

A: The reason that I didn't wish to go—

Q: The reason why you did not wish to leave your own room and go into his room?

A: Yes; because May, meaning his wife, might catch on.

Q: Yes.

A: And because I didn't want to.

Q: Yes. Now, then, you told him the reason why you didn't want to go into his room was because May, his wife, might catch on?

Q: It was not the only reason.

A: Well, but that is the reason you gave him.

Q: One of them.

A: Yes.

Q: Yes.

A: And that was the principal reason why you did not want to go into that room?

Q: I didn't say that it was the principal reason.[115]

The defense attorney led Cole to admit that he was hesitant to enter Bushnell's room because he might get caught, not because he objected to

what they were going to do. If the moral implications of his behavior concerned Cole, then he would not have placed in the foreground his worry
about the wife discovering the situation. Cole's description of the encounter
with Bushnell hinted that Bushnell coerced him by grabbing his hands and
forcing him to have sex, but the questions of consent in the trial did not
revolve around the use of force in the bedroom. Instead, the pivotal moment
was Cole's decision to walk through the doorway. Bushnell's defense attorney
recognized this weakness in his story and pressed him further:

> *Defense Attorney Amos Evans*: Now, you knew what was going to
> take place if you went in there?
>
> *Daniel Cole*: Well, I surmised that something would.
>
> *Q*: Yes. And notwithstanding your surmise that a thing of this
> kind was going to take place you went in?
>
> *A*: Yes, sir.
>
> *Q*: Now, do you mean to say that you went in against your will?
>
> *A*: No, because I controlled my own will.
>
> *Q*: Yes. Then when you went in, you surmised what was going
> to take place, and notwithstanding that, you went in there vol-
> untarily yourself, didn't you? He didn't pick you up and carry
> you in, did he?
>
> *A*: No.
>
> *Q*: Well, that was not against your will, was it?
>
> *A*: What?
>
> *Q*: That you went into his room?
>
> *A*: Well, that is a ridiculous question.
>
> *Q*: Well, it may seem so to you. It might not to others. It was
> not against your will that you went into his room, was it?

A: Well, no. If a man says that he is going to do a thing and makes up his mind to do it, it is not against his will.[116]

Daniel Cole's stubbornness revealed the contradictory quality of his sexual consent. While he described the force that the defendant mustered against him, it was a moment of resistance underneath an assumed agreement between the two men that they would have sexual relations in the room and then conceal it from Bushnell's wife. Cole consented to the encounter but tried to deflect questions about why he, too, was not complicit. At one point, Cole laughed at the defense attorney's questions, prompting the judge to admonish him. Daniel Cole pleaded with the judge, "But, your Honor, this man makes such outrageous accusations. The whole thing is an amusing farce."[117] The judge assured him of the seriousness of the situation.

After Cole stepped down, May Bushnell, the defendant's wife, took the stand and described during the opening of direct examination her relationship with her husband. She said that she was at the home of her husband's uncle in Richmond Hill and returned home Sunday afternoon. The prosecutor questioned her about the linen in their bedroom and she variously described it as "filthy, soiled," and "unmentionable."[118] The remaining questions from the prosecutor revolved around the stained bedroom linen, drawing protests from the defense attorney who thought that her descriptions were too vague to be admissible.

Following the testimony of the defendant's wife, Anthony Comstock took the witness stand on behalf of the prosecution. Comstock testified that he had a lengthy and revealing conversation with Bushnell wherein the defendant admitted to having sex with younger men. Bushnell's defense attorney objected to the admission of this conversation into the legal record because the rights of the defendant were not properly secured, an issue he later raised on appeal. He said, "There is no evidence, nothing to show, that the defendant knew why he came there, knew why this conversation took place as between Mr. Comstock and himself, or was apprised in regard to his rights, or told that the evidence or any statements that he might make at that time would be used against him."[119] The judge overruled his objections, and Comstock recited the conversation he had with the defendant in great detail, describing the conversation as if it were drawn from his memory word-for-word.[120] Comstock's testimony placed jurors in his office and gave them a front-row look at the supposedly damning conversation the suspect had with Comstock. In his re-creation of the conversation, Comstock remarked on a series of details that had not yet been previously introduced: that Bushnell recruited new sex partners through his religious charity work, the hospitalization of a second victim, two prior arrests, and a large debt he owed to his wife. Bushnell's admissions of guilt built into the recited dialogue allowed Comstock to add to Bushnell's list of victims and crimes without formally accusing him of anything. Bushnell's frequent references to his wife's betrayal rhetorically worked as admissions of guilt by tacitly acknowledging that his wife knew the truth and exposed it. Ultimately, Comstock testified that Bushnell violated his pledge to lead a pure life. Comstock discovered that Bushnell had invited a young man named Charles Walters to his apartment and he had him arrested.

The judge instructed the jury to consider two questions. First, they were to determine whether Bushnell had "unnatural connection" with Cole.[121] Next, the judge asked them to determine whether Cole's participation in the act was a "voluntary submission."[122] If Cole voluntarily had sex with Bushnell, the judge explained, there must be evidence corroborating the complaining witness for the jury to arrive at a proper guilty verdict. The jury found him guilty after deliberating for an hour.

George Bushnell appealed the decision on the grounds that Comstock's conversation was incompetent evidence coming five months after the commission of the crime. They contended that admission of Comstock's testimony created reasonable doubt as to the legality of the conviction. The application of the appeal was granted. The granting judge noted that Comstock was allowed to give hearsay and opinion evidence about criminal acts that were not specifically connected to the offense charged. The appellant court ruled that "it was not only sufficient to require the submission of the case to the jury, but that any other verdict than one of guilty would have been a miscarriage of justice."[123] The court noted that the entire conversation between Bushnell and Comstock, particularly the talk about similar crimes, should not have been received by the judge and that some of the evidence, therefore, was not proper. But, ultimately, the appeals court ruled that the judge did not err in overruling the objections and affirmed Bushnell's guilty verdict.

"He didn't ask for no girl"

Harlem became New York City's predominant black neighborhood in the 1900s and 1910s.[124] Although Greenwich Village had a larger reputation as a gay enclave, the social networks of Harlem men who had sex with other men were just as robust. Gays in Harlem were in many ways more open than they were in the Village. Harlem's racial divide gave it different meaning, as a site of sexual exchange, for black men and white men. Chauncey noted, "It was easier for white interlopers to be openly gay in their brief visits to Harlem than for the black men who lived there round the clock. But black men nonetheless turned Harlem into a homosexual mecca."[125] Historian Kevin Mumford describes Harlem as an urban "interzone" where different racial groups met and shared cultural practices. Mumford documented that in the sexual relationships between men before 1900, black men typically adopted the "female" role in the sexual act. The growing distinction between hetero- and homosexuals paralleled the sharp racial divide.[126]

Interracial homosexual clubs and speakeasies were located in a block that ran from 126th to 152nd streets between 5th and St. Nicholas avenues. Many of these "black and tans" were located in tenement apartments, while the more accessible clubs drew a greater heterosexual clientele. Reformers regarded these clubs as the worst of the worst, combining sexual immorality with miscegenation.[127] For white men, Harlem nightlife was a site of interracial sexual exchange occurring both inside and outside of the black and tans. The sex trade in the form of street solicitation flourished outside the black and tans as well.

Jurors in the 1914 trial *People v. Schiff* were afforded a glimpse into Harlem's interracial sex trade. Prosecutors asked them to convict a man for paying a black man to perform oral sex on him. Herman Schiff was the son of German immigrants Simon and Amelia Schiff. Census records from 1900 indicate that Herman worked as an office clerk and, in 1910, he worked in his father's shop.[128]

Harry Jackson, an eighteen-year-old African American elevator operator, testified to standing outside of a Harlem building at three in the morning. Herman Schiff walked past him and they said "Good morning" to each other. Schiff continued past him for several feet, turned around, and asked him if he wanted to make five dollars. "I said 'How?' He said, 'Come inside and I'll show you.'"[129] Jackson walked inside the sitting room of the building with Schiff. He sat in a chair while Schiff stood against a table and pulled out his penis. He balked at the invitation to fellate Schiff, but the defendant assured him that he would not get caught and reminded him of the promised money. According to Jackson's testimony, "I started in, and just as I started in, the officers walked in."[130] During their arraignment, at the 121st Street courthouse, Schiff urged Jackson to plead not guilty and to not betray him. According to Jackson's testimony, Schiff both threatened Jackson and promised him money if he cooperated. Jackson pleaded guilty to second degree assault and cooperated as a witness for the prosecution.

Herman Schiff claimed that he sought a prostitute and was too drunk to account his time with the young man. This defense strategy conceded his moral weakness, but not his alleged sexual depravity. During the opening of Jackson's cross-examination, Schiff's defense attorney asked the witness a number of questions to suggest that Schiff was "staggering home" having spent the evening drinking.[131] Schiff's attorney asked the elevator operator if Jackson spoke to Schiff first and if he had asked him during their early morning exchange of pleasantries whether or not he wanted a prostitute. "No I didn't," the witness replied. "Well," the attorney reached, "do you remember that he said that?" "No, he didn't ask for no girl."[132] Despite the blunt denial, the attorney pressed on with the characterization of Jackson approaching the drunk and vulnerable defendant with the offer of a "girl." The statements embedded in the attorney's questions insisted on Schiff's identity as a carousing bachelor. Through repetition, the attorney reinforced the idea that Jackson negotiated the price of a prostitute. In the span of two transcript pages—likely representing no more than a few minutes of time—the attorney inserted a rhetorical girl into the story of the two men: "he wanted a girl"; "you could get a girl for him"; "talking about what you could get a girl for him for"; "get a girl for him for"; "you getting a girl for him"; "to get him the girl"; "to get a girl"; "to pay to get a girl"; and "to have a girl."[133]

The arresting officer had a different memory of the event. Officer James Bishop was on a fixed post during the early morning when he noticed Schiff and Jackson acting in a "peculiar manner."[134] They embraced each other in front of a house, "placing their arms around the neck and body," and on three different occasions they went inside the building.[135] At 2:55 in the morning, an officer named Joseph Conden arrived at the post to relieve Bishop of his duty. Bishop pointed out the two suspicious men, and the officers followed them after Jackson and Schiff returned inside the building for a third time. They found the two engaged in oral sex, separated them, and then Bishop checked Jackson's mouth to see if Schiff had completed the act.[136] The police officer asked the suspect, "Why did you put your penis in Jackson's mouth?" and Schiff answered, "You know when a man gets passionate, he is liable to do anything."[137]

Herman Schiff's defense attorney emphasized two central details during his cross-examination of the police officer: Schiff wanted a prostitute and he was drunk. He asked the first officer, "Did the Negro boy say, in the police court, in the morning, that he had tried to get a girl for Mr. Schiff in the house, but couldn't, and was trying to get one in 136th Street?" Officer Bishop denied it. The attorney asked the second officer if the defendant looked drunk and suggested to the jurors, over the sustained objections of the prosecutor, how that could give proper grounds for acquittal:

Q: Had he been drinking at all?

Police Officer Bishop: He had drink in him, but he wasn't intoxicated in any way. He had been drinking.

Q: And do you think that the question of whether he was or was not intoxicated would have any effect upon the verdict in this case. As to his guilt or innocence?

A: I do not.

Q: You know that, under the law, this defendant must voluntarily submit himself to such an act, before he can be found guilty, don't you?

[objection—sustained—exception]

Q: Do you understand that you are charging him with having voluntarily submitted to this act?

[objection—sustained—exception].[138]

Finally, Herman Schiff took the stand for his defense. He testified that he was down on Broadway with a friend visiting a number of restaurants and cafés. Schiff and the dentist Dr. John B. Sennesac went to a picture show, the Knickerbocker Café, the Astor, and Claridge's. Schiff made a point to note his friend's profession, even though the attorney did not ask for it. The list of high-profile and expensive locations they visited rhetorically worked to placed Schiff as a member of New York's upper or upper-middle class. Schiff testified that they ended the evening at the Garden Restaurant, where they stayed until about 2:30.[139] As he walked home, he passed by Harry Jackson, who mumbled something at him. Schiff turned around and asked him what he said. Jackson asked him if he wanted a woman. Schiff testified that he was in a "groggy condition and as I came along, and as this boy accosted me, I only, as I say, remember indistinctly, vaguely as to the nature of what took place."[140] The prosecutor asked him during cross-examination, "And yet you thought it was a moral and decent thing to do at three A.M., to have a colored man solicit you to get a prostitute for you?" He said, "Well, under the circumstances coming home at that hour, and being a bit beside myself, when the boy accosted me that way, I didn't think it was anything out of the ordinary, under the circumstances."[141] The prosecutor questioned him about the connection between his intoxication and sense of morals:

> *Koenig*: And in the condition that you were in, that night, do you believe that your moral senses were deadened?

> *Schiff*: Now, as I recall back, they were deadened then.

> *Koenig*: And were they deadened then to the extent that you would resort to immoral and degenerate practices?

> *Schiff*: Well, I don't know whether you call that—

> *Posner*: Well, it depends upon what you call immoral and degenerate. This man is drawing a distinction between sleeping with a woman, and having this act practiced upon him.

> *Koenig*: I use the word "degenerate" to characterize the act testified to by the officers as degenerate.

> *Schiff*: Oh, I draw a line at degeneracy.[142]

The remainder of Schiff's defense consisted of character witnesses, including the testimony of John Sennesac, the dentist friend who attested to Schiff's drunken state. Schiff's witnesses stated that he lived a moral life and had a decent reputation, but the colloquy between the attorneys and the defendant suggested a qualitative distinction between immorality (sleeping with a prostitute) and degeneracy (sodomy). The prosecutor used the term "degenerate" to refer to the specific sex act, but the term also invoked a larger set of meanings about race and civilization.

"Degeneracy" in the turn-of-the-century United States meant more than individual sexual immorality. It referred to a broad understanding of civilization that linked sexuality with national health. The publication of Max Nordau's *Degeneration*, the first English version of which appeared in 1895 (the year of Oscar Wilde's trials), fueled the public discussion of degeneracy. While Wilde's trial provided an example of so-called degeneration, Nordau's text offered pseudoscientific explanations from which to understand the example. Nordau argued that the fate of Western civilization depended as much on its aesthetic and cultural dimensions as it did on its proper governance and economic production. A *New York Times* article titled "Are We Degenerating?" critiqued Nordau's "much-talked-of book."[143] What the attorneys precisely had in mind when clashing over the word "degeneracy" is impossible to discern, but the Wilde scandal and the connections it invoked among sex, degeneration, and civilization loomed in the background of this small courtroom skirmish over word choice.

≈

In modern usage, "sodomy" refers to oral or anal sex. From the eighteenth century through most of the nineteenth century, however, sodomy laws criminalized a wide range of sexual conduct, often falling under proscriptions against "crimes against nature" or against "unspeakable acts": bestiality, public masturbation, and pedophilia. A wealth of historical evidence suggests that sodomy laws did not target sexual intimacy among same-sex couples in particular. Colonial authorities considered sodomy a capital offense, but they did not view sodomy as linked to an offender's sexual orientation. A concern with nonreproductive sexual acts and sex between parties of vastly different social statuses (adult-child or master-servant) characterized the law's statutory scope and enforcement. Police and prosecutors typically pursued sodomy charges in instances where men sexually preyed upon children, but the enforcement of the law changed coinciding with the growth of gay subcultures in the early twentieth century.

The dominant understandings of sexuality and same-sex desire radically changed in the late nineteenth and early twentieth century, and the policing and surveillance of sodomy changed in response. During these years of sexual upheaval—revealed in the growth of scientific understandings of human sexuality, a selective erosion of Victorian sexual mores, and shifting norms of courtship—prosecutors made more frequent use of sodomy laws and they used them to target gay men. In the early twentieth century, sodomy prosecutions soared in cities like Boston, Philadelphia, St. Louis, and Los Angeles. Whereas the older use of the sodomy law primarily addressed men's coercive sex with weaker or nonconsenting parties, the twentieth-century use of the law increasingly tied nonnormative sex with a homosexual status group.[144]

With a new understanding of sodomy and homosexual identity in place, police and courts mounted a large intervention into the private lives of gays and lesbians. The net of sexual surveillance expanded during the first half of the twentieth century, as some anti-vice and anti-crime organizations were given quasi-police powers to investigate and secure evidence of sexual immorality. Following the repeal of Prohibition, vibrant urban gay subcultures were effectively crushed by the State Liquor Authority and other state agencies that made saloon licensing contingent on owners' cooperation in excluding supposed sexual degenerates from their businesses. During the Cold War, the state surveillance of gays and lesbians intensified and the US government launched an extensive attack on suspected gays and lesbians in civil service.[145] Moreover, sodomy laws disproportionately affected the less fortunate. The greatest number of sodomy arrests occurred in impoverished sections of US cities. George Chauncey notes that the primary targets of sodomy arrests in New York City during the 1940s and '50s were Puerto Rican and African American.[146]

In the words of legal scholar William Eskridge, "The modern regulatory state cut its teeth on gay people."[147] These efforts were buoyed by the modern conflation of gay identity and sodomy. The seemingly inseparable link between "sodomy" and same-sex desire broadly affected sexual privacy by cementing a connection between deviant sexual practices and gays and lesbians. Earlier medical, legal, and cultural understandings of sodomy variously positioned it as a vice, addiction, or human failing. Likewise, men in the nineteenth century could have sex with other men without impugning their masculinity or respectable status. In the modern age, however, sodomy was seen as an index of a particular sexual self. Sodomy trials in the early twentieth century show how the practice of sodomy marked individuals *prima facie* as deviant or criminal, while gays and lesbians were simultaneously marked as deviant for presumably engaging in the practice of sodomy.

Chapter 6

Conclusion

Rethinking Sexual Revolution

The double-edged qualities of the first sexual revolution revealed themselves within New York City's criminal courthouse. On the one hand, trial testimony revealed strong signs that New York City was undergoing the "first sexual revolution." Signs of sexual revolution abound in sex crime trial testimony. Jurors were told about lustful acts in darkened movie houses, automobile seats, and late-night cafés. Other jurors heard testimony about men who had sex with other men in steamy bathhouses. Trial testimony underscored the connection between sexual expression and structural changes in home life, work, and leisure. The trials occurred in an economic environment where twenty-two year-old Sadie Marsa was able to earn money away from home as a sales clerk, and where twenty-three-year-old Margaret Peters earned a living as an office worker. New York City offered Lillian Schlosser a place to relocate and find refuge with an older couple after the death of her parents. Yet, all three were exploited and abused in their new positions in the city.

The narratives of sexual violence and legal injustice voiced in early twentieth-century sex crime trials contradict the image of early twentieth-century America as a time of sexual revolution and progress. Felony criminal trials for sexual assault show that men exercised violence against women who took advantage of new economic and social opportunities in New York City. Trials for criminal seduction often uncovered accounts of acquaintance rape. In first degree rape cases, the Court of General Sessions received testimony about women attacked in a dentist chair, on the street, and on a date. Compulsory prostitution trials uncovered situations where young women were pulled into sex-for-money exchanges because of trickery and force. Trial testimony recounted in the previous chapters showed how law enforcement and the court system reacted to proliferating sexual freedoms and opportunities, and the stories demonstrate how lateral power relations within working-class and immigrant communities were crucial to the trajectory of sex crime prosecutions in the Progressive Era. Police and courts often served the interests of the upper classes, men, and racial and ethnic majorities. The trial transcripts, however, expose power dynamics that fall outside of the competing images of sexual revolution and social control. Court transcripts reveal the considerable extent to which members of working-class and immigrant communities used the machinery of law enforcement for their own ends. Jurors represented neighborhood values about proper manhood and womanhood. They did not passively receive two competing stories presented by the prosecutor and the defense. Rather, jurors played a dynamic role in shaping how the prosecution and the defense told their stories. Jurors in early twentieth-century courts routinely interrupted the flow of cross-examination to ask questions that were neither solicited by attorneys nor screened by judges. They asked questions that altered prosecution or defense strategies and prompted judges to intervene and offer a more elaborate explanation of the crime or the relevant law.

Trials for the different criminal offenses were similar insofar as they captured the contradictions of sexual revolution in turn-of-the-century New York City. In the context of the criminal courtroom, these contradictions revolved around competing notions of social and sexual respectability. For example, seduction prosecutions opened opportunities for women to restore their good name and social respectability. In some instances, these prosecutions redressed sexual assault and did so in an era decades before "date rape" was a commonly understood phenomenon. But complainants were constrained by assumptions about sexual respectability embedded in the law, primarily the restriction of the law only to victims of "chaste character." The complainants' prior chastity (as a physical fact and a moral condition) shaped the outcome of seduction prosecutions.

First degree rape trials often punished sexual offenders and provided a measure of justice to victims, but complainants were trapped in double binds created by prevailing ideas of femininity and masculinity. If women testified to being unconscious or under mental duress during the attack, defense attorneys pilloried them for being unreliable narrators. Yet, women were accused of consenting to intercourse if they testified that they were conscious during the attack, because unconsciousness was perceived as one of the few definitive signs of nonconsent. Also, defense attorneys criticized rape complainants if they did not fight against their attacker with substantial force, but fighting was perceived as unladylike.

Finally, compulsory prostitution trials reflected tensions and ambiguities of early urban New York City. These trials occurred during the national outcry over forced prostitution, so-called "white slavery." "White slaves" in early twentieth-century popular culture were native-born white women who lacked sexual agency, and the "white slavers" were conniving immigrants (typically, Russians or Italians) who ensnared their prey with false promises, drugging, and physical force. Compulsory prostitution trials, however, generated stories of coercion that frequently failed to fit the prevailing white slavery narrative. The criminalization of compulsory prostitution invariably delivered justice to some women coerced into sex-for-money exchanges. Similar to seduction and rape trials, however, jurors and other court actors expected complainants to fit an expected standard of respectability. Testimony from forced prostitution victims on the witness stand often clashed with the image of the archetypal white slave and the whiteness and naïvety that it implied. Women were kept not under lock and key or threats of violence but by economic and familial circumstances that—to courtroom participants—implied some measure of sexual consent.

Sodomy trials exposed spaces of sexual freedom: bathhouses and late-night hustling. These trials also displayed an intensified crackdown against sexual practices that fell outside heterosexual middle- and upper-class norms of respectability. Whereas sodomy prosecutions before the twentieth century primarily targeted men who raped and sexually exploited children, prosecutors in the first few decades of the twentieth century used the law to target illicit nightlife and sexual minorities and subcultures. Sodomy trials hint at a sexual revolution replete with explicit performances and anonymous sexual exchanges, but the transcripts of those trials also expose the power of the state to enforce heteronormative ideas of sexual propriety.

The first sexual revolution in New York City opened up spaces of sexual possibility, but it fell short of ensuring sexual autonomy. New York City criminal courts allowed acts of sexual violence to go unpunished by erecting institutional barriers that undermined justice-producing functions of criminal justice. Despite the material and ideological changes occurring in the lives of young men and women, sexual modernity failed to eradicate many of the problems women faced. The rise of dating allowed young men and women unparalleled privacy and opportunity for sexual expression, but the shift away from supervised courtship allowed men greater economic control over their dates.[1] The freedom afforded by the sexual revolution arguably contributed to a drastic increase in premarital pregnancy rates and, in many cases, this reflected the sexual desires of unmarried men and women.[2] Historians of sexuality have noted that this also reflected violence and coercion, as young women were unable to resist the sexual demands of employers and suitors once away from the protection of their families and communities.[3] In short, the first sexual revolution facilitated what we would now call "date rape" as much as it facilitated dating. The first sexual revolution promised to remove the shackles of Victorian sexual repression, but it did not end the sexual double standard, pervasive sexual violence, and gender inequality in the home and at work. In this setting, men and women stood on unequal footing despite women's gains in work, politics, and social life.

Sexual Consent and Sexual Agency

Sex crime prosecutions in early twentieth-century New York City prompt a rethinking of the historical time period by complicating characterizations of the era as either a time of sexual progress or regression. Analysis of sex crime trials also points to the interlocking relationship between gender ideology and the law. Sex crimes trial testimony clarifies the joint role of legal institutions and gender and sexual ideologies in mitigating and shoring up inequality between men and women, and between sexual majorities and sexual minorities. Sex crime trials show the embedded relationship between law and culturally constructed notions of gender. The examples marshaled in this book demonstrate how criminal trials simultaneously consist of micro-social interactions and underlying social and historical processes. Trial participants exercise power through courtroom talk, but their language games occur in a structured social space saturated with rules and constraints. Sex crime trials reveal how gender ideology—enduring ideas about the differences between masculinity and femininity, and men and women—finds its way into the courtroom and is amplified or subverted through the give-and-take of courtroom testimony.

The courtroom conflicts about seduction, pimping, prostitution, and sodomy center on the question of sexual consent, which is embedded in wider understandings of human agency. Sexual agency—the ability or capacity for humans to organize freely their sexual identities and practices—is a necessary precondition for authentic sexual consent. A cultural imagination populated by white slaves and seduced virgins lends itself to different story-telling strategies compared to a cultural imagination populated by villainous prostitutes and New Women.

The term "agency" in social science and humanities scholarship denotes humans' capacity for critical reflection and individual action. As an abstract capacity, theorists conceive of agency as something we have by virtue of being human. Historian and social theorist William Sewell Jr. argues that agency "is inherent in the knowledge of cultural schemas that characterizes all minimally competent members of a society."[4] Like the use of the term "structure," scholars place agency in the center of theoretical arguments and expositions about how people use culture to resist hegemonic political, legal, and economic arrangements. Agency is seen as a countervailing humanistic force against the varied determinisms of social position, economic constraint, and socialization, but it is a force that is also enabled by those structural factors.[5] In this context, some scholars use the phrase "sexual agency" to refer to the ability to order one's sexual life and meaningfully consent to sex.

Historian Pamela Haag argues that sexual consent is a historical construct. She writes, "Consent, especially, is an abstraction in the historical imagination most typically invoked by feminists to mark an imagined sexual agency or to designate an ideal of sexual agency."[6] To say that "sexual consent" is socially constructed does not deny sexual violence, but it suggests that what we perceive as violent or unacceptable changes over time and in response to institutional, political, and other group-level social forces. The critique implied by Haag's phrase "imagined sexual agency" is not that feminists believe in a wrongheaded idea of consent, but that not recognizing agency and consent as constructs leads to a lack of recognition of the unequal and multivalent power relations that create the very possibility for sexual agency or sexual consent.

The sex crime trials considered in this book show how the legal sphere creates and constructs agency. On one level, judges, jurors, police, and other legal agents create laws that enable capacities for action and build incentives and sanctions for different practices and social strategies. Law's structures enable and constrain agents; courts, laws, and judges impose themselves from above. Yet this appearance of autonomy conceals the more subtle ways that law constructs agency and sexual agency.

At the level of courtroom talk, witnesses and attorneys pursued lines of discourse that formed patterns across the cases, but they were not following a blueprint of action. Within the rules and norms of testimony and witness questioning, trial actors made unpredictable conversational moves. Sadie Marsa, who accused a man of seduction, refused to act like a seduced maiden on the witness stand when she mocked the defense attorney's questions. Daniel Cole, who was a "victim" of sodomy, put his attorneys in a difficult situation by revealing his complicity. Various complainants in "white slavery" trials discussed their active involvement in the prostitution trade despite the popular image of prostitution as innocent women abducted by immigrant procurers. The verbal exchanges between the attorneys, witnesses, judges, and jurors created the grist of trial stories through a process of social interaction. Close consideration of the way individuals use words in the courtroom, including an examination of question format and syntax, allows for an analysis that considers and accounts for agency and purposive action.

At the level of culture and shared meaning, stories provide the foundation upon which experiential details can be meaningfully sorted, arranged, and communicated to others. Culture, defined as shared systems of meaning, give stories their coherence and intelligibility. Trial strategies drew strength from themes, images, and characters in broader culture. As Amsterdam and Bruner explain, legal categories make factual and logical distinctions, but "even for the most studious law student or the most experienced criminal practitioner, 'murderer' will almost surely also call to mind, most of the time and for most purposes, images that have nothing to do with the Penal Code and everything to do with Jack the Ripper or Jimmy Cagney or Horror Comics."[7] Trial participants do not work solely within the ambit of formal law; rather, formal law exists in dialogue with norms, doxa, and relevant cultural codes. Analyses of the cultural and discursive bases of law recognize that formal law does not impose itself from a hermetically sealed position of autonomy but is negotiated in interactions made as much from popular knowledge as from codified rules. Criminal sex crime trials engaged topics and uncovered details deemed too indecent to print in a newspaper, and the relative obscurity of the courtroom participants all but ensured their absence from the historical record. The recovery and retelling of these stories cast a bright light outside the courtroom as well as within it.

Notes

Introduction

1. *People v. Bloch*, 15.
2. Ibid., 83.
3. Ibid., 283.
4. Ibid., 351.
5. Clement, *Love for Sale*, 49.
6. See Israel, *Bachelor Girl*, 120.
7. McGovern, "The American Woman's Pre-World War I Freedom in Manners and Morals," 333.
8. The phrase "first sexual revolution" refers to large-scale transformations that occurred in American sexual practices and ideologies from approximately 1900 to 1920. See Haag, *Consent*, 121–142; Smith, "Dating of the American Sexual Revolution"; White, *First Sexual Revolution*; White, *Sexual Liberation or Sexual License?* On the complications of dating "sexual revolution," see Martin, "Structuring the Sexual Revolution."
9. Hobson, *Uneasy Virtue*, 161.
10. Liu, *The Chinatown Trunk Mystery*.
11. Ullman, *Sex Seen*, 8.
12. Flood, *Rape in Chicago*, 15.
13. Ewick and Silbey, "Subversive Stories and Hegemonic Tales," 209.
14. Anthony Amsterdam and Jerome Bruner observe that "[l]aw lives on narrative, for reasons both banal and deep. For one, the law is awash in storytelling. Clients tell their stories to lawyers, who must figure out what to make of what they hear. As clients and lawyers talk, the client's story gets recast into plights and prospects, plots and pilgrimages into possible worlds." Amsterdam and Bruner, *Minding the Law*, 110.
15. Robertson, "What's Law Got to Do with It?"
16. Nixon and Landman, "Turning Our Minds to *Minding the Law*," 175.
17. The history of the Transcript Collection is recounted in Belcher and Sexton, "Digitizing Criminals." General information about the collection is found in Faber and Rowland, *Trial Transcripts of the Court of New York, 1883–1927*.

18. See "Demand for Good Stenographers," *New York Times*, Sept. 29, 1901, 15; "Great Demand for Women Stenographers," *New York Times*, March 11, 1901, 5.

19. My sample includes almost all of the seduction and sodomy trials in the Transcript Collection, but due to the large number of rape and compulsory prostitution transcripts, I systematically employed selection criteria that limited the cases by year and age of the complaining witness. For compulsory prostitution cases, I collected only those from 1908 (the first case appealed under the new law) to 1915. For similar reasons, I collected only rape and sodomy trial transcripts where the complainant, or complaining witness, was over sixteen years old. For rape cases, I excluded trials where "abduction" was included in the indictment. All of the trials involve complainants, or complaining witnesses, sixteen years of age or older. I imposed this age threshold to make the transcript set more manageable in size, but also because sexual violence against children often invoked different understandings of age, agency, crime, and respectability and activated different parts of the law and legal machinery. How men and women in the early twentieth century made sense of the boundaries between childhood and adulthood is important for understanding the motivations of different legal actors in sex crime trials, but a sustained analysis of trials involving sexual crimes against children is beyond the scope of this book and is a topic expertly handled by others. See Robertson, *Crimes against Children*.

20. I have used the Transcript Collection in a number of published works. See Donovan, *White Slave Crusades*, 89–109; Donovan and Barnes-Brus, "Narratives of Sexual Consent and Sexual Coercion"; Donovan, "Gender Inequality and Criminal Seduction"; Donovan, "The Sexual Basis of Racial Formation."

21. Scholars influenced by poststructuralism positioned gender as a relational concept that describes ideologies about sex difference. For Scott, gender "provides a way to decode meaning and to understand the complex connections among various forms of human interaction." Scott, *Gender and the Politics of History*, 45–46. See Benhabib et al., *Feminist Contentions*; Kelly, *Critique and Power*. Poststructuralists like Joan Scott and Mary Poovey located power in language, narrative, discourse, ideology, and systems of meaning. Critics charged that the focus on language and ideology obscures power instead of exposing it; the "descent into discourse" detracted historians and their readership from the real experiences of real people. See Palmer, *Descent into Discourse*.

22. In an influential piece on feminine respectability in the Caribbean, Peter J. Wilson defined respectability as "a value derived from conformity to the ideals of the total society or the legal society." Wilson, "Reputation and Respectability," 78. Discussions of respectability feature prominently in recent historical scholarship on Britain and the United States. See Green, "Between Respectability and Self-Respect"; Balos and Fellows, "A Matter of Prostitution"; Cordery, "Friendly Societies and the Discourse of Respectability in Britain"; Higginbotham, *Righteous Discontent*. For use of the respectability concept in sociology, see Duneier, *Slim's Table*; Phipps, "Rape and Respectability"; Schalet et al., "Respectability and Autonomy."

23. Skeggs, *Formations of Class and Gender.*

24. Ibid., 15.

25. Green distinguishes between "imposed respectability and asserted self-respect." Green, "Between Respectability and Self-Respect," 2.

26. Davidson, "The Goosing of Violet Nye and Other Tales," 450.

27. Higginbotham also explains how black women's respectability discourse acted as a constraint. See Higginbotham, *Righteous Discontent.*

28. Boyer, "Place and the Politics of Virtue," 265.

29. Ibid., 268.

30. Phipps, "Rape and Respectability," 678.

31. Biernacki, "Method and Metaphor," 63. Biernacki critiques new cultural history for its selective reading of Geertz. See Biernacki, "Method and Metaphor"; Lacquer, "Credit, Novels, and Masturbation"; Darton, *Great Cat Massacre.*

32. Maza, "Stories in History," 1497. Amy Srebnick observed: "Not the least of these changes has been the legitimization of unusual or even fanciful topics as viable subjects for the historian. Cat massacres, penopticism, the carnevalesque, the stories of social outcasts and criminals have proven to be not only engaging topics for study, but, more important, useful pathways into our understanding of what the French have identified as *mentalités*." See Strebnick, *Mysterious Death of Mary Rogers,* xv.

33. Davis, *Fiction in the Archives.*

34. Conley and O'Barr, *Just Words,* 119.

35. Davis explains her approach: "After exploring the crafting of the tales, I will circle back to their fidelity to 'real events,' or at least to the same event as recounted by others, and ask what relation truth-telling had to the outcome of the stories and what truth status they enjoyed in society at large." Davis, *Fiction in the Archives,* 5.

36. Walkowitz, *City of Dreadful Delight,* 218.

37. McLaren, *Trials of Masculinity,* 10.

38. Strebnick, *Mysterious Death of Mary Rogers,* xv.

39. Duggan, *Sapphic Slashers,* 5; Cohen, *Murder of Helen Jewett*; Trotti shows Patricia Cline Cohen's powerful study of the murder of nineteenth-century prostitute Helen Jewett "recreating the world of meaning illuminated by a single violence crime." See Trotti, "Review Essay."

40. See White, *Content of the Form.*

41. Hutchby and Wooffitt, *Conversation Analysis,* 8.

42. Ibid., 5–6.

43. Ibid., 4.

44. Conley, *Just Words*; Ehrlich, *Representing Rape*; Matoesian, *Law and the Language of Identity*; Matoesian, *Reproducing Rape.*

45. See also Drew, "Contested Evidence in Courtroom Cross-Examination."

46. Sanday, *Woman Scorned,* 216.

47. Matoesian, *Reproducing Rape,* 33.

48. Cotterill, *Language and Power in Court*, 67.

49. Wittgenstein, *Philosophical Investigations*. For an example of Wittgenstein's language game concept applied to the legal domain, see Leader-Elliott and Naffine, "Wittgenstein, Rape Law and the Language Games of Consent."

50. Hutchby and Wooffitt, *Conversation Analysis*, 93.

51. Travers, "Understanding Talk in Legal Settings."

52. Sociologist and conversation analyst John Manzo argues that "'law' consists, in the first place, of concerted work by real persons in real time." Manzo, "Ethnomethodology, Conversation Analysis, and the Sociology of Law," 10.

53. Built environments mediate our social existence by constraining and enabling human action. Sewell writes that our built environment shapes and organizes our "daily routines, whom we will interact with, how we can earn our living, our sense of limits of the manipulatable world, the means of bringing people together for coordinated action." Sewell, *Logics of History*, 363; Unlike what is often conjured by the word "structure," which implies a stasis that often substitutes for explanation, built environments have a built-in capacity for change. This connection shows how those language games build and comprise what social scientists call "social structure." Social structure is neither reducible to the built environment and its grand motors of change (like economics and political power), nor is it reducible to semiotic practices.

54. Silvernail, *Penal Code* 122.

55. *Consolidated Laws*, 2821.

56. Ibid., 85.

57. Blank, *Straight*.

58. The first freedom guaranteed by sexual citizenship entails freedoms of sexual refusal. Individuals with full sexual autonomy have the right and ability to refuse sex with anyone for any reason or no reason at all. The second facet is a freedom to make choices about one's life, associations, and activities with other consenting adults. These rights create sexual citizens. See Cossmann, *Sexual Citizens*; Schulofer, *Unwanted Sex*, 99.

Chapter 1. Trials of the First Sexual Revolution

1. Guterl, *Color of Race in America*, 15. On the discourse of "civilization" during the Progressive Era, see Bederman, *Manliness and Civilization*.

2. Antoniazzi, *Wayward Woman*, 1.

3. Blake, *How New York Became American*, 5.

4. Bodnar, *Transplanted*, xviii.

5. Guterl, *Color of Race in America*, 31.

6. Blake, *How New York Became American*, 6. In the decade leading up to World War I, approximately thirteen million immigrants arrived in the United States. Daniels, *Not Like Us*, 58.

7. See Dinnerstein et al., *Natives and Strangers*, 179–180; Roediger, *Working Toward Whiteness*.

8. Dinnerstein et al., *Natives and Strangers*, 71.

9. Glazer and Moynihan, *Beyond the Melting Pot*, 137–142; Gurock, *When Harlem Was Jewish*, 36.

10. Glazer and Moynihan, *Beyond the Melting Pot*, 185.

11. Osofsky, *Harlem*.

12. Ibid., 105.

13. Ibid., 105–110.

14. Osofsky, "Race Riot." See also Reitano, *The Restless City*, 114.

15. See Chauncey, *Gay New York*. It is important to note that use of the term "gay" to refer to men who had sex with other men is a relatively recent appellation introduced in the 1940s. As I explain in chapter 4, men and women in the early twentieth century had a different vocabulary for describing same-sex relations.

16. White, *Sexual Liberation*, 25.

17. Reitano, *Restless City*, 109.

18. Kushner, "Nineteenth-Century Sexuality," 35.

19. See Foucault, *History of Sexuality*. In 1978, the year the English translation of *The History of Sexuality* became available to US historians, Kushner wrote: "Such an outpouring of warnings of the dangers of sexuality in children and adults, however, does not necessarily prove that most Americans led sexually repressed lives in the nineteenth century. It may be proof of just the opposite. After all, one would not continually warn the nation of the dangers of sexual excesses if no one were being sexually excessive." See Kushner, "Nineteenth-Century Sexuality and the 'Sexual Revolution' of the Progressive Era," 35.

20. Horowitz, *Rereading Sex*, 4. See also Cocks, "Rethinking Sexuality in the Progressive Era."

21. John D'Emilio and Estelle Freedman give the clearest exposition of the structural origins of the first sexual revolution in *Intimate Matters*. Their book synthesizes a large body of historical research on sexual norms, attitudes, and practices from colonial times to the 1960s.

22. D'Emilio and Freedman, *Intimate Matters*, 58.

23. Lystra, *Searching the Heart*, 77–80.

24. Davis, "Not Marriage at All." See also, Cott, *Public Vows*; Seidman, *Romantic Longings*. On how the companionate marriage model contributed to rising divorce rates, see May, *Great Expectations*.

25. McGovern notes, "The great leap forward in women's participation in economic life came between 1900 and 1910; the percentage of women who were employed changed only slightly from 1910 to 1930." McGovern, "The American Women's Pre–World War I Freedom in Manners and Morals," 320.

26. Kessner and Caroli, "New Immigrant Women at Work."

27. Odem, *Delinquent Daughters*. See also Hunt, "Regulating Heterosocial Space"; Meyerowitz, *Women Adrift*; Peiss, *Cheap Amusements*. By 1910, New York had

160 clubs for girls and young women. See Friedman-Kasaba, *Memories of Migration*, 152.

28. On the growth of US amusements from the nineteenth to twentieth centuries, see Ashby, *Amusement for All*.

29. According to Hobson, the overt sexuality of young women in the cities contradicted the "conventional view of women as asexual, passive, and primarily interested in the ideals of domesticity, the management of home, care of husband, and rearing of children." Hobson, *Uneasy Virtue*, 16.

30. Stelzle, "How One Thousand Workingmen Spend Their Spare Time."

31. Friedman, *Prurient Interests*, 26.

32. Peiss, *Cheap Amusements*, 88. See also Piott, *Daily Life in the Progressive Era*, 109.

33. Israels, "Diverting a Pastime."

34. Julia Schoenfeld, "The Social and Moral Aspects of Amusements of Working Girls in New York City," 1914. Quoted in Edwards, *Popular Amusements*, 78.

35. "Hotel Trotting Bad, Says Grand Jury," *New York Times*, March 28, 1913, 7.

36. Quoted in Erenberg, *Steppin' Out*, 83.

37. Knowles, *The Wicked Waltz*, 129.

38. Erdman, *Blue Vaudeville*, 107–113.

39. Ibid., 110.

40. "The Vulgarization of Salome," 439.

41. Erdman, *Blue Vaudeville*, 110.

42. Golden, *Vernon and Irene Castle's Ragtime Revolution*.

43. Ibid., 2.

44. Castle and Castle, *Modern Dancing*.

45. On the opposition to popular dance in the early twentieth century, see Wagner, *Adversaries of Dance*, 236–291. On the role of the Castles in popularizing partner dancing, see Ashby, *With Amusement for All*, 207–210.

46. Peiss observes, "Although most adolescent working-class women lived at home, a sizable number—as many as 68,000 in 1910—lived alone, lodging in boardinghouses or renting rooms." Peiss, *Cheap Amusements*, 74.

47. Of the 343,000 wage-earning women in New York, four-fifths were single, and nearly one-third were aged sixteen to twenty. See Peiss, *Cheap Amusements*, 34.

48. The YWCA in New York City led the way to create the first boarding home in 1856. By 1898 there were at least ninety boarding homes in forty-five cities.

49. Weiner, *From Working Girl to Working Mother*.

50. Ibid., 55.

51. Meyerowitz, *Women Adrift*, 108–115.

52. Peiss, *Cheap Amusements*; Clement, *Love for Sale*.

53. Clement, *Love for Sale*, 47.

54. Jenkins, *Moral Panic*; Odem, *Delinquent Daughters*; Weeks, *Sex, Politics, and Society*.

55. McAdoo, *Guarding a Great City*, 93.

56. Lardner and Reppetto, *NYPD*, 131.

57. Bingham, "Foreign Criminals in New York."

58. Lardner and Reppetto, *NYPD*, 141–142.

59. On Maude Miner, see Odem, *Delinquent Daughters*, 113–114.

60. Fineman, *Women in the Criminal Justice System*, 95.

61. Hicks, *Talk with You Like a Woman*, 159–162.

62. Fineman, *Women in the Criminal Justice System*.

63. Gilfoyle, "The Moral Origins of Political Surveillance," 637.

64. Lardner and Reppetto, *NYPD*, 90.

65. Parkhurst, *Our Fight with Tammany*, 161.

66. Lardner and Reppetto, *NYPD*; Welch, *King of the Bowery*.

67. Page, "Power and Importance of the Magistrates' Court," 635.

68. One commenter referred to the magistrate's court, as "a very real factor in Americanization." See, Paddon, "Inferior Criminal Courts of New York City," 8.

69. McAdoo, "Administrative Organization of the Courts," 682.

70. Bingham, *Annals of the American Academy*, 12.

71. Ferrari, "Immigrant in New York County Criminal Courts," 194.

72. McAdoo, "Administrative Organization of the Courts," 679.

73. Ibid., 678.

74. Robertson, *Crimes against Children*, 31.

75. See Claghorn, *Immigrant's Day in Court*, 124–128.

76. Ibid. See also DeVille, "New York Attorneys and Ambulance Chasing"; Ferrari, "Immigrant in New York County Criminal Courts."

77. Claghorn, *Immigrant's Day in Court*, 128–132.

78. "279-Year-Old General Sessions Losing Identity in Court Overhaul," *New York Times* April 6, 1962, 21.

79. Robertson, *Crimes against Children*, 31.

80. Ferrari, "Immigrant in New York County Criminal Courts," 214.

81. Henry Dexter, "Better Jurors Needed," *New York Times*, Oct. 15, 1905, 8.

82. Train, *Prisoner at the Bar*, 206.

83. Rosen explains: "As they view the entire body of evidence and begin to discuss the case among themselves jurors work towards a collective narrative, one that necessarily depends on the ways in which narratives are generally created in their culture." Rosen, *Law as Culture*, 148.

Chapter 2. Date Rape and the Crime of Seduction

1. Whiteaker, *Seduction, Prostitution, and Moral Reform in New York*.

2. Thirteen states did not have criminal seduction laws, including Delaware, Florida, Idaho, Louisiana, Maine, Maryland, Massachusetts, Nevada, New Hampshire, Tennessee, Utah, Vermont, and West Virginia. See Humble, "Seduction as a Crime."

See also Haag, *Consent*, 188. Canada as well passed a "Bill for the Better Protection of Women and Girls" that criminalized the seduction of previously chaste women. Backhouse, *Petticoats and Prejudice*, 40–80; Broode, *Courted and Abandoned*, 88–92.

3. *Laws of the State of New York*, 493.

4. Ibid.

5. The three elements of seduction are articulated in McKinney, *Consolidated Laws*, 748.

6. "Seduction as a Crime," in *Criminal Law Magazine*, 339.

7. Humble, "Seduction as a Crime," 151.

8. Friedman, "Name Robbers," 1097.

9. Stearns, "Reform Periodicals and Female Reformers, 1830–1860"; Ginzberg, "Moral Suasion Is Moral Balderdash."

10. Hobson, *Uneasy Virtue*, 56.

11. See Cohen, *Murder of Helen Jewett*; Hobson, *Uneasy Virtue*; Gilfoyle, *City of Eros*; Odem, *Delinquent Daughters*, 16–20.

12. Mass communication scholar Guy Reel described the *Gazette* as "one of the most lurid and sensational journals of the era." Reel, "This Wicked World."

13. *Beautiful Victim*, 13, 15. This pamphlet is reprinted in Van Every, *Sins of America*.

14. Ibid, 15.

15. Ibid, 15.

16. Ibid., 6.

17. Ibid., 18.

18. After she complained of stomach pain, he gave her a reddish liquid and "Golden Pills," which were compared to Madame Restell's pills, the famous product of the nineteenth century's best-known abortionist. The liquid ate the sides of her mouth.

19. *Beautiful Victim*, 24.

20. For an insightful analysis of this case and what it says about notions of autonomy and liberalism in nineteenth-century America, see Haag, *Consent*, 19–21.

21. For analysis of purity crusades as a strategy of conservative social control, see Odem, *Delinquent Daughters*. For an analysis that considers different strands of feminist thinking in Victorian social reform, see Pleck, "Feminist Responses to 'Crimes against Women,' 1868–1896."

22. Larson, "Women Understand So Little, They Call My Good Nature 'Deceit.'"

23. Marilley, "Frances Willard and the Feminism of Fear."

24. Cott, "Passionlessness," 233.

25. Cott contends, "The positive contribution of passionlessness was to replace that sexual/carnal characterization of women with a spiritual/moral one, allowing women to develop their human faculties and their self-esteem. The belief that women lacked carnal motivation was the cornerstone of the argument for women's

moral superiority, used to enhance women's status and widen their opportunities in the nineteenth century." Cott, "Passionlessness," 233. See Baker, "The Domestication of Politics."

26. Larson, "Women Understand So Little," 303.

27. Haag, *Consent*; VanderVelde, "Legal Ways of Seduction."

28. As Haag explains, "the project for the protofeminists was to articulate a single woman's public status and value in terms distinct from the feudal bond of master and servant." Haag, *Consent*, 11.

29. Law professor Lea VanderVelde demonstrates how the trajectory of seduction, the change from its tortious to criminal status, mirrored a similar transition in rape law. VanderVelde, "Legal Ways of Seduction."

30. Ibid., 862–863.

31. Hartog, *Man and Wife in America*.

32. Ibid., 96–98.

33. *People v. Bogden*, 57.

34. Pretrial statement, Sophie Gregorwich, Feb. 28, 1914, *People v. Weintraub*, CGSCF, New York Municipal Archives.

35. *People v. Abraham Cohen*.

36. Ibid., 6.

37. Ibid.

38. Mills, *New York Criminal Reports*, 62.

39. *People v. Brennan*, 258.

40. Train, *Courts, Criminals*, 165.

41. Ibid., 167.

42. Ibid.

43. *People v. Krakauer*, 11.

44. Ibid., 17.

45. Ibid., 13.

46. Ibid., 16.

47. Ibid., 14.

48. Ibid.

49. Ibid., 30.

50. Ibid., 16.

51. Ibid., 17.

52. Ibid.

53. Ibid., 17A.

54. Ibid.

55. Ibid., 17–18, 50–52.

56. Ibid., 19.

57. Reagan, *When Abortion Was a Crime*, 23.

58. Ibid.

59. *The Penal Code of the State of New York in Force December 1, 1882*, 83.

60. Ibid.

61. *People v. Krakauer*, 64.

62. Ibid., 67.

63. Ibid., 68.

64. Ibid., 160.

65. Klapper, *Jewish Girls Coming of Age in America*, 28.

66. Klapper, *Jewish Girls Coming of Age in America*, 231–237. See also Clement, *Love for Sale*, 32–38.

67. Klapper, *Jewish Girls Coming of Age in America*, 231.

68. Clement, *Love for Sale*, 23–24.

69. Binder and Reimers, *All Nations Under Heaven*.

70. *People v. Handsman*, 8.

71. Statement of Sadie Marsa, CGSCF, 3.

72. *People v. Handsman*, 10.

73. Ibid.

74. Ibid., 14.

75. Ibid., 14.

76. Statement of Sadie Marsa, 6.

77. Statement of Sadie Marsa, 6. For greater clarity, I removed phrases like "He said" and "I said" from the transcript, and I identified the speakers.

78. Statement of Sadie Marsa.

79. Statement of Sadie Marsa, 8.

80. *People v. Isaac Cohen*, 13.

81. Ibid., 14.

82. Ibid., 17.

83. Sara Habif, deposition, CGSCF, 2.

84. Mrs. Jessurun, deposition, CGSCF, 1.

85. *People v. Isaac Cohen*, 85.

86. *People v. Handsman*, 32–33.

87. Matoesian, *Reproducing Rape*, 148–157; Matoesian, *Law and the Language of Identity*, 71–79.

88. LeMoncheck describes this as the "continuum model of sexual violence." LeMoncheck, "When Good Sex Turns Bad."

89. See VanderVelde, "Legal Ways of Seduction," 864–865.

90. *People v. Bogden*.

91. Ibid., 57.

92. *People v. Sochinsky*.

93. Ibid., 31.

94. Nicholas's police record, investigated by E. W. France, CGSCF.

95. *People v. Nicholas*, 14.

96. Ibid., 9.

97. Ibid., 28.

98. Ibid., 27–28.

99. Ibid., 57.

100. Ibid., 64–65.

101. *People v. Brennan.*

102. Ibid., 14.

103. Ibid., 64.

104. Matoesian, *Law and the Language of Identity*, 70–79.

105. *People v. Brennan*, 77.

106. Ibid., 101.

107. Estrich, *Real Rape*, 50–53.

108. Haag, *Consent*, 12–13.

109. Humble, "Seduction as a Crime," 146.

110. *People v. Mandel Weinstock*, March 2, 1912, in Mills, *New York Criminal Reports*, 53–77.

111. *People v. Brennan*, 255.

112. See *People v. Lynx; People v. Weintraub; People v. Rosen; People v. Handsman*, 43; *People v. Millinger*, 14; *People v. Nicholas*, 11; *People v. Brennan*, 17.

113. *People v. Cozzens*, 57; *People v. Nicholas; People v. Lynx*, 91–92.

114. *People v. Handsman*, 56.

115. Ibid., 56.

116. Ibid., 106.

117. Meyerowitz, *Women Adrift*, 108–115.

118. *People v. Brennan*, 125, 139–142, 164.

119. Ibid., 164–165.

120. Ibid., 255.

121. Pretrial statement, Sadie Cohen, Jan. 5, 1903, CGSCF.

122. *People v. Rosenberg*, 14.

123. Ibid., 15.

124. Ibid., 48.

125. Ibid., 48. I deleted "I said" (twice) and "she said" from this excerpt for better readability.

126. Ibid., 51.

127. Ibid.

128. Ibid., 43.

129. Ibid., 40–41.

130. Ibid., 41.

131. Ibid., 48.

132. Ibid., 55.

133. *People v. Hawkins.*

134. Ibid., 20.

135. Mary C. Keegan's deposition, April 5, 1918, CGSCF, 1.

136. *People v. Hawkins*, 49–56.

137. Ibid., 186.

138. Ibid., 290.

139. Ibid., 288.

140. Ancestry.com, 1920 Census, Manhattan Assembly District 23, New York, New York; Roll: T625 1226; 13B; Enumeration District: 1495; Image: 939.

141. Dunlap, "The Reform of Rape Law and the Problem of White Men"; Larson, "Even a Worm Will Turn at Last."

142. Larson, "Even a Worm Will Turn at Last."

143. Ibid., 19.

144. See, for example, Jane Larson's call for a more positive appraisal of nineteenth-century sex reform and its legislative outcomes. Larson, "Even a Worm Will Turn at Last"; Larson, "Women Understand So Little."

145. Kandiyoti, "Bargaining with Patriarchy."

146. Dubinsky, *Improper Advances*; Dubois and Gordon, "Seeking Ecstasy on the Battlefield"; Marilley, "Frances Willard and the Feminism of Fear"; Odem, *Delinquent Daughters*; Whiteaker, *Seduction, Prostitution, and Moral Reform*.

147. Dubinsky, *Improper Advances*; Jenkins, *Moral Panic*; Weeks, *Sex, Politics, and Society*.

148. This phrase is credited to social theorist Orville Lee, who derives it from James C. Scott's book *Weapons of the Weak*. See Lee, "Legal Weapons for the Weak?," 26.

149. Russell, *Politics of Rape*. The chapter entitled "Lovers Rape, Too" in Diana Russell's *The Politics of Rape* attempted to broaden the taken-for-granted category of rape beyond stranger rape. Working against a legal and popular culture that minimizes the seriousness and prevalence of date rape, second-wave feminists fought to change both the legal processing of rape cases and the prevailing public image of the crime. See Sanday, *Woman Scorned*; Rose, "Rape as a Social Problem"; Marsh et al., *Rape and the Limits of Law Reform*. Published in 1975, Susan Brownmiller's landmark study *Against Our Will* was the first feminist work to use the term "date rape" to refer to acts of forced intercourse where the people involved know one another, and where physical coercion may be less of a factor than in stranger rape. The 1970s anti-rape movement recognized that rape was perpetrated not solely by psychologically deranged deviants but by men whom victims trusted and considered normal. Leaders in the anti-rape movement have argued that rape is not an aberration of heterosexual courtship but is the product of a rape culture wherein men define the terms of sexual access for women. Sanday, *Woman Scorned*; Miller and Biele, "Twenty Years Later"; Rose, "Rape as a Social Problem."

150. Larson, "Women Understand So Little," 394.

151. McLaren, *Sexual Blackmail*.

152. Ibid.

Chapter 3. Rape and the
Double Bind of Progressive-Era Femininity

1. Freedman, *Redefining Rape*, 3.

2. Flood, *Rape in Chicago*, 15.

3. Cook, *Code of Criminal Procedure and Penal Code of the State of New York*, 136.

4. Freedman, *Redefining Rape*, 145–151.

5. Robertson, *Crimes against Children*, 33.

6. Ibid.

7. None of the trials involved instances of what legal scholar Susan Estrich would term "simple rape." Estrich, *Real Rape*.

8. *Penal Code of the State of New York*, 1902, 74.

9. Ibid.

10. *People v. Abbott*, 19 Wend. 192, 195 (NY. *1838*).

11. Brownmiller, *Against Our Will*, 360; Plummer, *Telling Sexual Stories*, 66.

12. *People v. Roy*, 3.

13. Ibid., 10.

14. Ibid., 68–69.

15. Ibid., 85.

16. Ibid., 85.

17. Ibid., 15.

18. Ibid., 15.

19. Smith-Rosenberg, *Disorderly Conduct*, 206.

20. Ibid.

21. *People v. Roy*, 21.

22. Ibid., 68–69, 85.

23. Ibid., 50.

24. Ibid., 102.

25. Ibid., 147.

26. Ibid., 196.

27. Ibid.

28. Ibid., 17.

29. Ibid., 45.

30. Ibid., 18–19.

31. Ibid., 42–43.

32. Kellor, *Out of Work*; see also, Katzman, *Seven Days a Week*, 101–105.

33. *People v. Costanis*, 11–13.

34. Ibid., 17.

35. Ibid., 18.

36. Ibid.

37. Matoesian, *Law and the Language of Identity*, 57.

38. *People v. Costanis*, 19.
39. Ibid.
40. Ibid., 22.
41. Ibid., 42.
42. Ibid., 43.
43. Ibid.
44. Ibid., 46–47.
45. Cooper, *Once a Cigar Maker*, 18–20, 306
46. Schneider, *Trade Unions and Community*, 50–73.
47. *People v. Bloch*, 3.
48. The second question the defense attorney asked during *voir dire* foreshadowed his defense strategy. He asked potential jurors if their judgment would be affected if "the prosecutrix might claim that she was a virtuous girl, up to that time?" *People v. Bloch*, 4.
49. Ibid., 15.
50. Ibid., 53.
51. Ibid., 43.
52. Ibid., 53
53. Ibid., 48.
54. Ibid., 71.
55. Ibid.
56. Ibid., 83.
57. Ibid., 218.
58. Ibid., 224.
59. Ibid., 228.
60. Ibid., 246, 256.
61. Ibid., 255.
62. Ibid., 234.
63. Ibid., 277.
64. Ibid., 278.
65. Ibid., 278.
66. Ibid., 319.
67. Ibid., 350.
68. Ibid., 351.
69. Ibid., 264.
70. Tori Barnes-Brus and I elaborate on the active role played by jurors in "Narratives of Sexual Consent and Sexual Coercion."
71. Ibid., 357.
72. Ibid., 358–360.
73. Ibid., 369.
74. Ibid., 381, 382.

75. Ibid., 391.
76. *People v. Schonland*, 10.
77. Ibid., 40.
78. Ibid.
79. Ibid., 78.
80. Ibid.
81. Ibid.
82. Ibid., 80.
83. Ibid., 92.
84. Ibid., 116.
85. Ibid., 117.
86. Ibid., 124–125.
87. Ibid., 131.
88. Ibid., 147.
89. Ibid., 167–168.
90. Ibid., 167.
91. Ibid., 168.
92. Ibid.
93. Ibid., 171
94. Ibid., 169.
95. Ibid., 170.
96. Ibid., 171.
97. Ibid., 174–175.
98. Ibid., 176.
99. Ibid., 177.
100. Ibid., 178.
101. Ibid., 179.
102. Ibid.
103. Ibid., 180.
104. Ibid., 187.
105. Ibid., 189.
106. Ibid., 183.
107. Ibid., 202.
108. Ibid., 204.
109. Ibid.
110. Ibid., 205.
111. Ibid.
112. *People v. Morrick*, 17.
113. Salwen, *Upper West Side*, 156.
114. *People v. Morrick*, 21.
115. Ibid., 113.

116. Ibid.
117. Ibid., 113–114.
118. Ibid., 22, 23.
119. Ibid., 6.
120. Ibid.
121. Ibid., 6–7.
122. Ibid., 7.
123. Ibid., 39.
124. Ibid., 47.
125. Flood, *Rape in Chicago*, 119–120, 161–163. Notably, Flood addresses the racial dimensions of sexual assault prosecutions.
126. Ibid., 55.
127. Ibid.
128. Ibid., 66.
129. Ibid., 65.
130. *Miranda v. Arizona*, 384 U.S. 436 (1966).
131. MacKinnon, *Sex Equality*, 800–856.
132. *People v. Morrick*, 7.
133. Ibid., 29.
134. Ibid.
135. Ibid., 36.
136. Estrich, *Real Rape*; Warshaw, *I Never Called It Rape*.
137. Frohmann, "Convictability and Discordant Locales."
138. Ibid.
139. Frohmann, "Discrediting Victims' Allegations."
140. Ehrlich, *Representing Rape*; Estrich, *Real Rape*; Matoesian, *Law and the Language of Identity* and *Reproducing Rape*.

Chapter 4. White Slaves and Ordinary Prostitutes

1. Gilfoyle, *City of Eros*, 23–31.
2. Clement, *Love for Sale*, 86–98.
3. Ibid., 98–113.
4. Ibid., 239–269.
5. Kneeland, *Commercialized Prostitution in New York City*.
6. Bell, *Fighting the Traffic in Young Girls*, 442.
7. Ibid., 266. The book eventually sold over four hundred thousand copies including seventy thousand within the first seven months of its publication.
8. Gilfoyle, *City of Eros*, 296. In general, scholars have argued that the public attention to white slavery constituted a scare or panic. See Diffee, "Sex and the City"; Morone, *Hellfire Nation*; Soderlund, "Covering Urban Vice."

9. Stamp, *Movie-Struck Girls*, 52

10. Beckman, "The White Slave Traffic Act."

11. Donovan, *White Slave Crusades*, 1–2.

12. See Soderlund, "Covering Urban Vice"; Morone, *Hellfire Nation*, 257–280; Diffee, "Sex and the City."

13. Rosen, *Lost Sisterhood*, 1982

14. See McKinney, *Consolidated Laws of New York*, 814.

15. Waterman, *Prostitution and Its Repression*.

16. Ibid.

17. *People v. Drenka*, 60.

18. *People v. Spano*, 321.

19. *People v. Dix*, 163.

20. See, for example, "White Slave's Story Stirs Up the Court," *New York Times*, Oct. 20, 1911, 9; "34 Years in Prison for 'White Slaver,'" *Evening Mail*, Oct. 27, 1911, 1; "White Slaver Is Guilty," *Evening World*, Oct. 23, 1911, 16 (*People v. Solow*); "Four 'White Slaves' Bought in New York," *New York Daily Tribune*, April 20, 1910, 1; "'White Slave' Sales Described in Court," *New York Times*, May 19, 1910, 5 (*People v. Moore*); "'White Slave' Offender Sentenced," *New York Times*, Feb. 7, 1911, 6 (*People v. Rubin*); "Stir in White Slave Case," *New York Times*, Sept. 21, 1913 (*People v. Walker*). Most trials, however, received little or no press coverage.

21. Waterman, *Prostitution and Its Repression*, 16. For instance, in 1917, of the fifty-one Section 2460 felony cases, there were only seventeen convictions. Section 2460 fell into greater disuse during the next decade. In 1929, the district attorney's office processed only five cases and three were dismissed.

22. Mann Act 1910 (18 U.S.C. §§ 2421–2424).

23. Ward, *Unforgivable Blackness*, 304.

24. See *Caminetti v. United States*, 1917.

25. Beckman, "The White Slave Traffic Act."

26. Peiss, *Cheap Amusements*.

27. Clement, *Love for Sale*, 47.

28. *People v. Cilento*, 128.

29. Ibid., 137.

30. This is consistent with Robertson's study of early twentieth-century sex crime trials involving youthful victims. He writes that "throughout the period of this study [1880–1960], jurors showed themselves willing to nullify laws, to make decisions based on their own sense of what constituted a crime or an appropriate punishment, rather than on an assessment of how far the evidence satisfied the legal requirements." Robertson, *Crimes against Children*, 5.

31. For instance, in *People v. Mercury* the judge offered the following instructions: "[W]hatever may have been the purpose or the primary object of Section 2460 of the Penal Law, it is operative as well in the case of a woman who is unchaste as in the case of a pure virgin, in the sense that it is legally possible for a person

to be guilty of the commission of their crime as charged in this indictment who induces, entices or procures a woman who has already fallen from virtue, to do any one of the things brought to your attention, as forming parts of the section in question." *People v. Mercury*, 134.

32. Antoniazzi, *Wayward Woman*, 91–105.

33. Turner, "Daughters of the Poor," 55.

34. Ibid.

35. Donovan, *White Slave Crusades*, 101.

36. By the 1910s the "black Tenderloin" ran from 28th to 30th Street between 7th and 8th avenues. See Heap, *Slumming*, 37.

37. "More White Slave Arrests Coming Soon," *New York Times*, May 1, 1910, 20; "Raider Deserted Girl, May Be Slain, in 'White Slave' Den," *New York Evening World*, May 3, 1910, 1. See Donovan, *White Slave Crusades*, 89–109; Donovan, "The Sexual Basis of Racial Formation," 708–728.

38. Donovan, *White Slave Crusades*, 95–98.

39. *People v. Moore*, 13–14.

40. *New York Times*, May 5, 1910, 20.

41. "Belle Moore Guilty of Selling Girls," *New York Times*, May 20, 1910, 18.

42. Donovan, *White Slave Crusades*, 89–109; Soderlund, "Covering Urban Vice," 447.

43. *People v. Moore*, 49.

44. "Thomas C. T. Crain, Ex-Justice, Dies, 82," *New York Times*, May 30, 1942.

45. *People v. Moore*, 265.

46. Ibid.

47. Ibid., 269.

48. Ibid., 288.

49. Ibid., 289.

50. "Belle Moore Guilty of Selling Girls: Verdict against the Mulatto Caught in Whitman's 'White Slave' Net," *New York Times*, May 20, 1910, 18. Alexander Karlin appealed the case, but was unsuccessful. See *The New York Supplement*.

51. *People v. Dix-a*, 20.

52. Ancestry.com, 1910 Federal Census, Manhattan Ward 12, New York, New York; Roll: T624 1018; 12B; Enumeration District: 422.

53. Ibid.

54. *People v. Dix-b*, 326.

55. *People v. Dix-b*, 326.

56. US passenger ship lists made available by the US Immigration and Naturalization Department do not list Katie Howboto and her aunt arriving under those names. This is not unusual because immigrants often altered their names when they arrived, and immigration and customs officials often entered names in their record books phonetically (the name appears as Katy Howboto in police court

records). Moreover, as the transcripts show, Katie used at least one pseudonym since arriving in the United States.

57. "Statement of Katy Howboto," *People v. Dix*, July 8, 1914, District Attorney's Papers, box 858, case 100212, New York Municipal Archives, 1.

58. Ibid.

59. *People v. Dix*, 7.

60. Ibid.

61. "Statement of Katy Howboto," 1.

62. Ibid., 2.

63. *People v. Dix-a*, 8.

64. *People v. Dix-a*, 11.

65. Pretrial Statement of Officer McGuirk, *People v. Dix*, July 20, 1914, District Attorneys Papers, box 858, case 100212, New York Municipal Archives, 1.

66. *People v. Dix-b*, 112.

67. "Statement of Sadie Smith," July 6, 1914, New York Municipal Archives.

68. Ibid., 7.

69. Ibid. 7.

70. "Statement of Officer James J. McGuirk," July 20, 1914, 1; *People v. Dix-b*, 197.

71. *People v. Dix-b*, 166.

72. Ibid.

73. "Statement of Officer James J. McGuirk," July 20, 1914, 1.

74. Ibid.

75. *People v. Dix-b*, 169.

76. "Statement of Officer James J. McGuirk," July 20, 1914, 2.

77. *People v. Dix-b*, 163.

78. Ibid., 191.

79. Ibid.

80. Ibid., 197.

81. Ibid., 208.

82. Ibid., 224.

83. Ibid., 225.

84. Ibid., 121–122.

85. Ross, *Working-Class Hollywood*, 19. In Manhattan, about 72 percent of movie audiences in 1910 were from the blue-collar sector, 25 percent from the clerical workforce, and 3 percent from what the creators of the survey called "the leisure class."

86. Ibid., 7.

87. Ibid.

88. Stamp, *Movie-Struck Girls*, 48. Historian Christina Simmons adds, "In movie theaters and dance halls working-class couples set an example of sexually

integrated amusement followed quickly by middle-class youth." Simmons, "The
Myth of Victorian Repression," 159.

89. Ullman, *Sex Seen*, 42. She writes: "The movies and popular stage made
clear that women were deeply interested in expressions of erotic desire. Women on
the screen initiated sexual contact, took responsibility for its development, and often
enjoyed its pleasures without ill consequences." See Ullman, *Sex Seen*, 3. Israel writes,
"The finalized flapper icon was likewise a product of the war years. By 1918, there
were more than three hundred films circulating the country at any given time, many
of them featuring well-defined flapper characters." See Israel, *Batchelor Girl*, 130.

90. Stamp, *Movie-Struck Girls*, 47

91. Hazard, "The Moral Havoc Wrought by Moving Picture Shows," 290.

92. Ross describes how "[l]ocal theaters also doubled as neighborhood social
centers where people went to meet their friends, gossip, flirt, vent frustrations, and
discuss politics." Ross, *Working-Class Hollywood*, 26

93. Diffee, "Sex and the City"; Stamp, *Movie-Struck Girls*, 41–101.

94. Stamp, *Movie-Struck Girls*, 42.

95. *People v. DiMattio*, case 1993, roll 251, 1914, 7–8.

96. *People v. DiMattio*, 76.

97. *People v. DiMattio*, 116–117.

98. *People v. DiMattio*, 83.

99. *People v. Orlick*, 154.

100. Ibid., 231.

101. Ibid., 155.

102. *People v. DiMattio*, 57.

103. Ibid.

104. Ibid., 70–71.

105. *People v. Orlick*, 109.

106. Ibid., 103.

107. Ibid., 270–271.

108. *People v. Belkin-a*, 109.

109. *People v. Belkin-a*, 110.

110. *People v. Belkin-b*, 116.

111. Ibid., 120, 121.

112. Ibid., 169.

113. Ibid., 387.

114. *People v. Belkin-a*, 430. To counter this image of a rundown apartment
with a bolted cell, the defense attorney made the unusual move of calling on himself
to testify for the defense, asking and answering his own questions. He stated that
"there was nothing of newness" about the bolt. *People v. Belkin-a*, 430.

115. See, for example, D. F. Suthlerland's "The True Story of Estelle Ramon of
Kentucky." Ramon allegedly escaped a brothel when her rescuer tied sheets togeth-

er and escaped through a window (in Bell, *Fighting the Traffic*, 80–97). Another reformer (Ophelia Amigh) recounted a white slavery story where a newsboy heard tapping on a window that led to the rescue of a white slave (in Bell, *Fighting the Traffic*, 117–126). In *Panders and Their White Slaves*, Roe described a story of a white slave's rescue after she threw a note from a brothel window (1910, 158–175). Bell titled an essay about the beginnings of his anti-vice crusade "Barred Windows: How We Took Up the Case of the White Slaves." Bell, *Fighting the Traffic*, 190.

116. *People v. Belkin-b*, 112–113.

117. Donovan, *White Slave Crusades*, 73–78.

118. For example, New York City's first female probation officer, Maude Miner, stated, "Nothing more inhuman and brutal can be imagined than the methods of violence employed by procurers in obtaining girls whom they cannot secure in less forcible ways. They drug them, criminally assault them, starve them into submission and threaten to cut or kill them." Miner, *Slavery of Prostitution*, 102.

119. Friedman, "Name Robbers"; Robertson, *Crimes against Children*, 115–179.

120. *People v. Belkin-b*, 49.

121. Ibid.

122. Ibid.

123. Ibid.

124. Ibid., 272.

125. Ibid.

126. Ibid., 200.

127. Ibid.

128. *People v. Russo*, 7.

129. Ibid., 47.

130. Ibid., 46.

131. Ibid.

132. Ibid.

133. Ibid.

134. Ibid., 44–45.

135. Ibid., 48.

136. Ibid.

137. Ibid., 49.

138. *People v. Spano*, 270.

139. Ibid., 274.

140. Ibid., 283

141. Ibid., 291.

142. Ibid., 328–329.

143. Ibid., 212.

144. "White Slaver Convicted," *New York Times*, Dec. 18, 1912, 2.

145. *People v. Belkin-b*, 725.

146. Ibid.
147. Ibid., 12.
148. Ibid.
149. Ibid., 412.
150. Ibid., 413.
151. Ibid., 627.
152. *People v. Brown*, 90.
153. Roe, *Panders and White Slaves*, 39.
154. Quoted in Bell, *Fighting the Traffic*, 146.
155. Quoted in Bell, *Fighting the Traffic*, 55.
156. Ewick and Silbey, "Subversive Stories and Hegemonic Tales."

Chapter 5. Sodomy, Manhood, and Consent

1. I use the phrase "perceived biological sex" because individuals who identify as queer, transgender, or intersexed are erased by a notion of "biological sex" as
somehow more true or authentic than gender identity.
2. "Senators Loudly Debate Gay Ban," *New York Times*, May 8, 1993, 9.
3. As Godbeer explains, "The notion of sexual orientation had no place in
their discourse; nor did they evoke desire as an independent agency that gave rise
to sexual acts." Godbeer, "'The Cry of Sodom,'" 265.
4. D'Emilio and Freedman, *Intimate Matters*.
5. Eskridge, *Gaylaw*, 25
6. Robertson, *Crimes against Children*, 58.
7. Ibid., 57–71.
8. Eskridge, *Gaylaw*.
9. Ibid., 374.
10. Katz, *Invention of Heterosexuality*, 24.
11. Chauncey, *Gay New York*, 8–9.
12. On the role of Wilde in creating new ways to understand sexuality, see
Sinfield, *Wilde Century*. On the literary importance of Wilde, see Robbins, *Oscar
Wilde*. For an analysis of the trials, see Foldy, *Trials of Oscar Wilde*.
13. Fronc, *New York Undercover*, 20–21.
14. Ibid., 20. See also Heap, *Slumming*, 259.
15. Lardner and Reppetto, *NYPD*, 102.
16. Ibid., 111.
17. Ibid., 104–107.
18. Ibid., 112.
19. Walsh did not officially assume the position of police inspector until
June because he failed the civil services examination after the police commissioner

promoted him on January 9. "Four New Police Inspectors," *The Sun* (New York), June 24, 1903, 12. During the Ariston raid, Walsh acted in the capacity of "Acting-Inspector," although the court records refer to him simply as "Inspector Walsh."

20. Sacks, "To Show Who Was in Charge," 806.

21. Gaynor, "Lawlessness of the Police in New York," 24.

22. *People v. Bushnell*, 2.

23. "The Vulgarization of Salome," 439.

24. Fronc, *New York Undercover*.

25. *People v Schaumloeffel*, 20.

26. Ibid.

27. Ibid., 22.

28. Ibid., 23.

29. Ibid., 24.

30. The judged asked the detective, "Were those his words?," and he replied that they were. *People v Schaumloeffel*, 24.

31. Ibid.

32. Ibid., 26. The lyrics of "Goodbye Eliza Jane" were written by Andrew B. Sterling and the music composed by Harry Von Tilzer. See http://www.bluegrass-messengers.com/master/goodbyemissliza1.html, accessed December 8, 2010.

33. *People v Schaumloeffel*, 62.

34. Ibid., 47.

35. Ibid., 52.

36. Ibid., 120.

37. Ibid., 141.

38. Ibid., 154.

39. Ibid., 136.

40. Ibid., 148.

41. Hanaford and Hines, *Who's Who in Music and Drama*, 372.

42. Williams, *Washing "The Great Unwashed."*

43. *New York Times*, Feb. 14, 1901, 2.

44. Tenement bathhouses were developed by the New York Association for the Improvement of the Conditions of the Poor in the 1890s. Chauncey, *Gay New York*, 208.

45. Ibid., 207.

46. Ibid., 219.

47. Chauncey, *Gay New York*, 207.

48. *People v. Bennett*. Four other transcripts from the transcript collection involve defendants from the Ariston Bathhouse case: *People v. Casson*; *People v. Galbert*; *People v. Kregel*; *People v. Schnittel*.

49. *People v. Bennett*, 51.

50. *New York Times*, Feb. 23, 1903, 12.

51. *New York Times*, Feb. 25, 1903, 6.

52. *New York Times*, March 17, 1903, 6.

53. *New York Times*, Feb. 23, 1903, 12.

54. *New York Times*, June 26, 1903, 2.

55. *New York Press*, Feb. 23, 1903.

56. Bérbué, "History of Gay Bathhouses," 187–220; Chauncey, *Gay New York*.

57. *People v. Casson*, 63.

58. *People v. Galbert*, 298. In *People v. Bennett* Judge Goff urged jurors not to be unjustly biased against the defendant given the "revolting and disgusting character of the charge." *People v. Bennett*, 195.

59. *People v. Bennett*, 170.

60. *People v. Galbert*, 175.

61. *People v. Casson*, 7.

62. Ibid., 45.

63. *People v. Casson*, 73.

64. Ibid., 69.

65. *People v. Schnittel*, 137.

66. One of the diagrams is reproduced in Chauncey, *Gay New York*, 213. Officers Robert Hibbard and Norman Fitzsimmons each created diagrams of the bathhouse. The police drawings were accepted into evidence in all five trials and provoked little controversy. In *People v. Bennett* (117), the defendant disputed the accuracy of the illustration and offered his own that he had drawn in the Tombs. The prosecutor did not protest the counter-drawing being offered into evidence, stating that both drawings were "about the same."

67. *People v. Kregel*, 71.

68. Ibid., 74.

69. Robertson, *Crimes against Children*.

70. *People v. Kregel*, 82.

71. Ibid., 96.

72. Robertson, *Crimes against Children*, 43.

73. *People v. Kregel*, 107.

74. *People v. Kregel*, 110.

75. *People v. Kregel*, 113.

76. *People v. Galbert*, 117.

77. Ibid.

78. *New York Tribune*, June 23, 1903, 11.

79. *People v. Galbert*, 191.

80. Ibid., 192.

81. Ibid., 177.

82. "J. M. Carrere Dies of His Injuries," *New York Times*, March 2, 1911, 9.

83. *People v. Galbert*, 280.

84. Ibid., 277.

85. He said, "I ask your Honor to charge the jury that, no matter how conclusive the testimony may appear to be, the character of the accused may be such as to create a doubt in the minds of the jury, and lead them to believe, in view of the improbabilities that such a person, of such character, would not be guilty of the offense charged, that the other evidence in the case is false, or the witnesses mistaken." *People v. Galbert*, 307.

86. *People v. Galbert*, 334.

87. Ibid., 93.

88. Ibid., 92.

89. Ibid., 238.

90. Ibid., 269.

91. Bederman, *Manliness and Civilization*.

92. *People v. Bennett*, 12.

93. Ibid., 86.

94. Ibid., 94.

95. Chauncey, *Gay New York*.

96. *People v. Bennett*, 16–17.

97. Ibid., 130.

98. Ibid., 173.

99. Ibid., 172.

100. Ibid., 136.

101. Ibid., 191–192.

102. *People v. Bushnell*, 65.

103. Ibid., 10.

104. Ibid.

105. Ibid., 15.

106. Ibid., 14–15.

107. Ibid., 15.

108. Ibid., 18–19.

109. Ibid., 22.

110. Ibid., 59.

111. On the culture of obscene book sales in nineteenth-century New York City, see: Dennis, *Licentious Gotham*. On the class- and gender-based motivations behind the New York Society for the Suppression of Vice and Comstock's anti-obscenity crusade, see Beisel, *Imperiled Innocents*.

112. Beisel, *Imperiled Innocents*, 34–39.

113. Ibid., 38.

114. Eskridge, *Dishonorable Passions*, 46.

115. *People v. Bushnell*, 41–42.

116. Ibid., 43–44.

117. Ibid., 57.

118. Ibid., 67.

119. Ibid., 84.

120. The New York State Supreme Court agreed with the judge. When the case was eventually appealed, it declared that "it is manifest that these objections were without merit." *People v. Bushnell*, 7.

121. *People v. Bushnell*, 110.

122. Ibid.

123. The People of the State of New York, Respondent, v. George W. Bushnell, Appellant. Supreme Court of New York, Appellate Division, First Department 86 A.D. 5, 83 N.Y.S. 403, 1903 N.Y. App. Div.

124. By the mid-1910s, Harlem housed 80 percent of New York City's black population. Osofsky, *Harlem*; Chauncey, *Gay New York*, 245.

125. Chauncey, *Gay New York*, 244.

126. Mumford writes, "If placed in their urban context—of white supremacist backlash against interracial socializing—it does not seem unreasonable to suggest that inverts drew on the stigmatized, socially dangerous culture of miscegenation to invent their sexual practices and construct their sexual subjectivities. To that extent the invert's performance of polarized gender roles—the exaggeration of the difference between the extremely feminine female roles and the masculine male roles—was paralleled by the constructed opposition between blackness and whiteness." Mumford, *Interzones*, 77.

127. Ibid., 80–92.

128. Ancestry.com, Federal Census, 1900, Schiff, Herman, 1900, Manhattan, New York, New York; Roll: T623 1121, Page: 25B, Enumeration District: 901; Federal Census, 1910, Schiff, Herman, 1910; Manhattan Ward 12, New York, New York; Roll: T624 1026; 1A; Enumeration District: 702.

129. *People v. Schiff*, 5.

130. Ibid.

131. Ibid., 12.

132. Ibid., 10.

133. Ibid., 12–13.

134. Ibid., 26.

135. Ibid., 36.

136. Ibid., 47.

137. Ibid., 67.

138. Ibid., 84.

139. Ibid., 99.

140. Ibid., 14.

141. Ibid., 111–112.

142. Ibid., 113.

143. "Are We Degenerating? Dr. Nordau's Book Discussed at Nineteenth Century Club," *New York Times*, April 17, 1895, 5.

144. Eskridge, *Gaylaw*.

145. Johnson, *Lavender Scare*.

146. Chauncey, *Gay New York*.

147. Eskridge, *Gaylaw*, 43.

Chapter 6. Conclusion: Rethinking Sexual Revolution

1. Bailey, *From Front Porch to Back Seat*, 14–20.

2. Having reached a low of 10 percent in the nineteenth century, premarital pregnancy rates rose to about 23 percent from 1880 to 1910. D'Emilio and Freedman, *Intimate Matters*, 199.

3. D'Emilio and Freedman, *Intimate Matters*, 200. Immigrant women from Southern and Eastern Europe were especially vulnerable to sexual and economic exploitation. During this era when Jews, Italians, Greeks, and Russians fell outside of the category of "white," female immigrants from those countries often faced a triple burden of poverty, racial bigotry, and gender discrimination. See Jacobson, *Whiteness of a Different Color*; Bederman, *Manliness and Civilization*.

4. Sewell, "A Theory of Structure," 18.

5. Shapiro, "Agency Theory."

6. Haag, *Consent*, 187, n. 16.

7. Amsterdam and Bruner, *Minding the Law*, 31.

Bibliography

Archival Sources

Trial Transcript Collection, Lloyd Sealy Library, John Jay College of Criminal Justice
Court of General Sessions Case Files (CGSCF), New York City Municipal Archives,
New York City.

Published Primary Sources

Newspapers

New York Daily Tribune
New York Evening World
New York Sun
New York Times

The Beautiful Victim. New York: National Police Gazette, n.d.
Bell, Ernest. *Fighting the Traffic in Young Girls*. Chicago: G. S. Ball, 1910.
Bingham, Theodore. "Administration of Criminal Law: Third Degree System." *Annals of the American Academy of Political and Social Science* 36 (Jan. 1910): 11–15.
———. "Foreign Criminals in New York." *North American Review* 188 (September 1908).
———. *The Girl That Disappears: The Real Facts about the White Slave Traffic*. Boston: Gorham Press, 1911.
Castle, Vernon, and Irene Castle. *Modern Dancing*. New York: World Syndicate, 1914.
Claghorn, Kate Holladay. *The Immigrant's Day in Court*. New York: Harper and Brothers, 1923.
Committee of Fifteen. *The Social Evil: With Special Reference to Conditions Existing in the City of New York*. New York: Putnam's Sons, 1902.

Cook, John Thomas. *The Code of Criminal Procedure and Penal Code of the State of New York*. New York: H. B. Parsons, 1893.

Edwards, Richard Henry. *Popular Amusements*. New York: Association Press, 1915.

Ferrari, Robert. "The Immigrant in New York County Criminal Courts." *Journal of the American Institute of Criminal Law and Criminology* 3, no. 2 (1912).

Gaynor, William. "Lawlessness of the Police in New York." *North American Review* (January 1903): 23–29.

Hanaford, Harry Prescott, and Dixie Hines. *Who's Who in Music and Drama*. New York: H. P. Hanaford, 1914.

Hazard, Mrs. Barclay. "The Moral Havoc Wrought by Moving Picture Shows." *Current Opinion* (April 1914): 290.Humble, H. W. "Seduction as a Crime." *Columbia Law Review* 21 (1921): 144–154.

Israels, C. H. "Diverting a Pastime." *Leslie's* (July 27, 1911).

Kellor, Frances A. *Out of Work: A Study of Unemployment*. New York: Putnam's Sons, 1915.

Kneeland, George. *Commercialized Prostitution in New York City*. New York: Century Co., 1913.

Mayer, Joseph. *The Regulation of Commercialized Vice: An Analysis of the Transition from Segregation to Repression in the United States*. New York: Klebold Press, 1922.

McAdoo, William. "The Administrative Organization of the Courts." *Proceedings of the Academy of Political Science in the City of New York* 5, no. 3 (1915): 198–208.

———. *Guarding a Great City*. New York: Harpers, 1906.

McKinney, William. *McKinney's Consolidated Laws of New York, Annotated*. New York: West, 1917.

Mills, Charles H. *The New York Criminal Reports: Reports of Cases Decided in All Courts of the State of New York*. Albany: W. C. Little, 1912.

Miner, Maude. *The Slavery of Prostitution: A Plea for Emancipation*. New York: Garland, 1916.

New York Society for the Suppression of Vice. *Annual Report 1878, 1880–1913*. New York: The Society.

Paddon E, Mary. "The Inferior Criminal Courts of New York City." *Journal of the American Institute of Criminal Law and Criminology* 11, no. 1 (1920).

Page, Alfred A. "The Power and Importance of the Magistrates' Court." *Proceedings of the Academy of Political Science in the City of New York* 1, no. 4 (1911).

Parkhurst, Charles. *Our Fight with Tammany*. New York: Scribner's, 1895.

Pretrial Statement of Sadie Cohen, Jan. 5, 1903, CGSCF, New York Municipal Archives.

Pretrial Statement of Sadie Marsa, CGSCF, New York Municipal Archives.

Pretrial Statement of Sophie Gregorwich, Feb. 28, 1914, CGSCF, New York Municipal Archives.

Research Committee of the Committee of Fourteen. *The Social Evil in New York City*. New York: G. P. Putnam's Sons, 1910.

Roe, Clifford. *Panders and White Slaves*. New York: Fleming and Revell, 1910.

Stelzle, Charles. "How One Thousand Workingmen Spend Their Spare Time." *The Outlook* (April 4, 1914): 762–766.

Train, Arthur C. *Courts, Criminals, and the Camorra*. New York: Scribner's, 1912.

———. *The Prisoner at the Bar: Sidelights on the Administration of Criminal Justice*. New York: Scribner's, 1908.

Van Every, Edward. *Sins of America as "Exposed" by the Police Gazette*. New York: Frederick A. Stokes, 1931.

Secondary Sources

Books

Amsterdam, Anthony, and Jerome Bruner. *Minding the Law: How Courts Rely on Storytelling, and How Their Stories Change the Ways We Understand the Law and Ourselves*. Cambridge: Harvard University Press, 2001.

Antoniazzi, Barbara. *The Wayward Woman: Progressivism, Prostitution, and Performance in the United States, 1888–1917*. Lanham: Rowman & Littlefield, 2014.

Arnold, Marybeth H. "The Life of a Citizen in the Hands of a Woman: Sexual Assault in New York City, 1790–1820." In *Passion and Power: Sexuality in History*, ed. K. Peiss and C. Simmons, 35–56. Philadelphia: Temple University Press, 1989.

Ashby, LeRoy. *Amusement for All: A History of American Popular Culture*. Lexington: University Press of Kentucky, 2006.

Backhouse, Constance. *Petticoats and Prejudice: Women and Law in Nineteenth-Century Canada*. Toronto: Osgoode Society, 1991.

Bailey, Beth. *From Front Porch to Back Seat: Courtship in Twentieth-Century America*. Baltimore: Johns Hopkins University Press, 1989.

Bederman, Gail. *Manliness and Civilization*. Chicago: University of Chicago Press, 1995.

Beisel, Nicola. *Imperiled Innocents: Anthony Comstock and Family Reproduction in Victorian America*. Princeton: Princeton University Press, 1997.

Benhabib, Seyla, Judith Butler, Drucilla Cornell, and Nancy Fraser. *Feminist Contentions: A Philosophical Exchange*. New York: Routledge, 1994.

Bérbué, Allan. "The History of Gay Bathhouses." In *Policing Public Sex*, ed. E. Glenn Colter et al., 187–220. Boston: South End Press, 1996.

Biernacki, Richard. "Method and Metaphor after New Cultural History." In *Beyond the Cultural Turn*, ed. Victoria E. Bonnell and Lynn Hunt, 62–94. Berkeley: University of California Press, 1998.

Binder, Frederick and David Reimers. *All Nations Under Heaven: An Ethnic and Racial History of New York City*. New York: Columbia University Press, 1995.

Blake, Angela M. *How New York Became American, 1890–1924*. Baltimore: Johns Hopkins University Press, 2006.

Bodnar, John. *Transplanted: A History of Immigrants in Urban America.* Bloomington: Indiana University Press, 1985.

Bonnell, Victoria E., and Lynn Hunt. *Beyond the Cultural Turn.* Berkeley: University of California Press, 1998.

Bontatibus, Donna R. *The Seduction Novel of the Early Nation: A Call for Socio-Political Reform.* East Lansing: Michigan State University Press, 1999.

Broode, Patrick. *Courted and Abandoned: Seduction in Canadian Law.* Toronto: University of Toronto Press, 2002.

Brownmiller, Susan. *Against Our Will: Men, Women, and Rape.* New York: Simon and Schuster, 1975.

Burgess-Jackson, Keith. *A Most Detestable Crime: New Philosophical Essays on Rape.* Oxford: Oxford University Press, 1999.

Chauncey, George. *Gay New York: Gender, Urban Culture, and the Making of the Gay Male World, 1890–1940.* New York: Basic Books, 1994.

Clement, Elizabeth. *Love for Sale: Courting, Treating, and Prostitution in New York City, 1900–1945.* Chapel Hill: University of North Carolina Press, 2006.

Cohen, Patricia Cline. *The Murder of Helen Jewett.* New York: Vintage, 1998.

Collins, Patricia Hill. *Black Feminist Thought: Knowledge, Consciousness, and the Politics of Empowerment.* New York: Routledge, 1990.

Conley, John M., and William M. O'Barr. *Just Words: Law, Language, and Power.* Chicago: University of Chicago Press, 1998.

Cooper, Patricia Ann. *Once a Cigar Maker: Men, Women, and Work Culture in American Cigar Factories, 1900–1919.* Urbana: University of Illinois Press, 1987.

Cossmann, Brenda. *Sexual Citizens: The Legal and Cultural Regulation of Sex and Belonging.* Stanford: Stanford University Press, 2007.

Cott, Nancy F. *Public Vows: A History of Marriage and the Nation.* Cambridge: Harvard University Press, 2000.

Cotterill, Janet. *Language and Power in Court: A Linguistic Analysis of the O. J. Simpson Trial.* New York: Palgrave, 2003.

Daniels, Roger. *Not Like Us: Immigrants and Minorities in America, 1890–1924.* Chicago: Ivan R. Dee, 1997.

Darton, Robert. *The Great Cat Massacre: And Other Episodes in French Cultural History.* New York: Vintage, 1984.

Davis, Natalie Zemon. *Fiction in the Archives: Pardon Tales and Their Tellers in Sixteenth-Century France.* Stanford: Stanford University Press, 1987.

D'Emilio, John, and Estelle Freedman. *Intimate Matters: A History of Sexuality in America.* New York: Harper and Row, 1988.

Dennis, Donna. *Licentious Gotham: Erotic Publishing and Its Prosecution in Nineteenth-Century New York.* Cambridge: Harvard University Press, 2010.

Dinnerstein, Leonard, Roger L. Nichols, and David M. Reimers. *Natives and Strangers: A History of Ethnic Americans.* Sixth edition. Oxford: Oxford University Press, 2015.

Donovan, Brian. *White Slave Crusades: Race, Gender, and Anti-Vice Activism, 1887–1917.* Urbana: University of Illinois Press, 2006.

Drew, Paul. "Contested Evidence in Courtroom Cross-Examination: The Case of a Trial for Rape." In *Talk at Work: Interaction in Institutional Settings*, ed. Paul Drew and John Heritage, 470–520. Cambridge: Cambridge University Press.

Dubinsky, Karen. *Improper Advances: Rape and Heterosexual Conflict in Ontario, 1880–1929.* Chicago: University of Chicago Press, 1993.

Dubois, Ellen Carol, and Linda Gordon. "Seeking Ecstasy on the Battlefield: Danger and Pleasure in Nineteenth-Century Feminist Sexual Thought." In *Pleasure and Danger: Exploring Female Sexuality*, ed. C. Vance. 31–49. Boston: Routledge, 1984.

Duggan, Lisa. *Sapphic Slashers: Sex, Violence, and American Modernity.* Durham: Duke University Press, 2000.

Duneier, Mitchell. *Slim's Table: Race, Respectability, and Masculinity.* Chicago: University of Chicago Press, 1992.

Dunlap, Leslie K. "The Reform of Rape Law and the Problem of White Men: Age of Consent Campaigns in the South, 1885–1910." In *Sex, Love, Race: Crossing Boundaries in North American History*, ed. Martha Hodes, 352–371. New York: New York University Press, 1999.

Ehrlich, Susan. *Representing Rape: Language and Sexual Consent.* New York: Routledge, 2001.

Erdman, Andrew L. *Blue Vaudeville: Sex, Morals, and the Mass Marketing of Amusement, 1895–1915.* Jefferson: McFarland & Company, 2004.

Erenberg, Lewis A. *Steppin' Out: New York Nightlife and the Transformation of American Culture, 1890–1930.* Chicago: University of Chicago Press, 1981.

Eskridge, William N. *Gaylaw: Challenging the Apartheid of the Closet.* Cambridge: Harvard University Press, 1999.

Estrich, Susan. *Real Rape.* Cambridge: Harvard University Press, 1987.

Faber, Eli, and Eileen Rowland. *Trial Transcripts of the Court of New York, 1883–1927: A Historical Introduction.* New York: John Jay Press, 1989.

Fineman, Clarice. *Women in the Criminal Justice System.* New York: Praeger, 1994.

Flood, Dawn. *Rape in Chicago: Race, Myth, and the Courts.* Urbana: University of Illinois Press, 2012.

Foldy, Michael. *The Trials of Oscar Wilde: Deviance, Morality, and Late-Victorian Society.* New Haven: Yale University Press, 1997.

Foucault, Michel. *The History of Sexuality.* Vol. 1. New York: Vintage, 1984.

Freedman, Estelle. *Redefining Rape: Sexual Violence in the Era of Suffrage and Segregation.* Cambridge: University of Harvard Press, 2013.

Friedman, Andrea. *Prurient Interests: Gender, Democracy, and Obscenity in New York City, 1909–1945.* New York: Columbia University Press, 2000.

Friedman-Kasaba, Kathie. *Memories of Migration: Gender, Ethnicity, and Work in the Lives of Jewish and Italian Women in New York, 1870–1924.* Albany: State University of New York Press, 1996.

Fronc, Jennifer. *New York Undercover: Private Surveillance in the Progressive Era.* Chicago: University of Chicago Press, 2009.

Garton, Stephen. *Histories of Sexuality: Antiquity to Sexual Revolution.* London: Equinox, 2004.

Gilfoyle, Timothy. *City of Eros: New York City, Prostitution, and the Commercialization of Sex, 1790–1920.* New York: Norton, 1994.

Glazer, Nathan, and Daniel Patrick Moynihan. *Beyond the Melting Pot: The Negroes, Puerto Ricans, Jews, Italians, and Irish of New York City.* Cambridge: MIT Press, 1970.

Golden, Eve. *Vernon and Irene Castle's Ragtime Revolution.* Lexington: University of Kentucky Press, 2007.

Gurock, Jeffrey. *When Harlem was Jewish, 1870–1930.* New York: Columbia University Press, 1979.

Guterl, Matthew. *The Color of Race in America, 1900–1940.* Cambridge: Harvard University Press, 2001.

Haag, Pamela. *Consent: Sexual Rights and the Transformation of American Liberalism.* Ithaca: Cornell University Press, 1999.

Hanne, Blank. *Straight: The Surprisingly Short History of Heterosexuality.* New York: Beacon Press, 2012.

Hartog, Henrik. *Man and Wife in America: A History.* Cambridge: Harvard University Press, 2000.

Heap, Chad. Slumming: *Sexual and Racial Encounters in American Nightlife, 1885–1940.* Chicago: University of Chicago Press, 2008.

Hicks, Cheryl. *Talk with You Like a Woman: African American Women, Justice, and Reform in New York, 1890–1935.* Chapel Hill: University of North Carolina Press, 2010.

Higginbotham, Evelyn Brooks. *Righteous Discontent: The Women's Movement in the Black Baptist Church, 1880–1920.* Cambridge: Harvard University Press, 1993.

Hobson, Barbara Meil. *Uneasy Virtue: The Politics of Prostitution and the American Reform Tradition.* Chicago: University of Chicago Press, 1987.

Horowitz, Helen Lefkowitz. *Rereading Sex: Battles over Sexual Knowledge and Suppression in Nineteenth-Century America.* New York: Knopf, 2002.

Hutchby, Ian, and Robin Wooffitt. *Conversation Analysis.* New York: Polity Press, 1999.

Israel, Betsy. *Bachelor Girl: The Secret History of Single Women in the Twentieth Century.* New York: William Morrow, 2002.

Jacobson, Matthew Frye. *Whiteness of a Different Color: European Immigrants and the Alchemy of Race.* Chicago: University of Chicago Press, 1998.

Jenkins, Philip. *Moral Panic: Changing Conceptions of the Child Molester in Modern America.* New Haven: Yale University Press, 1998.

Johnson, David K. *The Lavender Scare: The Cold War Prosecution of Gays and Lesbians in the Federal Government.* Chicago: University of Chicago Press, 2006.

Katz, Jonathan N. *The Invention of Heterosexuality.* New York: Dutton, 1995.

Katzman, David. *Seven Days a Week: Women and Domestic Service in Industrializing America.* Urbana: University of Illinois Press, 1981.

Kelly, Michael. Critique and Power: Recasting the Foucault/Habermas Debate. Cambridge: MIT Press, 1994.

Klapper, Melissa R. *Jewish Girls Coming of Age in America, 1860–1920.* New York: New York University Press, 2005.

Knowles, Mark. *The Wicked Waltz and Other Scandalous Dances: Outrage at Couple Dancing in the 19th and Early 20th Centuries.* New York: McFarland, 2009.

Lacquer, Thomas. "Credit, Novels, and Masturbation." In *Choreographing History*, ed. Susan Foster, 119–128. Bloomington: University of Indiana Press, 1995.

Lardner, James, and Thomas Reppetto. *NYPD: A City and Its Police.* New York: Holt, 2000.

Lebsock, Suzanne. *A Murder in Virginia: Southern Justice on Trial.* New York: Norton, 2003.

LeMoncheck, Linda. "When Good Sex Turns Bad: Rethinking a Continuum Model of Sexual Violence against Women." In *A Most Detestable Crime: New Philosophical Essays on Rape*, ed. K. Burgess-Jackson, 159–182. Oxford: Oxford University Press, 1999.

Liu, Mary Ting Yi. 2007. *The Chinatown Trunk Mystery: Murder, Miscegenation, and Other Dangerous Encounters in Turn-of-the-Century New York City.* Princeton: Princeton University Press.

Lystra, Karen. *Searching the Heart: Women, Men, and Romantic Love in Nineteenth-Century America.* New York: Oxford University Press, 1989.

MacKinnon, Catharine. *Sex Equality.* New York: Foundation Press, 2001.

Manzo, John. "Ethnomethodology, Conversation Analysis, and the Sociology of Law." In *Law in Action: Ethnomethodological and Conversation Analytic Approaches to Law*, ed. Max Travers and John Manzo, 1–24 Brookfield: Ashgate, 1997.

Marsh, Jeanne, Alison Geist, and Nathan Caplan. *Rape and the Limits of Law Reform.* Westport: Greenwood, 1982.

Matoesian, Gregory. *Law and the Language of Identity: Discourse in the William Kennedy Smith Rape Trial.* Oxford: Oxford University Press, 2001.

———. *Reproducing Rape: Domination through Talk in the Courtroom.* Chicago: University of Chicago Press, 1993.

May, Elaine Tyler. *Great Expectations: Marriage and Divorce in Post-Victorian America.* Chicago: University of Chicago Press, 1980.

McLaren, Angus. *Sexual Blackmail: A Modern History*. Cambridge: Harvard University Press, 2002.

———. *The Trials of Masculinity: Policing Sexual Boundaries, 1870–1930*. Chicago: University of Chicago Press, 1999.

Meyerowitz, Joanne. *Women Adrift: Independent Wage Earners in Chicago, 1880–1930*. Chicago: University of Chicago Press, 1988.

Miller, Peggy, and Nancy Biele. "Twenty Years Later: The Unfinished Revolution." In *Transforming a Rape Culture*, ed. E. Buchwald, P. Fletcher, and M. Roth, 49–54. Minneapolis: Milkweed, 1993.

Morone, James A. *Hellfire Nation: The Politics of Sin in American History*. New Haven: Yale University Press, 2003.

Mumford, Kevin. Interzones: *Black/White Sex Districts in Chicago and New York in the Early Twentieth Century*. New York: Columbia University Press, 1997.

Odem, Mary. *Delinquent Daughters: Policing Adolescent Female Sexuality in the United States, 1885–1920*. Chapel Hill: University of North Carolina Press, 1995.

Osofsky, Gilbert. *Harlem: The Making of a Ghetto*. Chicago: Ivan R. Dee, 1996 [1963].

Palmer, Bryan. *Descent into Discourse: The Reification of Language and the Writing of Social History*. Philadelphia: Temple University Press, 1990.

Peiss, Kathy. *Cheap Amusements: Working Women and Leisure in Turn-of-the-Century New York*. Philadelphia: Temple University Press, 1986.

Philips, Jim, and Rosemary Gartner. *Murdering Holiness: The Trials of Franz Creffield and George Mitchell*. Vancouver: University of British Columbia Press, 2003.

Piott, Steven. *Daily Life in the Progressive Era*. Westport: Greenwood Press, 2011.

Plummer, Kenneth. *Telling Sexual Stories: Power, Change and Social Worlds*. New York: Routledge, 1995.

Poovey, Mary. *Uneven Developments: The Ideological Work of Gender in Mid-Victorian England*. Chicago: University of Chicago Press, 1988.

Reagan, Leslie J. *When Abortion Was a Crime: Women, Medicine, and Law in the United States, 1867–1973*. Berkeley: University of California Press, 1997.

Reitano, Joanne. *The Restless City: A Short History of New York from Colonial Times to the Present*. New York: Routledge, 2006.

Robbins, Ruth. *Oscar Wilde*. New York: Continuum Press, 2011.

Robertson, Stephen. *Crimes against Children: Sexual Violence and Legal Culture in New York City, 1880–1960*. Chapel Hill: University of North Carolina Press, 2005.

Roediger, David R. 2006. *Working Toward Whiteness Working Toward Whiteness: How America's Immigrants Became White*. New York: Basic.

Rosen, Lawrence. *Law as Culture: An Invitation*. Princeton: Princeton University Press, 2006.

Rosen, Ruth. *The Lost Sisterhood: Prostitution in America, 1900–1918*. Baltimore: Johns Hopkins University Press, 1982.

Ross, Steven J. *Working-Class Hollywood*. Princeton: Princeton University Press, 1999.

Russell, Diana. *The Politics of Rape*. New York: Stein and Day, 1974.

Salwen, Peter. *Upper West Side: A History and Guide*. New York: Cross River Press, 1989.

Sanday, Peggy Reeves. *A Woman Scorned: Acquaintance Rape on Trial*. New York: Doubleday, 1996.

Schneider, Dorothee. *Trade Unions and Community: The German Working Class in New York City, 1870–1900*. Urbana: University of Illinois Press, 1994.

Schulofer, Stephen J. *Unwanted Sex: The Culture of Intimidation and the Failure of Law*. Cambridge: Harvard University Press, 2000.

Scott, Joan Wallach. *Gender and the Politics of History*. New York: Columbia University Press, 1999.

"Seduction as a Crime." *Criminal Law Magazine* 3 (1882): 331–347.

Seidman, Stephen. *Romantic Longings: Love in America, 1830–1980*. New York: Routledge, 1991.

———. The Social Construction of Sexuality. New York: W. W. Norton, 2003.

Sewell Jr., William. 2005. *Logics of History: Social Theory and Social Transformation*. Chicago: University of Chicago Press.

Sinfield, Alan. *The Wilde Century: Effeminacy, Oscar Wilde, and the Queer Moment*. New York: Columbia University Press, 1994.

Shuy, Roger W. "Discourse Analysis in the Legal Context." In *The Handbook of Discourse Analysis*, ed. Deborah Schiffrin, Deborah Tannen, and Heidi E. Hamilton, 437–452. New York: Blackwell, 2001.

Simmons, Christina. "The Myth of Victorian Repression." In *Passion and Power: Sexuality in History*, ed. Kathy Peiss and Christina Simmons, 157–178. Philadelphia: Temple University Press, 1989.

Skeggs, Beverley. *Formations of Class and Gender: Becoming Respectable*. London: Sage, 1997.

Smith, Daniel S. "The Dating of the American Sexual Revolution: Evidence and Interpretation." In *The American Family and Social-Historical Perspective*, ed. Michael Gordon, 321–335. New York: St. Martin's Press, 1978.

Smith-Rosenberg, Carroll. *Disorderly Conduct: Visions of Gender in Victorian America*. Oxford: Oxford University Press, 1985.

Stamp, Shelley. *Movie-Struck Girls: Women and Motion Picture Culture after the Nickelodeon*. Princeton: Princeton University Press, 2000.

Stansell, Christine. *City of Women: Sex and Class in New York, 1789–1860*. Urbana: University of Illinois Press, 1986.

Strebnick, Amy Gilman. *The Mysterious Death of Mary Rogers: Sex and Culture in Nineteenth-Century New York*. Oxford: Oxford University Press, 1995.

Taslitz, Andrew E. *Rape and the Culture of the Courtroom*. New York: New York University Press, 1999.

Ullman, Sharon. *Sex Seen: The Emergence of Modern Sexuality in America*. Berkeley: University of California Press, 1998.

Vance, Carol. *Pleasure and Danger: Exploring Female Sexuality*. Boston: Routledge, 1992.
Wagner, Ann. *Adversaries of Dance: From the Puritans to the Present*. Urbana: University of Illinois Press, 1997.
Walkowitz, Judith R. *City of Dreadful Delight*. Chicago: University of Chicago Press, 1992.
Ward, Geoffrey. *Unforgivable Blackness: The Rise and Fall of Jack Johnson*. New York: Random House, 2010.
Warshaw, Robin. *I Never Called It Rape: The Ms. Report on Recognizing, Fighting, and Surviving Date Rape*. New York: HarperTrade, 1994.
Waterman, Willoughby Cyrus. *Prostitution and Its Repression in New York City, 1900–1931*. New York: Columbia University Press, 1932.
Weeks, Jeffrey. *Sex, Politics, and Society: The Regulation of Sexuality since 1800*. New York: Longman, 1981.
Weiner, Lynn Y. *From Working Girl to Working Mother: The Female Labor Force in the United States, 1920–1980*. Chapel Hill: University of North Carolina Press, 1985.
White, Hayden. *The Content of the Form: Narrative Discourse and Historical Representation*. Baltimore: Johns Hopkins University Press, 1990.
White, Kevin. *The First Sexual Revolution: The Emergence of Male Heterosexuality in Modern America*. New York: New York University Press, 1992.
———. *Sexual Liberation or Sexual License? The American Revolt against Victorianism*. Chicago: Ivan R. Dee, 2000.
Whiteaker, Larry. *Seduction, Prostitution, and Moral Reform in New York, 1830–1860*. New York: Garland, 1997. Williams, Marilyn. *Washing "The Great Unwashed": Public Baths in Urban America, 1840–1920*. Columbus: Ohio State University Press, 1992.
Wittgenstein, Ludwig. *Philosophical Investigations*. New York: Prentice Hall, 1973.

Articles

Baker, Paula. "The Domestication of Politics: Women and American Political Society, 1780–1920." *American Historical Review* 89 (1984): 620–647.
Balos, Beverly, and Mary Louise Fellows. "A Matter of Prostitution: Becoming Respectable." *NYU Law Review* 74 (1999): 1220–1303.
Beckman, Marlene D. "The White Slave Traffic Act: Historical Implications of a Federal Crime Policy on Women." *Women and Politics* 4 (1984): 85–101.
Belcher, Ellen, and Ellen Sexton. "Digitizing Criminals: Web Delivery of a Century on the Cheap." *OCLC Systems and Services* 24, no. 2 (2007): 116–132.
Berkowitz, Jeffrey S. "Breaking the Silence: Should Jurors Be Allowed to Question Witnesses during Trial?" *Vanderbilt Law Review* 44 (1991): 118–147.

Boyer, Kate. "Place and the Politics of Virtue: Clerical Work, Corporate Anxiety, and Changing Meanings of Public Womanhood in Early Twentieth-Century Montreal." *Gender, Place & Culture* 5 (1998): 261–275.

Burnham, John. "The Progressive Era Revolution in American Attitudes toward Sex." *Journal of American History* 59 (1973): 899–900.

Cocks, Catherine. "Rethinking Sexuality in the Progressive Era." *Journal of the Gilded Age and Progressive Era* 5 (2006): 94–118.

Cordery, Simon. "Friendly Societies and the Discourse of Respectability in Britain, 1825–1875." *Journal of British Studies* 34 (1995): 35–58.

Cott, Nancy. "Passionlessness: An Interpretation of Victorian Sexual Ideology, 1790–1850." *Signs* 4 (1978): 219–236.

Davidson, Janet F. "The Goosing of Violet Nye and Other Tales: White Women and Sexual Respectability on the Pennsylvania Railroad." *Labor History* 41 (2000): 437–452.

Davis, Rebecca L. "'Not Marriage at All, but Simple Harlotry': The Companionate Marriage Controversy." *Journal of American History* 94, no. 4 (March 2008): 1137–1163.

DeVille, Kenneth. "New York Attorneys and Ambulance Chasing in the 1920s." *Historian* (1997): 290–310.

De Young, Mary. "Help, I'm Being Held Captive: The White Slave Fairy Tale of the Progressive Era." *Journal of American Culture* 6 (1983): 96–99.

Diamond, Shari, Mary R. Rose, and Beth Murphy. "Jurors' Unanswered Questions." *Court Review* 41 (2004): 20–29.

Diffee, Christopher. "Sex and the City: The White Slavery Scare and Social Governance in the Progressive Era." *American Quarterly* 57 (2005): 411–437.

Donovan, Brian. "Gender Inequality and Criminal Seduction: Prosecuting Sexual Coercion in the Early Twentieth Century." *Law and Social Inquiry* 30 (2005): 61–88.

———. "The Sexual Basis of Racial Formation: Anti-Vice Activism and the Creation of the Twentieth-Century Color Line." *Ethnic and Racial Studies* 26 (2003): 708–728.

Donovan, Brian, and Tori Barnes-Brus. "Narratives of Sexual Consent and Sexual Coercion: Forced Prostitution Trials in Progressive-Era New York City." *Law and Social Inquiry* 36 3 (2011): 597–619.

Ehrlich, Susan. "The Discursive Reconstruction of Sexual Consent." *Discourse and Society* 9, no. 2 (1998): 149–171.

Ewick, Patricia, and Susan Silbey. "Narrating Social Structure: Stories of Resistance to Legal Authority." *American Journal of Sociology* 106 (2003): 1328–1372.

———. "Subversive Stories and Hegemonic Tales: Toward a Sociology of Narrative." *Law and Society Review* 29 (1995): 197–226.

Feinsinger, Nathan P. "Legislative Attack on 'Heart Balm.'" *Michigan Law Review* 33 (1935): 979–1009.

Friedman, Lawrence. "Name Robbers: Privacy, Blackmail, and Assorted Matters in Legal History." *Hofstra Law Review* 30 (2002): 1093–1132.

———. "Popular Legal Culture: Law, Lawyers, and Popular Culture." *Yale Law Journal* 98 (1989): 1579–1606.

Frohmann, Lisa. "Convictability and Discordant Locales: Reproducing Race, Class, and Gender Ideologies in Prosecutorial Decisionmaking." *Law and Society Review* 31 (1997): 531–555.

———. "Discrediting Victims' Allegations of Sexual Assault: Prosecutorial Accounts of Case Rejections." *Social Problems* (1991): 213–226.

Gilfoyle, Timothy. "The Moral Origins of Political Surveillance: The Preventative Society in New York City, 1867–1918." *American Quarterly* 38, no. 4 (1986): 637–652.

Ginzberg, Lori D. "'Moral Suasion Is Moral Balderdash': Women, Politics, and Social Activism in the 1850s." *Journal of American History* 73, no. 3 (December 1986): 601–622.

Godbeer, Richard. "'The Cry of Sodom': Discourse, Intercourse, and Desire in Colonial New England." *William and Mary Quarterly* 52 (1995): 259–286.

Green, Cecilia A. "Between Respectability and Self-Respect: Framing Afro-Caribbean Women's Labour History." *Social and Economic Studies* 55 (2006): 1–31.

Haag, Pamela. "Power and the New Cultural History." *Radical History Review* 63 (1995): 200–205.

Hunt, Alan. "Regulating Heterosocial Space: Sexual Politics in the Early Twentieth Century." *Journal of Historical Sociology* (March 2002): 1–34.

Johnson, Val Marie. "Protection, Virtue, and 'the Power to Detain': The Moral Citizenship of Jewish Women in New York City, 1890–1920." *Journal of Urban History* 31 (2005): 655–684.

Kandiyoti, Deniz. "Bargaining with Patriarchy." *Gender and Society* 2 (1988): 274–290.

Kessner, Thomas, and Betty Caroli. "New Immigrant Women at Work: Italians and Jews in New York City, 1880–1905." *The Journal of Ethnic Studies* 5, no. 4 (1978): 19–31.

Kushner, Howard. "Nineteenth-Century Sexuality and the 'Sexual Revolution' of the Progressive Era." *Canadian Review of American Studies* 9 (Spring 1978): 34–49.

Larson, Jane. "'Even a Worm Will Turn at Last': Rape Reform in Late Nineteenth-Century America." *Yale Journal of Law and the Humanities* 9 (1997): 1–71.

———. "Women Understand So Little, They Call My Good Nature 'Deceit': A Feminist Rethinking of Seduction." *Columbia Law Review* 93 (1993): 375–472.

Leader-Elliott, Ian, and Ngaire Naffine. "Wittgenstein, Rape Law and the Language Games of Consent." *Monash University Law Review* 26 (2000): 48–71.

Lee, Orville. "Legal Weapons for the Weak? Democratizing the Force of Words in an Uncivil Society." *Law and Social Inquiry* 26 (2001): 847–891.

Marilley, Suzanne. "Frances Willard and the Feminism of Fear." Feminist Studies 19 (1993): 123–145.

Martin, Jon. "Structuring the Sexual Revolution." *Theory and Society* 25 (1996):105–151.

Maza, Sarah. "Stories in History: Cultural Narratives in Recent Works in European History." *American Historical Review* (Winter 1996): 1493–1515.

McGovern, James R. "The American Woman's Pre–World War I Freedom in Manners and Morals." *Journal of American History* 55 (September 1968): 315–333.

Mumford, Kevin. "Homosex Changes: Race, Cultural Geography, and the Emergence of the Gay." *American Quarterly* 48 (1996): 395–413.

Nixon, Cheryl, and Janet Landman. "Turning Our Minds to *Minding the Law*." *Social Justice Research* 16, no. 2 (2003): 169–189.

Osofsky, Gilbert. "Race Riot, 1900: A Study of Ethnic Violence." *The Journal of Negro Education* 32, no. 1 (1963): 16–24.

Phipps, Alison. "Rape and Respectability: Ideas about Sexual Violence and Social Class." *Sociology* 43 (2009): 667–683.

Pleck, Elizabeth. "Feminist Responses to 'Crimes against Women,' 1868–1896." *Signs* 8 (1983): 451–470.

Reel, Guy. "This Wicked World: Masculinities and the Portrayals of Sex, Crime, and Sports in the *National Police Gazette*, 1879–1906." *American Journalism* 22, no. 1 (Winter 2005): 61–94.

Robertson, Stephen. "Seduction, Sexual Violence, and Marriage in New York City, 1886–1955." *Law and History Review* (2006): 331–373.

———. "What's Law Got to Do with It? Legal Records and Sexual Histories." *Journal of the History of Sexuality* 14 (2005): 161–185.

Rose, Vicki McNickle. "Rape as a Social Problem: A Byproduct of the Feminist Movement." *Social Problems* 25 (1977): 75–89.

Sacks, Marcy S. "'To Show Who Was in Charge': Police Repression of New York City's Black Population at the Turn of the Twentieth Century." *Journal of Urban History* 31 (September 2005): 799–819.

Schalet, Amy, Geoffrey Hunt, and Karen Joe-Laidler. "Respectability and Autonomy: The Articulation and Meaning of Sexuality among the Girls in the Gang." *Journal of Contemporary Ethnography* 32 (2003): 108–143.

Sewell, William, Jr. "A Theory of Structure: Duality, Agency, and Transformation." *American Journal of Sociology* 98 (1992): 1–29.

Shapiro, Susan. "Agency Theory." *Annual Review of Sociology* 31 (2005): 263–284.

Stearns, Bertha-Monica. "Reform Periodicals and Female Reformers, 1830–1860." *American Historical Review* 37, no. 4 (July 1932): 678–699.

Travers, Max. "Understanding Talk in Legal Settings: What Law and Society Studies Can Learn from a Conversation Analyst." *Law and Social Inquiry* (Spring 2006): 447–463.

Trotti, Michael. "Review Essay: The Lure of the Sensational Murder." *Journal of Social History* (Winter 2001): 429–443.

Umphrey, Martha Merrill. "The Dialogics of Legal Meaning: Spectacular Trials, the Unwritten Law, and Narratives of Criminal Responsibility." *Law and Society Review* 33 (1999): 393–423.

VanderVelde, Lea. "The Legal Ways of Seduction." *Stanford Law Review* 48 (1996): 818–901.

Welter, Barbara. "The Cult of True Womanhood: 1820–1860." *American Quarterly* 18 (1966): 151–174.

Wilson, Peter J. "Reputation and Respectability: A Suggestion for Caribbean Ethnology." *Man* 4 (1969): 70–84.

State Penal Codes, Legal Texts, and Decisions

Caminetti v. United States, 242 U.S. 470 (*1917*)

Cook, John Thomas. *Code of Criminal Procedure and Penal Code of the State of New York*. New York: H. B. Parsons, 1893.

Consolidated Laws of the State of New York. New York: J. B. Lyon Company, 1909.

Laws of the State of New York. New York: J. B. Lyon Company, 1916.

McKinney William M. *Consolidated Laws of New York, Annotated*. Northport: Edward Thompson Company, 1917.

Mills, Charles H. *New York Criminal Reports*. Albany: W. C. Little, 1914.

Miranda v. Arizona, 384 U.S. 436 (1966).

New York Supplement: Supreme and Lower Courts of Record, vol. 127. St. Paul: West Publishing, 1911.

The Penal Code of the State of New York in Force December 1, 1882, as Amended by Laws of 1882, 1883, 1884, 1885, 1886, 1887, 1888, 1889, 1890, 1891, and 1892, with Notes of Decisions to Date. 1892. Eleventh revised edition. New York and Albany: Banks and Brothers.

People v. Abbott, 19 Wend. 192, 195 (NY. *1838*). The People of the State of New York, Respondent, v. George W. Bushnell, Appellant. Supreme Court of New York, Appellate Division, First Department 86 A.D. 5, 83 N.Y.S. 403, 1903 N.Y. App. Div.

Silvernail, William H. *Penal Code and Code of Criminal Procedure of the State of New York*. Albany: W. C. Little, 1905.

Sex Crime Trials in the Trial Transcript Collection, John Jay College of Criminal Justice

People v. Belkin, trial 1748, reel 223, 1913 (*People v. Belkin-a*).

People v. Belkin, trial 1768, reel 225, 1913 (*People v. Belkin-b*).

People v. Bennett, trial 369, reel 66, 1903.

People v. Bloch, trial 557, reel 91, 1906.

People v. Bogden, trial 1291, reel 167, 1910.

People v. Brennan, trial 2650, reel 327, 1918.

People v. Brown, trial 1651, reel 212, 1912.

People v. Bushnell, trial 260, reel 47, 1901.

People v. Casson, trial 350, reel 64, 1903.

People v. Cilento, trial 1830, reel 231, 1914.

People v. Abraham Cohen, trial 2212, reel 279, 1916.

People v. Isaac Cohen, trial 1812, reel 228, 1913.

People v. Costanis, trial 2037, reel 256, 1915.

People v. Cozzens, trial 657, reel 103, 1907.

People v. DiMattio, trial 1993, reel 251, 1914.

People v. Dix, trial 1922, reel 243, 1914 (*People v. Dix-a*).

People v. Dix, trial 1935, reel 245, 1914 (*People v. Dix-b*).

People v. Drenka, trial 1093, reel 145, 1910.

People v. Galbert, trial 373, reel 66, 1903.

People v. Handsman, trial 2695A, reel 331, 1918.

People v. Hawkins, trial 2517, reel 315, 1918.

People v. Krakauer, trial 491, reel 83, 1905.

People v. Kregel, trial 353, reel 353, 1903.

People v. Lynx, trial 1702, reel 219, 1913.

People v. Mercury, trial 1527, reel 197, 1912.

People v. Millinger, trial 2468, reel 311, 1917.

People v. Moore, trial 1169, reel 153, 1910.

People v. Morrick, trial 2313, reel 294, 1917.

People v. Nicholas, trial 1970, reel 248, 1914.

People v. Orlick, trial 2049, reel 258, 1914.

People v. Rosen, trial 2435, reel 308, 1917.

People v. Rosenberg, trial 343, reel 62, 1903.

People v. Roy, trial 1811, reel 228, 1914.

People v. Rubin, trial 1303, reel 169, 1911.

People v. Russo, trial 2137, reel 269, 1908.

People v Schaumloeffel, trial 419, reel 73, 1904.

People v. Schiff, trial 1915, reel 242, 1914.

People v. Schonland, trial 668, reel 104, 1907 (*People v. Schonland-a*).

People v. Schonland, trial 686, reel 105, 1907 (*People v. Schonland-b*).

People v. Schnittel, trial 355, reel 64, 1903.

People v. Sochinsky, trial 2079, reel 261, 1915.

People v. Solow, trial 1423, reel 184, 1911.

People v. Spano, trial 1645, reel 211, 1912.

People v. Walker, trial 1754, reel 224, 1913.

People v. Weintraub, trial 1849, reel 233, 1913.

Index